# WHAT DO I DO WITH MY MONEY NOW?

# WHAT DO I DO WITH MY MONEY NOW?

*Answers for Any Market from*
*Warren Buffett, Peter Lynch*
*and Other Investors You Can Trust*

EDITED BY CLINT WILLIS

Marlowe & Company
New York

WHAT DO I DO WITH MY MONEY NOW?: *Answers for Any Market from Warren Buffett, Peter Lynch and Other Investors You Can Trust.*

Compilation Copyright © 2003 by Clint Willis
Introductions Copyright © 2003 by Clint Willis

Published by Marlowe & Company
An Imprint of Avalon Publishing Group Incorporated
161 William Street, 16th floor
New York, NY 10038

Library of Congress Catalog-in-Publication Data

What Do I Do with My Money Now?: Answers for Any Market from Warren Buffett, Peter Lynch and Other Investors You Can Trust. / edited by Clint Willis.
     p. cm.
  ISBN 1-56924-479-0
     1. Investments. 2. Investment analysis. 3. Portfolio management.
     I. Willis, Clint.

HG4521.13855 2003
332.6--dc21                                                      2003043049


Book design: Simon S. Sullivan

Printed in the United States of America

Distributed by Publishers Group West

*for Mark Boyar*
*one of the best*

# CONTENTS

*xi* | INTRODUCTION
by Clint Willis

*1* | THE CLAY PEDESTAL OF SUPERANALYST ✓
by Burton G. Malkiel
from *A Random Walk Down Wall Street*

*39* | THE SUPERINVESTORS OF GRAHAM-AND-DODDSVILLE
by Warren E. Buffett

*57* | THE TWO WISE MEN
by Robert G. Hagstrom, Jr.
from *The Warren Buffett Way*

*87* | THE PERFECT STOCK, WHAT A DEAL!
by Peter Lynch with John Rothchild
from *One Up on Wall Street*

*111* | WILLIAM MILLER
by Kirk Kazanjian
from *Value Investing with the Masters*

*137* | THE EGO TRAP
by Gary Belsky and Thomas Gilovich
from *Why Smart People Make Big Money Mistakes—and How to Correct Them*

*161* | TULIPOMANIA
by Charles Mackay
from *Extraordinary Popular Delusions and the Madness of Crowds*

*173* | MISTAKES OF THE FIRST TWENTY-FIVE YEARS
by Warren E. Buffett
from *Berkshire Hathaway 1989 Annual Report*

*179* | BEN GRAHAM: IDEAS AS MEMENTOS
by Charles D. Ellis

*193* | ON SIMPLICITY
by John C. Bogle
from *Common Sense on Mutual Funds*

*221* | PERSPECTIVES ON STOCKS AS INVESTMENTS
by Jeremy J. Siegel
from *Stocks for the Long Run*

*235* | MARKET TIMING
by Roger C. Gibson
from *Asset Allocation*

*245* | THE MAN WHO NEVER LOST
by John Train

*249* | THE AMERICAN DREAM—ON A SHOESTRING
by Joe Dominguez and Vicki Robin
from *Your Money or Your Life*

*267* | THE VIRTUES OF INVESTING
by James H. Gipson
from *Winning the Investment Game*

*289* | TRUST NO ONE
by Andrew Tobias
from *The Only Investment Guide You'll Ever Need*

*299* | ACKNOWLEDGMENTS

*300* | PERMISSIONS

*302* | BIBLIOGRAPHY

# INTRODUCTION
## by Clint Willis


**M**OST BOOKS ABOUT investing are like lottery tickets. Both are designed to profit from our ignorance and our greed—but the books are more dangerous. Reasonable people aren't likely to blow their savings on lottery tickets, but a bad investment book can make mincemeat of a 401(k) plan.

A few investment books do what all good books do: They try to tell the truth. The very best investors—and the best investment writers—are men or women of intellectual integrity: the likes of Warren Buffett, John Bogle, Benjamin Graham, Burton Malkiel, Roger Gibson, Arthur Levitt. Like true artists and scholars, they try to see the world exactly as it is, and they succeed to an impressive degree.

The odds are against such success. Behavioral economists, psychologists and lately biologists have found that human beings are not wired for clarity. We tend to take mental and emotional short-cuts that lead us far astray. These short-cuts lead to household accidents, wars, broken hearts—and bad investment decisions. We chase hot funds and stocks; we take investment advice from strangers; we trust magazines and television programs that pander to our worst instincts; we ignore our greatest investment opportunities. Result: the average investor—amateur or professional—can't come close to keeping pace with the market averages.

What's more, we are bombarded with bad and dishonest advice. Magazines, newspapers, television programs, websites, newsletters and other media appeal to our greediest or our most fearful impulses. Brokers, financial planners, analysts and other advisors offer bad advice designed to boost their profits at our expense. Fund sponsors engage in deceptive sales practices and manage portfolios for their own benefit rather than the benefit of shareholders. Small wonder we make bad investment choices and obtain poor results.

These facts make it all the more striking that some investors do beat the averages—consistently and without taking unreasonable risks. Peter Lynch during his 13 years running Fidelity's Magellan fund beat the S&P 500 by an average of 13.4 percentage points annually. Warren Buffett during the past 36 years has steered Berkshire Hathaway to an annual return of more than 22%. Bill Miller beat the S&P during each of the 12 years through 2002.

Buffett has written that many of the world's best investors (including Buffett himself) draw insights from a common source: the teachings of Benjamin Graham and David L. Dodd. True enough. I would add that the best investors—and the best investment thinkers—succeed to the extent that they avoid the sin of self-deception: They try hard not to lie to themselves. That may be the most useful lesson any reader can draw from this book, and it's worth at least $16.95.

You will notice that the best money managers and investment thinkers don't arrive at the same conclusions about how to make money. Graham worries more about assets; Buffett and Miller are concerned with a firm's business model; Fisher worries about management. Gibson doesn't worry much about stock-picking because he thinks asset allocation is far more important. Bogle is fanatical about keeping investment fees and other costs low.

These investors are all different from one another, and none has it all figured out. Each man has strengths and weaknesses, and each has blind spots. Their collective wisdom is more useful (as well as more interesting) than what any one of them alone can tell us, which is one reason to read this collection.

Most investing advice comes wrapped in promises. The more glowing the promises, the worse the advice. The writers represented in this collection offer no guarantees. Some of them are pessimistic about the average investor's chances at making money on Wall Street.

Lacking the wisdom of restraint, I will go out on a limb and suggest that these writers' work will help you to become a more intellectually and emotionally honest investor. I'll add that while the results may not make you rich, they probably won't make you poor—but I'm not promising anything.

—Clint Willis

Princeton professor **Burton Malkiel** doesn't write like a
professor. Malkiel is a fan—within limits—of the efficient market and random walk theories. Both theories
hold that people can't predict stock price movements.
His classic book was first published in 1973.


# THE CLAY PEDESTAL OF
# SUPERANALYST
by Burton G. Malkiel

from *A Random Walk Down Wall Street* (1973)

*How could I have been so mistaken as to have trusted the experts?*
—John F. Kennedy (after the Bay of Pigs fiasco)

I N THE BEGINNING he was a statistician. He wore a white,
starched shirt and threadbare blue suit. He quietly put on his
green eyeshade, sat down at his desk, and recorded meticulously
the historical financial information about the companies he followed.
The result: writer's cramp.

But then a metamorphosis began to set in. He rose from his desk,
bought blue button-down shirts and gray flannel suits, threw away his
eyeshade, and began to make field trips to visit the companies that
previously he had known only as a collection of financial statistics. His
title now became security analyst.

As time went on, his stature continued to grow. Portfolio managers increasingly relied on his reports and recommendations in
deciding which stocks should be bought and sold. In recent years

his shirts acquired stripes and, yes, he even sprouted sideburns! He became . . . SuperAnalyst!

As a SuperAnalyst, he is a special person. His job is to divine the future. He is trained to evaluate all that he hears and reads. He studies his industries exhaustively, inspects the firms' plants and operations, asks penetrating questions of the companies' officers, and talks with their customers and suppliers. He plays golf on weekends with company presidents and flies down to Washington to check the political weather. But the supreme accolade is that SuperAnalyst, once the humble statistician, is now a bona fide *chartered financial analyst!*

## THE MYSTIQUE OF SUPERANALYST

Some of Wall Street's portfolio managers actually invest on the basis of charts and various technical schemes described in the last chapter. But even on Wall Street, technicians are considered a rather strange cult, and little faith is put in their recommendations. Thus the preceding studies casting doubt on the efficacy of technical analysis would not be considered surprising by most professionals. The really important question is whether fundamental analysis is any good. For most professional investment managers rely on an army of highly paid security analysts for their basic information—and SuperAnalyst is a fundamentalist.

Two extreme views have been taken in appraising the effectiveness of SuperAnalyst. One popularly held view regards him as almost omnipotent. Together with other SuperAnalysts he is known as They.

*They are the people who move stocks. They get the information first, maybe They even create the information; and They are about to put the stock up or down. They are mysterious, anonymous, powerful, and They know everything. Nothing fazes Them. They are the powers of the marketplace.*

"Adam Smith," who wrote that in *The Money Game*, goes on to suggest that professional portfolio managers and their teams of Super-Analysts are becoming more powerful and more skilled all the time. The individual has scarcely a chance against them.

An opposite-extreme view is taken by much of the academic community. Some academicians have gone so far as to suggest that a blindfolded monkey throwing darts at the *Wall Street Journal* could select stocks with as much success as SuperAnalyst. They have argued that fund managers and their SuperAnalysts can do no better at picking stocks than a rank amateur. Many have concluded that the value of professional investment advice is nil.

My own view of the matter is somewhat less extreme than that taken by many of my academic colleagues. Nevertheless, an understanding of the large body of research on these questions is essential for any intelligent investor. This chapter will recount the major battle in an ongoing war between academics and market professionals that has shaken Wall Street to its bedrock. Current field reports have the academics claiming victory and the professionals screaming "Foul."

## CAN SECURITY ANALYSTS SEE INTO THE FUTURE?

Forecasting future earnings is the security analysts' *raison d'être*. As a top Wall Street professional put it in his fraternity magazine, *The Institutional Investor*: "Expectation of future earnings is still the most important single factor affecting stock prices." As we have seen, growth (in earnings and therefore in the ability to pay dividends) is the key element needed to estimate a stock's firm foundation of value. The analyst who can make accurate forecasts of the future will be richly rewarded. "If he is wrong," *The Institutional Investor* puts it, "a stock can act precipitously, as has been demonstrated time and time again. Earnings are the name of the game and always will be."

To predict future directions, analysts generally start by looking at past wanderings. "A proven score of past performance in earnings growth is," one analyst told me recently, "a most reliable indicator of future earnings growth." If management is really skillful, there is no reason to think it will lose its Midas touch in the future. If the same adroit management team remains at the helm, the course of future earnings growth should continue as it has in the past, or so the argument goes.

Such thinking represents SuperAnalyst's first mistake, according to the academic world. Calculations of past earnings growth are no help in predicting future growth. If you knew the growth rates of all companies over, say, the 1950–60 period, this would not have helped you at all in predicting what growth they would achieve in the 1960–70 period. And knowing the fast growers of the sixties has not helped analysts find the fast growers of the early seventies. This startling result was first reported by British researchers for companies in the United Kingdom in an article charmingly titled "Higgledy Piggledy Growth." Learned academicians at Princeton and Harvard applied the British study to U.S. companies—and, surprise, the same was true here!

"IBM," the cry immediately went up. "Remember IBM." I do remember IBM: a steady high grower for decades. It is an exception (though for how much longer is open to question). I also remember Litton Industries and dozens of other firms that chalked up consistent large growth rates until the roof fell in. I hope you remember *not* the exception but rather the rule: there is no reliable pattern that can be discerned from past records to aid the analyst in predicting future growth.

A good SuperAnalyst will argue, however, that there's much more to predicting than just the past record. Rather than measure every factor that goes into the actual forecasting process, those of us at Princeton's Financial Research Center decided to concentrate on the end result: the prediction itself.

Donning our cloak of academic detachment, we wrote to nineteen major Wall Street firms engaged in fundamental analysis. The nineteen firms, which asked to remain anonymous, included some of the major brokerage firms, mutual fund management companies, investment advisory firms, and banks engaged in trust management. They are among the most respected names in the investment business.

We requested—and received—past earnings predictions on how these firms felt earnings for specific companies would behave over both a one-year and a five-year period. These estimates, made at several different times, were then compared with actual results to see how well the analysts forecast short-run and long-run earnings changes. Rude as it may seem, we wound up defrocking SuperAnalyst.

Bluntly stated, the careful estimates of security analysts (based on industry studies, plant visits, etc.) do little, if any, better than those that would be obtained by simple extrapolation of past trends, which we have already seen are no help at all. Indeed, when compared with actual earnings growth rates, the five-year estimates of security analysts were actually worse than the predictions from several naïve forecasting models.

For example, one placebo with which the analysts' estimates were compared was the assumption that every company in the economy would enjoy a growth in earnings of about 4 percent over the next year (approximately the long-run rate of growth of the national income). It turned out that if you used this native forecasting model you would make smaller errors in forecasting long-run earnings growth than by using the professional forecasts of the analysts.

Our method of determining the efficacy of the security analyst's diagnoses of his companies is exactly the same as was used before in evaluating the technicians' medicine. We compared the results obtained by following the experts with the results from some naïve mechanism involving no expertise at all. Sometimes these naïve predictors work very well. For example, if you want to forecast the weather tomorrow you will do a pretty good job by predicting that it will be exactly the same as today. It turns out that while this system misses every one of the turning points in the weather, for most days it is quite reliable. How many weather forecasters do you suppose do any better?

When confronted with the poor record of their five-year growth estimates, the security analysts honestly, if sheepishly, admitted that five years ahead is really too far in advance to make reliable projections. They protested that while long-term projections are admittedly important, they really ought to be judged on their ability to project earnings changes one year ahead.

Believe it or not, it turned out that their one-year forecasts were even worse than their five-year projections. It was actually harder for them to forecast one year ahead than to estimate long-run changes.

The analysts gamely fought back. They complained it was unfair to judge their performance on a wide cross section of industries, since earnings for electronics firms and various "cyclical" companies are notoriously hard to forecast. "Try us on utilities," one analyst confidently asserted. So we tried it, and They didn't like it. Even the forecasts for the stable utilities were far off the mark. Those the analysts confidently touted as high growers turned out to perform much the same as the utilities for which only low or moderate growth was pre-dicted. This led to the second major finding of our study: There is not one industry that is easy to predict.

Moreover, no analysts proved consistently superior to the others. Of course, in each year some analysts did much better than average, but there was no consistency in their pattern of performance. Analysts who did better than average one year were no more likely than the others to make superior forecasts in the next year.

Amidst all these accusations and counterassertions, there is a deadly serious message. It is this: Security analysts have enormous difficulty in performing their basic function of forecasting earnings prospects for the companies they follow. Investors who put blind faith in such forecasts in making their investment selections are in for some rude disappointments.

## WHY THE CRYSTAL BALL IS CLOUDED

It is always somewhat disturbing to learn that a group of highly trained and well-paid professionals may not be terribly skillful at their calling. Unfortunately, this is hardly unusual. Similar types of findings could be made for most groups of professionals. There is, for example, a classic example in medicine. At a time when tonsillectomies were very fashionable, the American Child Health Association surveyed a group of 1,000 children, eleven years of age, from the public schools of New York City, and found that 611 of these had had their tonsils removed. The remaining 389 were then examined by a group of physicians, who selected 174 of these for tonsillectomy and declared the rest had no tonsil problem. The remaining 215 were reexamined by another group of doctors, who recommended 99 of these for tonsillectomy. When the 116 "healthy" children were examined a third time, a similar percentage were told their tonsils had to be removed. After three examinations, only 65 children remained who had not been recommended for tonsillectomy. These remaining children were not examined further because the supply of examining physicians ran out.

Numerous other studies have shown similar results. Radiologists have failed to recognize the presence of lung disease in about 30 percent of the X-ray plates they read, despite the clear presence of the disease on the X-ray film. A recent experiment proved that professional staffs in psychiatric hospitals could not tell the sane from the insane. The point is that we should not take for granted the reliability and accuracy of any judge, no matter how expert. When one considers the low reliability of so many kinds of judgments, it does not seem too surprising that security analysts, with their particularly difficult forecasting job, should be no exception.

There are, I believe, four factors that help explain why security analysts have such difficulty in perceiving the future. These are: (1) the influence of random events; (2) the creation of dubious reported earnings through "creative" accounting procedures; (3) the basic incompetence of many of the analysts themselves; and (4) the loss of the best analysts to the sales desk or to portfolio management. Each factor deserves some discussion.

### 1. The Influence of Random Events

A company is not an entity unto itself. Many of the most important changes that affect the basic prospects for corporate earnings are essentially random, that is, unpredictable.

Take the utility industry, to which I referred earlier. Presumably it is one of the most stable and dependable groups of companies. During the early 1960s almost every utility analyst expected Florida Power and Light to be the fastest-growing utility. The analysts saw a continued high population growth, increased demands for electric power among existing customers, and a favorable regulatory climate.

Everything turned out exactly as forecast except for one small detail. The favorable Florida regulatory climate turned distinctly unfavorable as the sixties progressed. The Florida Public Utilities Commission ordered Florida Power and Light to make several substantial rate cuts and the utility was not able to translate the rapid growth in demand for electric power into higher profits. As a result, the company closed the decade with a mediocre growth record, far below the ebullient forecasts.

U.S. government budgetary and contract decisions can have enormous implications for the fortunes of individual companies. So can the incapacitation of key members of management, the discovery of a major new product, the finding of defects in a current product, natural disasters such as floods and hurricanes, etc. The stories of unpredictable events affecting earnings are endless.

### 2. The Creation of Dubious Reported Earnings through "Creative" Accounting Procedures

A firm's income statement may be likened to a bikini bathing suit—what it reveals is interesting but what it conceals is vital. National Student Marketing led the beauty parade in this regard. Andrew Tobias describes it all in *The Funny Money Game*.

In its fiscal 1969 report, National Student Marketing made generous use of terms such as "deferred new product development and start-up costs." These were moneys actually spent during 1969 but not charged against earnings in that year. "Unamortized costs of prepared sales programs" carried the ploy even further. These were advertising expenses that were not charged against earnings on the flimsy excuse that they would produce sales in the future. Subsidiary losses were easily handled: the companies were simply sold, removing their unfavorable results from the consolidated accounting statement. Actually it wasn't quite that simple, because the sales were consummated after the close of the fiscal year—but the accountants had no difficulty in arranging for the sale retroactively.

Since expenses were uncounted, why not count unearnings? No sooner said than done. These were duly noted in the sales column as unbilled receivables, on the justification that the actual billing of the sales could be expected to materialize in the future. Finally, came "the $3,754,103 footnote." Almost $4 million was added to net income in the form of earnings from companies whose acquisitions were "agreed to in principal and closed subsequent" to the end of fiscal 1969.

It turned out that even accepting the rest of the creative accounting, if you didn't count the earnings of companies that were not legally part of National Student Marketing in 1969, the company barely broke even. Of course, the imprimatur of a prestigious accounting firm was affixed to the bottom of a statement assuring the public that the accounts were prepared in accordance with "generally accepted accounting principles."*

The above is admittedly an extreme example, but the general problem is not uncommon. Seeming miracles can be accomplished

---

* In 1972 the Securities and Exchange Commission charged National Student Marketing Corp., its auditors, two law firms, and fifteen individuals with violations of federal securities laws. Included in the SEC suit was a charge that the company had issued "materially false and misleading" financial statements.

with depreciation; the peculiarities of conglomerate accounting; the franchise accounting game; and the special features of the reports of land-sales companies, computer leasing companies, and insurance companies. It is small wonder that security analysts have trouble estimating reported future earnings.

### 3. The Basic Incompetence of Many of the Analysts Themselves

The overall performance of analysts in many respects reflects the limit of their abilities. Their record with regard to STP Corporation is certainly a good example.

In early 1971, Andy Granatelli's STP was the darling of the Wall Street fraternity. Report after report indicated why it was likely to enjoy a large, long-term growth rate. Analysts pointed to its consistent pattern of growth over ten years. On the argument that the future would be more of the same, and that STP could continue to create its destiny through its marvelously successful advertising campaign, the Wall Street fraternity gave STP an estimated 20 percent growth rate for earnings in future years. As STP's stock price rose, analysts recommended the shares with greater and greater enthusiasm. Needless to say, but said nevertheless, STP management actively encouraged this enthusiasm.

Few analysts bothered to ask about the company's major product, STP oil treatment, which apparently accounted for three-quarters of the firm's revenues and earnings. What did the product really do? Could one really believe that STP helped cars start faster in winter and made engines run longer, quieter, and cooler in summer?

Admittedly, some analysts had a queasy feeling, but this was carefully reasoned away. For example, in the May 17 issue of the *Wall Street Transcript*, one analyst was quoted as saying: "The risk is that it is difficult to prove what exactly the product accomplishes, and people fear that the FTC might attack the company on an efficacy basis. We feel there is a very low probability of that happening and in the meantime consumers think the product works and that's the important thing. It is sort of a 'cosmetic company' for the car." If ever there was a castle in the air, STP certainly qualified.

While the above analyst was being quoted, *Consumer Reports* was completing its report on STP. This was published in July 1971 and stated that STP was a worthless oil thickener, not a panacea that would make ailing engines healthy again. Indeed, the consumer magazine reported that "STP can change the viscosity of a new car's oil to a considerably thicker grade than certain auto manufacturers recommend." The magazine went on to say that the major auto manufacturers positively discouraged the practice of using such additives, and suggested that STP might modify the properties of a car's engine oil so much that the new-car warranty terms might be affected.

The stock fell abruptly and the company's consistent record of past earnings growth came to an untimely end. As one analyst confided after the debacle, "I guess we just didn't ask the right questions."

To be perfectly blunt, many security analysts are not particularly perceptive, critical, or competent. I learned this early in the game as a young Wall Street trainee. In attempting to learn the techniques of the pros, I tried to duplicate some analytic work done by a metals specialist named Louie. Louie had figured that for each 1¢ increase in the price of copper, the earnings for a particular copper producer would increase by $1 per share. Since he expected a 3¢ increase in the price of copper, he reasoned that this particular stock was "an unusually attractive purchase candidate."

In redoing the calculation, I found that Louie had misplaced a decimal point. A penny increase in the price of copper would increase earnings by 10¢, not by $1. When I pointed this out to Louie (feeling sure he would want to put out a correction immediately) he simply shrugged his shoulders and declared, "Well, the recommendation sounds more convincing if we leave the report as is." Attention to detail was clearly not the forte of this particular analyst. From then on I referred to him as Sloppy Louie (not to denigrate the excellent fish restaurant of the same name near the New York financial district).

To balance this inattention to detail and careful work, we have those who glory in it. Take Railroad Roger, for example. Roger will accurately recount every conceivable statistic on track miles and freight carloadings for hours on end. But Roger does not have the faintest clue what the rails will earn next year, or which should be favored for purchase. Oil Analyst Doyle performs in a similar manner. His knowledge concerning refinery capacity and allowables in Texas is encyclopedic, but he lacks the critical acumen to translate this into judgments useful for investment decision-making.

Many analysts, however, emulate Louie. Generally too lazy to make their own earnings projections, they prefer to copy the forecasts of other analysts or to swallow the ones released by corporate managements without even chewing. Then it's very easy to know whom to blame if something goes wrong. "That ***!!! treasurer gave me the wrong dope." And it's much easier to be wrong when your professional colleagues had all agreed with you. As Keynes put it, "Worldly wisdom teaches that it is better for reputation to fail conventionally than to succeed unconventionally."

Corporate management goes out of its way to ease the forecasting task of the analyst. Let me give you a personal example: A two-day field trip was arranged by a major corporation to brief a whole set of Wall Street security analysts on its operations and future programs.

We were picked up in the morning by the company's private plane for visits and briefings at three of the company's plants. In the evening we were given first-class accommodations and royally wined and dined. After two more plant visits the next day, we had a briefing, replete with slide show, indicating a "most conservative five-year fore-cast" of robustly growing earnings.

At each stop we were showered with gifts—and not only the usual souvenir mock-ups of the company's major products. We also received a variety of desk accessories for the office, a pen and pencil set, ciga-rette lighter, tie bar, cuff links, and a tasteful piece of jewelry to "take home to the wife or mistress, as the case may be." Throughout each day liquor and wine flowed in abundance. As one bleary-eyed analyst confided at the end of the trip, "It's very hard not to have a warm feeling for this company."

I do not mean to imply that most Wall Street analysts typically receive payola for touting particular stocks. Indeed, from my own experience, I would judge that the standards of ethics in Wall Street are very high. Sure, there are crooks; but I would guess far fewer than in other professions.

I do imply that the *average* analyst is just that—a well-paid and usu-ally highly intelligent person who has an extraordinarily difficult job and does it in a rather mediocre fashion. Analysts are often misguided, sometimes sloppy, perhaps self-important, and at times susceptible to the same pressures as other people. In short, they are really very human beings.

## 4. The Loss of the Best Analysts to the Sales Desk or to Portfolio Management

My fourth argument against the profession is a paradoxical one: many of the best security analysts are not paid to analyze securities. They are either very high-powered institutional salesmen; efficient new-business getters, successful in bringing new underwriting business to their firms; or get promoted to be prestigious portfolio managers.

Brokerage houses that pride themselves on their research prowess project an aura of respectability by sending a security analyst to chaperone the regular salesman on a call to a financial institution. Institutional investors like to hear about a new investment idea right from the horse's mouth, and so the regular salesman usually sits back and lets the analyst do the talking. Thus most of the articulate analysts find their time is spent with institutional clients, not with financial reports and corporate treasurers. They also find that their monetary rewards are heavily dependent upon their ability to bring commission business to the firm.

Another magnet away from the study of stocks is the ability of some analysts to attract to their firm profitable underwriting clients, that is, companies who need to borrow money or sell new common stock to raise funds for expansion. The analyst on a field trip who is looking for new, small, expanding companies as potential investment recommendations may put a great deal of effort into selling his firm's investment banking services. I have seen many a security analyst make his reputation by his ability to attract such clients to the firm. He may not come up with good earnings forecasts or select the right stocks for investment, but he brings the bacon home to his firm and that is the name of the game.

Finally, both the compensation and prestige structures within the securities industry induce many analysts away from research work into portfolio management. It's far more exciting and remunerative to "run money" in the line position of portfolio manager than only to advise in the staff position of security analyst. Small wonder that many of the best-respected security analysts do not remain long in their jobs.

## DO SECURITY ANALYSTS PICK WINNERS? THE PERFORMANCE OF THE MUTUAL FUNDS

I can almost hear the chorus in the background as I write these words. It goes something like this: The real test of the analyst lies in the performance of the stocks he recommends. Maybe Sloppy Louie, the copper analyst, did mess up his earnings forecast with a misplaced decimal point; but if the stocks he recommended made money for his clients, his lack of attention to detail can surely be forgiven. "Analyze investment performance," the chorus is saying, "not earnings forecasts."

Fortunately, the records of one group of professionals the mutual funds—are publicly available. Better still for my argument, many of the men at the funds are the embodiment of the SuperAnalyst concept—they are the best and highest-paid analysts and portfolio managers in the business. They stand at the pinnacle of the investment profession.

"They" allegedly are the first to learn and act on any new fundamental information that becomes available. By their own admission "they" can clearly make above-average returns. As one investment manager recently put it: "It will take many years before the general level of competence rises enough to overshadow the startling advantage of today's aggressive investment manager." "Adam Smith" echoes a similar statement:

*All the players in the Game are getting rapidly more professional . . . The true professionals in the Game—the professional portfolio managers— grow more skilled all the time. They are human and they make mistakes, but if you have your money managed by a truly alert mutual fund or even by one of the better banks, you will have a better job done for you than probably at any time in the past.*

Statements like these are just too tempting to the lofty-minded men in the academic world. Given the wealth of available data, the time available to conduct such research, and the overwhelming desire to prove academic superiority in such matters, it was only natural that academia would zero in on the performance of SuperAnalyst.

### Mutual Funds Versus Randomly Selected Portfolios

Again the evidence from several studies, including a series conducted at the Wharton School of Finance, is remarkably uniform. Investors have done no better with the average mutual fund than they could have done by purchasing and holding an unmanaged broad stock index. In other words, over long periods of time mutual fund portfolios have not outperformed randomly selected groups of stocks.

When Nobel Prize-winning economist and M.I.T. professor Paul Samuelson testified to this effect before the powerful Senate Banking and Currency Committee, he aroused the curiosity of Senator Thomas McIntyre of New Hampshire, who decided to conduct a test. The senator tacked a listing of all stocks traded on the New York Stock Exchange to a dart board and proceeded to select his random portfolio by casually lofting darts in the direction of the board.

The result: his random portfolio had a better overall performance over a ten-year period than even the average of funds whose objective was maximum long-term capital growth.

The cost: 29½¢ per year. This included the dart board, dart, thumbtacks, newspaper, and brokerage fees, which were zero after the first year. The senator did admit to one problem, however. Being a fairly poor shot, he often missed the board completely and it took some time to select his portfolio.

### The Inconsistency of Performance

Many readers will say, politely and otherwise, that the senator's record was a fluke. It certainly doesn't jibe with the yearly performance rankings of mutual funds that one sees listed in financial magazines. These *always* show a substantial number of funds beating the averages each year—and some by significant amounts. What these rankings do not always make clear, however, is that occasionally superior performance is commonplace. Only consistency of performance can be accepted as evidence that SuperAnalyst clearly possesses superior powers. And the evidence points to the reverse—there seems to be no relationship between good performance in one period and superior returns in the next.

It turns out that the mutual fund portfolio managers as a group have as many bad years—that is, worse than average—as good years. And a mutual fund that has had one better-than-average year has only a 50 percent chance of repeating that record the next year. This is just what you would expect if mutual fund investing were a random process.

In compiling yearly rankings for thirty-nine funds over a ten-year period, Eugene Fama of the University of Chicago has nicely illustrated how inconsistent fund performance can actually be. The table below shows the yearly rankings for three funds over a period of ten years. These funds have gone back and forth from the top of the ranking (1) right to the bottom (39).

FUNDS AND THEIR RANKINGS

| Year | Keystone S-4 | Chemical Fund | International Resources |
|---|---|---|---|
| 1 | 29 | 1 | 10 |
| 2 | 1 | 39 | 37 |
| 3 | 38 | 14 | 39 |
| 4 | 5 | 27 | 22 |
| 5 | 3 (tied) | 3 (tied) | 35 |
| 6 | 8 | 33 | 1 |
| 7 | 35 | 1 | 37 |
| 8 | 1 | 27 | 39 |
| 9 | 1 (tied) | 4 | 1 (tied) |
| 10 | 36 | 23 | 11 |

Just as past earnings growth cannot predict future earnings, neither can past fund performance predict future results. Fund managements are also subject to random events—they may grow fat, become lazy, or break up. An investment approach that works very well for one period can easily turn sour the next. One is tempted to conclude that a very important factor in determining poll ranking is our old friend Lady Luck.

### Performance and Portfolio Turnover, Loading Fees, and Size

Another way to study the performance of SuperAnalyst is to examine the value of the buy and sell decisions made by portfolio managers directly. This is done by comparing the performance of each manager's actual portfolio with what he would have achieved if he had simply held his beginning-of-period portfolio throughout the time studied. Evidence indicates that portfolio managers succeeded in outperforming this buy-and-hold strategy only about 50 percent of the time. Thus their trades seem not to have improved their portfolio performance.

Other studies have asked whether fund managers have been able to predict market trends—buying at the bottom and selling off at the peak of speculative enthusiasm, thus both benefiting their shareholders and stabilizing the market. Again the mutual funds show no special abilities. They are just as likely to be buying at the top and selling on the way down. Bradbury K. Thurlow, a well-known professional, summed it up by noting, "The funds behaved like the worst of small investors, showing speculative exuberance at the top, dire forebodings at the bottom, and steadfast timidity during the recovery."

And how about that old maxim that you pay for what you get? Don't look for it in this area of Wall Street. There seems to be no relationship between performance and the fees paid to portfolio managers or the sales charge collected by many popular mutual funds. Load and no-load funds do just about the same. Nor is there a consistent relationship between size or portfolio turnover and average performance. The only dependable relationship that exists in explaining mutual fund performance is the tendency for funds assuming greater risks to earn, on average, a larger long-run rate of return.

## RISK HAS ITS REWARD

One of the best-documented propositions in the field of investment is that on average investors receive higher rates of return for bearing greater risk. Risk is considered to be the relative volatility of returns. An investment promising a stable and dependable 9 percent each year is less risky than (and preferable to) one that may return 36 percent in a year when the market is strong and lose 18 percent in a year when the market falls. At least this seems to be the view of the majority of investors. Return in this context is composed of both dividends and any appreciation (or depreciation) in the market value of the shares held.

I know that there are some mutual fund salesmen who will tell you not to worry about what happens in down markets because the major trend is up. The trouble is that every now and then stock markets have a habit of suffering fairly sharp setbacks and may not recover their former highs for a considerable period of time. And often investors are forced to sell during such a bear market because they need money and can't get it from the bank. It may be true that eventually their stocks will recover again, but that will be small consolation to them because other investors will be holding them.

Thus few, if any, investors can fail to be concerned with the downside risk of their investments. And because downside risk is so universally distasteful, investors who hold portfolios of riskier shares whose price swings are wider must be and actually are compensated with a somewhat higher long-run return.

The differences that exist in mutual fund returns can be explained almost entirely by differences in the risk they have taken. The following chart illustrates this relationship over the 1957–70 period for a representative group of mutual funds.

Risk is measured by the relative sensitivity of the fund's performance to swings in the general market. A volatility number of 1.2 suggests that the fund was 1.2 times as volatile as the market index—it tended to fluctuate about 20 percent more than the market. This relative volatility index also goes by the name "beta." A fund that tends to do

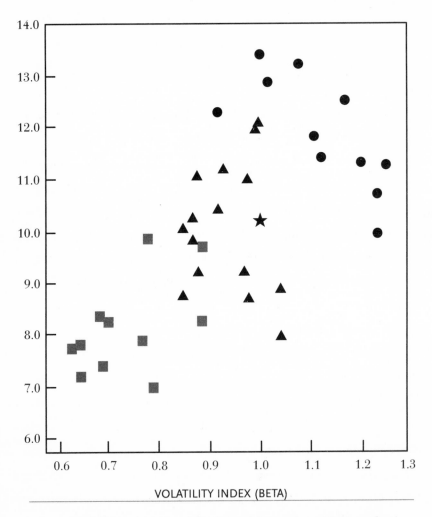

VOLATILITY INDEX (BETA)

[square] balanced income fund [triangle] growth and income fund
[circle] growth fund [star] standard and poor's 500-stock index

Performance of Selected Mutual Funds: 1957–1972

very well when the market goes up but falls out of bed when the market falters gets a high risk rating. A fund with more stable returns from year to year gets a low risk rating. The chart also shows the rate of return for the market as measured by the Standard & Poor's (S&P) 500 Stock Index, which by definition gets a volatility rating of one.

The chart shows that by and large the riskiest funds—the growth-oriented ones—have had the largest average return. But these are also the funds whose annual returns were most volatile and that fell most sharply when the market turned sour. The safest funds—those balanced with high-quality bonds—tended to have the lowest but most stable returns. To be sure, over the whole period (including up and down markets) the growth funds outdistanced their safer counterparts and even tended to do better than a broad stock-market average. But this was not a matter of skill—added risk was the price of that performance. Randomly selected portfolios of riskier stocks also tended to outdistance the market. Indeed, you could have bought the stocks making up the market average (say the Dow-Jones thirty industrials) on margin (that is, borrowing some of the funds needed to pay for the purchase) and increased both your return and your risk.

This last point is sufficiently important and so little understood—even by some market professionals—that I would like to provide an example of how this can be accomplished. Suppose that, on *average*, the return in the market—counting both dividends and capital gains—is somewhere around 9 percent per year. (A massive computer study financed by the Merrill Foundation and done at the University of Chicago suggests this is not far from the mark over reasonably long time periods.) Now suppose you have $1,000 to invest. This means that in a *typical* year you would make about 9 percent and would end up with $1,090.

But what if you wanted a bit more action for your $1,000? Just talk to your friendly broker and borrow an extra $1,000 at, say, 7 percent. (This is called buying on margin.) Now for your $1,000 investment (this is all you put up) you can buy $2,000 worth of stock; and in a typical year a 9 percent return will make your total portfolio grow to $2,180. At the end of this year you repay your broker the $1,070 you owe him (the borrowed $1,000 plus $70 interest) and you will have $1,110 ($2,180 minus $1,070). Through the magic of leverage you were able to increase the return on your $1,000 investment from 9 percent to 11 percent.

In general, leverage will tend to give you a larger average return. You will always increase your return if your borrowing rate is lower than what you earn on your investment. But if you get out your pencil and paper, you'll quickly see that in a year when the market doesn't do well you really can take a bath with your leveraged (and highly risky) investment stance. Leverage is a two-edged sword, which is exactly the point of the story. You were able to get a larger average return only by taking on more risk. There ain't no such thing as a free lunch. And don't let the mutual funds fool you. As the chart shows very clearly, the funds with the largest average returns also took on the most risk. If you held one of the supposedly better-performing but riskier funds, don't ascribe this to any genius on the fund manager's part. Your extra return was simply a just reward due you for bearing extra risk.

## CAN'T EVEN SOME OF THE ANALYSTS PICK SOME OF THE WINNERS?

The preceding paragraphs constitute rank heresy as far as Wall Street is concerned. My allegation that mutual funds generally do about the same as the market averages—with perhaps a bit of extra return for the particularly risky ones—flies in the face of its conventional (and convenient) wisdom. Is there not a group of "performance-oriented" funds whose whole *raison d'être* is the achievement of above-average returns and which, by their own admission, have clearly achieved their goals? All right, let's now see if these are exceptions to the generally mediocre performance I reported for the industry at large.

### Performance Investing

Performance investing was a product of the 1960s and became especially prominent during the 1967–68 strong bull market. This was the period when money managers changed their image. The old Scrooge-type image of the fiduciary counting his golden sovereigns with meticulous care and probity was out. Capital preservation gave way to capital productivity. The key word was "performance" and the financial press reported at frequent intervals the latest rank-ordered performance results for the funds, just like the daily horse-race results.

The fund managers who turned in the best results for the period were written up like sports celebrities in both the popular and professional organs. New public money no longer flowed to the old-line names in the fund game—only the new breed of money managers really did well in attracting new investments.

The star system had come to Wall Street. Everyone wanted to hitch his wagon to a SuperAnalyst—and Wall Street listened and brought forth well over a hundred new funds. Their names were reminiscent of the days of the South Sea Bubble: Explorer, Vanguard, Viking, Magellan, Polaris, and even New Era. But as one fund manager put it to a new salesman, "We aren't selling mutual funds, we're selling dreams," and those are the names on which dreams are dreamed. For a while it all worked. When the performance polls were published in 1967 and 1968, the go-gos with their youthful gunslingers as managers were right at the top of the pack, outgunning all the competition by a wide margin.

### Some Tricks of the Trade

How did the performance funds do it? By doing what comes naturally, of course. When the market is going up and you hold a portfolio of very risky (defined as very volatile) stocks, it follows that your portfolio can be expected to go up substantially more than the market. When the bulls are in command, risk can easily be forgotten. Thus it was that the performance-fund manager was honored and even believed in his own glory. After all, it was far easier to persuade himself that the big gains were the result of financial acumen than to admit they were the normal concomitant of holding volatile stocks in a rising market.

Self-delusion is a very human failing, but some fund managers indulged in practices that could not be so easily pardoned. These were the use of so-called "letter stock" and the buying up of large positions in very small and thinly capitalized companies. Such devices were among the unhealthiest developments of the performance era.

"Letter" or "restricted" stock is stock whose sale is subject to several restrictions, generally because it has not been registered with the Securities and Exchange Commission. This means that there is no prospectus to tell about the company's business, past record, etc. While unregistered stock may not be sold publicly, it may be sold privately. The buyer is required to sign an "investment letter" pledging that he bought the stock for investment purposes and indicating that he anticipates hanging onto the shares for a considerable period of time. Hence the name letter stock.

Companies often sold letter stock to large funds because it was a way of raising money quickly and of avoiding certain disclosures required by the SEC. The funds bought such stock at discounts of 20 percent to 50 percent. Now watch carefully for the trick. Suppose that a fund buys some letter stock at $50 per share, while the market price is $100. When the fund makes its next report, it might write the value of the stock to $75. Result: instant performance. On the next report, performance can be maintained simply by writing up the value even higher. Who cares if the stock is not readily marketable, as long as it boosts performance? Very few cared in the late 1960s.

Another performance trick involved the purchase of substantial blocks in companies with relatively few shares outstanding. The market for many of these issues was so thin (so few shares were available for trading) that a fund willing to take a big position could make the price almost anything it wished. It may be that in the long run these companies do, in fact, produce a higher return than the blue chips. (They should, because they are riskier.) But the funds interested in immediate performance were more concerned with what happened to the price in the short run when the next performance poll would be published. The better the record, the easier it was to sell new shares in the fund, and the more money would be available to buy up other small companies. Small wonder that many funds playing this game opened themselves to charges of market manipulation.

No one seemed to worry that these blocks of stock were not easily salable. But what would happen if the fund had to sell some of these shares—perhaps to meet redemptions during less favorable times? I am reminded of the classic story of the broker who suggested that his client, Sam, invest in some shares of a thinly capitalized company selling at fifty cents a share. Sam bought up several hundred shares, after which his friendly broker informed him that the price was now $1.00. "Excellent," Sam exclaimed, "buy more." Dutifully the broker executed his order and reported back that the price was now $1.50. "Fine," exclaimed our performance investor, "sell all my holdings." "Sure, Sam," the broker replied quizzically, "but to whom?"

## RISK HAS ITS PENALTY

The game ended unceremoniously with the bear market that commenced in 1969 and continued until 1971. The go-go funds suddenly went into reverse. It was fly now and pay later, for the performance funds with their portfolios of volatile stocks were no exception to the financial law of gravity. They went down just as sharply as they had gone up. The new breed of SuperAnalysts got clobbered in the 1969–71 period, as the fall of the performance funds was substantially sharper than for the averages as a whole. Perhaps the most dramatic way of describing the debacle is with the aid of the following table showing the rankings of the top funds in 1968 and their disastrous performance in the ensuing years. Even though most of the stock averages had recovered to their 1968 level by the end of 1972, most of the performance funds failed to reach their 1968 highs.

The Mates Fund led the pack in 1968, with a gain of 153.48 percent. (What performance!) Its net value, however, had to be calculated as of the close of business on December 19. On December 20, Mates temporarily stopped redeeming its shares and calculating their value. Twenty percent of Mates Fund was invested in thinly capitalized Omega Securities when the SEC announced the untimely suspension of trading in Omega (while it investigated for hanky-panky).

At the end of 1972, the Mates Fund sold at less than one-quarter of its 1968 value. Beware the mutual fund salesman who tries to build up your dreams by selling you the fund with the best recent performance! So many dreams have turned into nightmares that performance investing is now a dirty word on Wall Street.

## SOME RESULTS OF THE PERFORMANCE DERBY

| 1968 Rank | Fund | 1969 Rank** | 1970 Rank** | 1971 Rank** | 1972 Rank** | 1968 Net Asset Value* Per Share | 1972 Net Asset Value Per Share |
|---|---|---|---|---|---|---|---|
| 1 | Mates Investment Fund | 312 | 424 | 512 | 465 | 15.51 | 3.54 |
| 2 | Neuwirth Fund | 263 | 360 | 104 | 477 | 15.29 | 11.50 |
| 3 | Gibraltar Growth Fund (4) | 172 | 456 | 481 | | 17.27 | |
| 4 | Insurance Investors Fund (1) | 77 | 106 | 317 | 417 | 7.45 | 5.92 |
| 5 | Pennsylvania Mutual | 333 | 459 | 480 | 486 | 11.92 | 3.92 |
| 6 | Puerto Rican Investors Fund | 30 | 308 | 387 | 435 | 19.34 | 12.97 |
| 7 | Crown Western-Dallas | 283 | 438 | 207 | 244 | 13.86 | 8.10 |
| 8 | Franklin Dynatech Series | 342 | 363 | 112 | 120 | 14.47 | 10.83 |
| 9 | First Participating Fund (2) | 49 | 283 | 106 | 27 | 19.25 | 24.28 |
| 10 | Connecticut Western Mutual Fund (3) | 5 | 202 | | | 127.27 | |
| 11 | Enterprise Fund | 334 | 397 | 133 | 364 | 11.88 | 7.26 |
| 12 | Ivy Fund | 357 | 293 | 233 | 161 | 12.37 | 9.29 |
| 13 | Century Shares Trust | 120 | 55 | 62 | 62 | 13.09 | 16.31 |
| 14 | Mutual Shares Corporation | 284 | 272 | 152 | 452 | 22.18 | 16.51 |
| 15 | Putnam Equities Fund | 376 | 384 | 45 | 54 | 17.05 | 11.41 |
| 16 | Financial Industrial Income Fund | 244 | 222 | 277 | 231 | 8.40 | 6.44 |
| 17 | Consumers Investment (4) | 354 | | | | | |
| 18 | Columbia Growth Fund | 33 | 322 | 27 | 370 | 14.23 | 16.72 |
| 19 | Templeton Growth Fund | 1 | 241 | 163 | 1 | 4.00 | 8.95 |
| 20 | Schuster Fund | 129 | 231 | 253 | 425 | 12.29 | 11.32 |

(1) Insurance Investors Fund is now First Sierra Fund.

(2) First Participating Fund is now American General Growth Fund.

(3) Connecticut Western is now Channing Bond Fund, which is no longer surveyed by Lipper.

(4) No longer surveyed by Lipper.

* The net asset values for 1968 have been adjusted for all subsequent splits.
** Out of 381 funds surveyed in 1969; 463 in 1970; 526 in 1971; 537 in 1972.
Source: Arthur Lipper Corporation

## IS THERE ANYTHING GOOD TO BE SAID ABOUT PROFESSIONAL INVESTMENT MANAGEMENT?

Professionally managed mutual fund portfolios do not, on average, appear to perform any better than broad unmanaged indices of securities. While larger returns have been realized by investment funds specializing in riskier portfolios, the same is true of the returns from randomly selected portfolios of riskier stocks. It's true that a few funds have outperformed random portfolios with equivalent risk, but the number of funds with above-average records is no larger than might be attributed to chance.

In any activity in which large numbers of people are engaged, while the average is likely to predominate, the unexpected is bound to happen. The very small number of really good performers we find in the investment management business is not at all inconsistent with the laws of chance. Indeed, as I mentioned earlier, the fact that good past performance of a mutual fund is no help whatever in predicting future performance only serves to emphasize this point. The preceding table shows just how inconsistent fund performance can be.

Perhaps the laws of chance should be illustrated. Let's engage in a coin-tossing contest. Those who can consistently flip heads will be declared winners. The contest begins and 1,000 contestants flip coins. Just as would be expected by chance, 500 of them flip heads and these winners are allowed to advance to the second stage of the contest and flip again. As might be expected, 250 flip heads. Operating under the laws of chance, there will be 125 winners in the third round, 63 on the fourth, 31 on the fifth, 16 on the sixth, and 8 on the seventh.

By this time, crowds start to gather to witness the surprising ability of these expert coin-tossers. The winners are overwhelmed with adulation. They are celebrated as geniuses in the art of coin-tossing—

their biographies are written and people urgently seek their advice. After all, there were 1,000 contestants and only 8 could consistently flip heads. The game continues and there are even those who eventually flip heads nine and ten times in a row.* The point of this analogy is not to indicate that investment fund managers can or should make their decisions by flipping coins, but that the laws of chance do operate and they can explain some amazing success stories.

Some readers will complain that I am being unfair in using the performance of mutual funds to generalize about the quality of investment management. After all, mutual funds labor under some very severe handicaps. Many are so large that when they try to buy a position in a security the very activity of their purchase tends to move the price against them.

For example, I sit on the finance committee of a fund with assets of approximately $2½ billion. Whenever this fund tries to accumulate a position in a security it must anticipate that it may sometimes move the price of that security several points before its transaction is completed.

Some funds are also often forced to sell during market panics when redemptions are high. At such times the market is likely to be disorganized and large blocks of securities can be sold only at substantial discounts. Other readers may point out that mutual funds account for only about 20 percent of the stock holdings of institutional investors, and that it may not be fair to say their performance is typical of all professionals.

Academic researchers, curious souls that they are, have also

---

* If we had let the losers continue to play (as mutual fund managers do, even after a bad year) we would have found several more contestants who flipped eight or nine heads out of ten and were therefore regarded as expert tossers.

examined the performance of many other professional investors. The records of life insurance companies, property and casualty insurance companies, foundations, college endowments, state and local trust funds, personal trusts administered by banks, and individual discretionary accounts handled by investment advisors have all been studied, though not in nearly the same detail as mutual funds. This research suggests that there are no sizable differences in the investment performance of any of these professional investors or between the investment performance of these groups and that of the market as a whole. *No scientific evidence has yet been assembled to indicate that the investment performance of professionally managed portfolios as a group has been any better than that of randomly selected portfolios.*

Are there exceptions to this general rule? Of course there are. As I noted earlier, a few mutual funds have enjoyed outstanding long-run records. But many more had outstanding records through 1968.

The record of one major investment advisory service has, over a recent seven-year period, proved superior to random selection. But this service's longer-run record is only mediocre and it remains to be seen if it can beat the averages consistently in the future.

Another well-publicized success story concerns one of the major New York banks, which began a contest in early 1970, asking thirty-four brokerage firms to manage a fictitious $100 million common-stock portfolio. At the end of 1972 the average performance of the thirty-four contestants was considerably better than the Standard & Poor's index. Again, the time period is very short and the performance on paper should not be taken as a yardstick in the real world, where the attempt to purchase or sell substantial blocks of stock can have a large impact on the market price.

Isolated instances of success should not a SuperAnalyst make. As we examine more and more types of professional investors, we should expect more and more exceptions. So long as there are averages, some people will beat them. With large numbers of players in the money game, chance will—and does—explain some super performance records.

The very great publicity given occasional success in stock selection reminds me of the famous story of the doctor who claimed he had developed a cure for cancer in chickens. He proudly announced that in 33 percent of the cases tested remarkable improvement was noted. In another third of the cases, he admitted, there seemed to be no change in condition. He then rather sheepishly added, "And I'm afraid the third chicken ran away."

## THE BROAD FORM OF THE RANDOM-WALK THEORY

The academic world has rendered its judgment: Fundamental analysis is no more effective than technical analysis in beating the market. Security analysts may have difficulty perceiving the future, but we must readily concede that they are very good at interpreting whatever new information does become available and acting on it quickly. This is the fundamental problem preventing SuperAnalyst from beating the market. Information is disseminated too rapidly today, and it gets reflected almost immediately in market prices. By reacting so quickly, the analysts make it extremely difficult to realize a significant profit in the stock market on the basis of fundamental analysis.[*]

Professor Samuelson sums up the situation as follows:

---

[*] It might actually be very inconvenient for SuperAnalyst if it could be shown that he did make above-average returns. This would imply that some other group (presumably the public) was earning below-average returns. Think of the reformers who would press to restrict SuperAnalyst's activities so as to protect the public.

*If intelligent people are constantly shopping around for good value, selling those stocks they think will turn out to be overvalued and buying those they expect are now undervalued, the result of this action by intelligent investors will be to have existing stock prices already have discounted in them an allowance for their future prospects. Hence, to the passive investor, who does not himself search out for under- and overvalued situations, there will be presented a pattern of stock prices that makes one stock about as good or bad a buy as another. To that passive investor, chance alone would be as good a method of selection as anything else.*

This is the broad form of the random-walk theory. The narrow form of the theory said that technical analysis—looking at past stock prices—could not help investors. The broad form states that fundamental analysis is not helpful either. It says that all that is known concerning the expected growth of the company's earnings and dividends, all of the possible favorable and unfavorable developments affecting the company that might be studied by the fundamental analyst, are already reflected in the price of the company's stock. Thus throwing darts at the financial page will produce a portfolio that can be expected to do as well as any managed by professional security analysts. In a nutshell, the broad form of the random-walk theory states:

*Fundamental analysis of publicly available information cannot produce investment recommendations that will enable an investor consistently to outperform a buy-and-hold strategy in managing a portfolio.*

The random-walk theory does not, as some critics have proclaimed, state that stock prices move aimlessly and erratically and are insensitive to changes in fundamental information. On the contrary, the point of the random-walk theory is just the opposite: The market is so efficient—prices move so quickly when new information does arise—that no one can consistently buy or sell quickly enough to benefit. Indeed, the growing power and quickness of SuperAnalyst will help fulfill the random-walk theory by insuring that current prices reflect all known information. This theory believes that a random guess will enable you to predict the next market move with the same (or higher) degree of accuracy as the estimate provided through either technical or fundamental analysis. Needless to say, it is not popular in the brokerage houses.

The random-walk theory does recognize, however, that it is possible for insiders acting on the basis of information about an important mineral strike to make profits at the expense of public investors not privy to that information. Such things happened in the past with too much frequency. But Texas Gulf Sulphur situations, where insiders allegedly profited from news of mineral discoveries at the expense of the public, are now less likely to occur than in the past.

In recent years, the Securities Exchange Commission has taken an increasingly tough stand against anyone profiting from information not generally available to the public. The SEC has put the investment community on notice that corporate officials and anyone else acting on material nonpublic information do so at their own peril. More recently it has extended this warning to *any* investor acting on this information, even if he hears about it thirdhand—such as through his broker. It is small wonder that many a company president who thinks he has told a visiting security analyst some relevant piece of information he has not made available to others will immediately issue a public press release to rectify the situation.

Thus tightened rules on disclosure make time lags in the dissemi-
nation of new information much shorter than they may have been in
previous years. Of course, the more quickly information is disseminated to the public at large, the more closely the market may be
expected to conform to the random-walk model.

While the random-walk theory does recognize the potential disrup-
tiveness of inside information, it does not consider this to be of crucial
importance. Corporate insiders are so often wrong that it hardly seems
worth the legal risk involved to try to act on inside information. Many
professional investors would agree. Wall Street's legendary Armand
Erph was fond of citing a statement by Talleyrand that he had managed
to lose a fortune by never speculating except on inside information.
Bernard Baruch echoed this thought: "Given time, I believe that inside
information can break the Bank of England or the U.S. Treasury."

## A Personal Viewpoint

Just to show how truly contrary a former analyst turned academic can
be, I am now going to present my personal thoughts. But first, let's
briefly recap the diametrically opposed viewpoints. The view of many
of the managers themselves is that professionals have almost super-
natural powers—they are all-knowing, all-powerful, and can certainly
outperform all amateur and casual investors in managing money.
Much of the academic community believes that professionally managed investment portfolios cannot outperform randomly selected
portfolios of stocks with equivalent risk characteristics. Random
walkers claim that the stock market adjusts so quickly and perfectly to
new information that amateurs buying at current prices can do just as
well as the pros. Thus the value of professional investment advice is
nil—at least insofar as it concerns choosing a stock portfolio.

I walk a middle road. While I believe that investors must reconsider their faith in SuperAnalyst, I am not as ready as many of my academic colleagues to damn the entire field. I mentioned earlier that most of the evidence we have now concerns large funds, which operate under a variety of constraints. While it is true that there seems to be no difference in the performance of large and small funds, I still think it is necessary to round out the statistical picture with more evidence on many different kinds of investors.

I am also cautious because the random-walk theory rests on several fragile assumptions. The first is that there is perfect pricing in the market. As the quote from Paul Samuelson indicates, the random-walk theory holds that at any time stocks sell at the best estimates of their intrinsic values. Thus uninformed investors buying at today's structure of prices are really getting full value for their money, whatever securities they purchase.

The problem is that this line of reasoning is uncomfortably close to that used by proponents of the greater-fool theory. We have seen ample evidence that stocks sometimes do not sell on the basis of anyone's estimate of value (as hard as this is to measure) but are often swept up in waves of frenzy. To be sure, the market pros as a group do not seem to have the ability to recognize such periods of speculative excess or the independence and courage to take a contrary course. Professional managers were largely responsible for three major speculative waves of the 1960s and for more recent instances such as the Levitz furniture roller-coaster of 1972–73. But the existence of these broader influences on market prices at least raises the possibility that investors might not want to accept the current tableau of market prices as being the best reflection of intrinsic values.

There are other assumptions behind the random-walk theory that can also be questioned. News does not travel instantaneously, as the random walkers suggest, and I doubt that there will ever be a time in the future when all useful inside information is immediately disclosed to all. Moreover, the random-walk theory implies that no one possesses monopolistic power over the market and that stock recommendations based on unfounded beliefs do not lead to large buying.

Neither assumption is more than approximated in today's markets. Brokerage firms specializing in research services to institutions wield enormous power in the market and can direct tremendous money flows in and out of stocks. Many speculators (and indeed even fund managers) will rush to buy and sell a stock simply because they believe a large firm is about to recommend some action on it. In this environment it is quite possible that erroneous beliefs about a stock by some professionals can for a considerable time be self-fulfilling.

Finally, there is the enormous difficulty of translating known information about a stock into estimates of true value. We have seen that the major determinants of a stock's value concern the extent and duration of its growth path far into the future. Both the estimation of the growth path from known information and the translation of the growth path into a value estimate require art as much as science. In such an environment there is considerable scope for an individual to exercise superior intellect and judgment to turn in superior performance.

But while I believe in the possibility of superior professional investment performance, I must emphasize that the evidence we have thus far does not support the view that such competence in fact exists; and while I may be excommunicated from some academic sects because of my only lukewarm endorsement of the random walk, I make no effort to disguise my heresy in the financial church. It is clear that if there are exceptional financial managers they are very rare. This is a fact of life with which both individual and institutional investors will have to deal.

Proponents of the efficient market theory argue that no
one can consistently pick winning stocks because relevant information immediately shows up in share prices.
Superinvestor **Warren Buffett** tackled the theory in a
1984 talk he gave to celebrate the 50th anniversary of the
publication of *Security Analysis*, the textbook by David L.
Dodd and Buffett mentor Benjamin Graham.

# THE SUPERINVESTORS OF
# GRAHAM-AND-DODDSVILLE
by Warren E. Buffett

from *The Intelligent Investor* (1984)

I S THE GRAHAM and Dodd "look for values with a significant
margin of safety relative to prices" approach to security analysis
out of date? Many of the professors who write textbooks today say
yes. They argue that the stock market is efficient; that is, that stock
prices reflect everything that is known about a company's prospects and
about the state of the economy. There are no undervalued stocks, these
theorists argue, because there are smart security analysts who utilize all
available information to ensure unfailingly appropriate prices.
Investors who seem to beat the market year after year are just lucky. "If
prices fully reflect available information, this sort of investment adept-
ness is ruled out," writes one of today's textbook authors.

Well, maybe. But I want to present to you a group of investors who
have, year in and year out, beaten the Standard & Poor's 500 stock
index. The hypothesis that they do this by pure chance is at least
worth examining. Crucial to this examination is the fact that these
winners were all well known to me and pre-identified as superior

investors, the most recent identification occurring over fifteen years ago. Absent this condition—that is, if I had just recently searched among thousands of records to select a few names for you this morning—I would advise you to stop reading right here. I should add that all these records have been audited. And I should further add that I have known many of those who have invested with these managers, and the checks received by those participants over the years have matched the stated records.

Before we begin this examination, I would like you to imagine a national coin-flipping contest. Let's assume we get 22.5 million Americans up tomorrow morning and we ask them all to wager a dollar. They go out in the morning at sunrise, and they all call the flip of a coin. If they call correctly, they win a dollar from those who called wrong. Each day the losers drop out, and on the subsequent day the stakes build as all previous winnings are put on the line. After ten flips on ten mornings, there will be approximately 220,000 people in the United States who have correctly called ten flips in a row. They each will have won a little over $1,000.

Now this group will probably start getting a little puffed up about this, human nature being what it is. They may try to be modest, but at cocktail parties they will occasionally admit to attractive members of the opposite sex what their technique is, and what marvelous insights they bring to the field of flipping.

Assuming that the winners are getting the appropriate rewards from the losers, in another ten days we will have 215 people who have successfully called their coin flips 20 times in a row and who, by this exercise, each have turned one dollar into a little over $1 million. $225 million would have been lost, $225 million would have been won.

By then, this group will really lose their heads. They will probably write books on "How I Turned a Dollar into a Million in Twenty Days

Working Thirty Seconds a Morning." Worse yet, they'll probably start jetting around the country attending seminars on efficient coin-flipping and tackling skeptical professors with, "If it can't be done, why are there 215 of us?"

But then some business school professor will probably be rude enough to bring up the fact that if 225 million orangutans had engaged in a similar exercise, the results would be much the same—215 egotistical orangutans with 20 straight winning flips.

I would argue, however, that there *are* some important differences in the examples I am going to present. For one thing, if (a) you had taken 225 million orangutans distributed roughly as the U.S. population is; if (b) 215 winners were left after 20 days; and if (c) you found that 40 came from a particular zoo in Omaha, you would be pretty sure you were on to something. So you would probably go out and ask the zookeeper about what he's feeding them, whether they had special exercises, what books they read, and who knows what else. That is, if you found any really extraordinary concentrations of success, you might want to see if you could identify concentrations of unusual characteristics that might be causal factors.

Scientific inquiry naturally follows such a pattern. If you were trying to analyze possible causes of a rare type of cancer—with, say, 1,500 cases a year in the United States—and you found that 400 of them occurred in some little mining town in Montana, you would get very interested in the water there, or the occupation of those afflicted, or other variables. You know that it's not random chance that 400 come from a small area. You would not necessarily know the causal factors, but you would know where to search.

I submit to you that there are ways of defining an origin other than geography. In addition to geographical origins, there can be what I call an *intellectual* origin. I think you will find that a disproportionate number of successful coin-flippers in the investment world came from a very small intellectual village that could be called Graham-and-Doddsville. A concentration of winners that simply cannot be explained by chance can be traced to this particular intellectual village.

Conditions could exist that would make even that concentration unimportant. Perhaps 100 people were simply imitating the coin-flipping call of some terribly persuasive personality. When he called heads, 100 followers automatically called that coin the same way. If the leader was part of the 215 left at the end, the fact that 100 came from the same intellectual origin would mean nothing. You would simply be identifying one case as a hundred cases. Similarly, let's assume that you lived in a strongly patriarchal society and every family in the United States conveniently consisted of ten members. Further assume that the patriarchal culture was so strong that, when the 225 million people went out the first day, every member of the family identified with the father's call. Now, at the end of the 20-day period, you would have 215 winners, and you would find that they came from only 21.5 families. Some naive types might say that this indicates an enormous hereditary factor as an explanation of successful coin-flipping. But, of course, it would have no significance at all because it would simply mean that you didn't have 215 individual winners, but rather 21.5 randomly distributed families who were winners.

In this group of successful investors that I want to consider, there has been a common intellectual patriarch, Ben Graham. But the children who left the house of this intellectual patriarch have called their "flips" in very different ways. They have gone to different places and bought and sold different stocks and companies, yet they have had a combined record that simply can't be explained by random chance. It certainly cannot be explained by the fact that they are all calling flips identically because a leader is signaling the calls to make. The patriarch has merely set forth the intellectual theory for making coin-calling decisions, but each student has decided on his own manner of applying the theory.

The common intellectual theme of the investors from Graham-and-Doddsville is this: they search for discrepancies between the *value* of a business and the *price* of small pieces of that business in the market. Essentially, they exploit those discrepancies without the efficient market theorist's concern as to whether the stocks are bought on Monday or Thursday, or whether it is January or July, etc. Incidentally, when businessmen buy businesses—which is just what our Graham & Dodd investors are doing through the medium of marketable stocks—I doubt that many are cranking into their purchase decision the day of the week or the month in which the transaction is going to occur. If it doesn't make any difference whether all of a business is being bought on a Monday or a Friday, I am baffled why academicians invest extensive time and effort to see whether it makes a difference when buying small pieces of those same businesses. Our Graham & Dodd investors, needless to say, do not discuss beta, the capital asset pricing model, or covariance in returns among securities. These are not subjects of any interest to them. In fact, most of them would have difficulty defining those terms. The investors simply focus on two variables: price and value.

I always find it extraordinary that so many studies are made of price and volume behavior, the stuff of chartists. Can you imagine buying an entire business simply because the price of the business had been marked *up* substantially last week and the week before? Of course, the reason a lot of studies are made of these price and volume variables is that now, in the age of computers, there are almost endless data available about them. It isn't necessarily because such studies have any utility; it's simply that the data are there and academicians have worked hard to learn the mathematical skills needed to manipulate them. Once these skills are acquired, it seems sinful not to use them, even if the usage has no utility or negative utility. As a friend said, to a man with a hammer, everything looks like a nail.

I think the group that we have identified by a common intellectual home is worthy of study. Incidentally, despite all the academic studies of the influence of such variables as price, volume, seasonality, capitalization size, etc., upon stock performance, no interest has been evidenced in studying the methods of this unusual concentration of value-oriented winners.

I begin this study of results by going back to a group of four of us who worked at Graham-Newman Corporation from 1954 through 1956. There were only four—I have not selected these names from among thousands. I offered to go to work at Graham-Newman for nothing after I took Ben Graham's class, but he turned me down as overvalued. He took this value stuff very seriously! After much pestering he finally hired me. There were three partners and four of us at the "peasant" level. All four left between 1955 and 1957 when the firm was wound up, and it's possible to trace the record of three.

The first example (see Table 1 on page 53) is that of Walter Schloss. Walter never went to college, but took a course from Ben Graham at night at the New York Institute of Finance. Walter left Graham-Newman in 1955 and achieved the record shown here over 28 years.

Here is what "Adam Smith"—after I told him about Walter—wrote about him in *Supermoney* (1972):

*He has no connections or access to useful information. Practically no one in Wall Street knows him and he is not fed any ideas. He looks up the numbers in the manuals and sends for the annual reports, and that's about it.*

*In introducing me to [Schloss] Warren had also, to my mind, described himself. "He never forgets that he is handling other people's money and this reinforces his normal strong aversion to loss." He has total integrity and a realistic picture of himself. Money is real to him and stocks are real—and from this flows an attraction to the "margin of safety" principle.*

Walter has diversified enormously, owning well over 100 stocks currently. He knows how to identify securities that sell at considerably less than their value to a private owner. *And that's all he does.* He doesn't worry about whether it's January, he doesn't worry about whether it's Monday, he doesn't worry about whether it's an election year. He simply says, if a business is worth a dollar and I can buy it for 40 cents, something good may happen to me. And he does it over and over and over again. He owns many more stocks than I do—and is far less interested in the underlying nature of the business; I don't seem to have very much influence on Walter. That's one of his strengths; no one has much influence on him.

The second case is Tom Knapp, who also worked at Graham-Newman with me. Tom was a chemistry major at Princeton before the war; when he came back from the war, he was a beach bum. And then one day he read that Dave Dodd was giving a night course in investments at Columbia. Tom took it on a noncredit basis, and he got so interested in the subject from taking that course that he came up and enrolled at Columbia Business School, where he got the MBA degree. He took Dodd's course again, and took Ben Graham's course. Incidentally, 35 years later I called Tom to ascertain some of the facts involved here and I found him on the beach again. The only difference is that now he owns the beach!

In 1968 Tom Knapp and Ed Anderson, also a Graham disciple, along with one or two other fellows of similar persuasion, formed Tweedy, Browne Partners, and their investment results appear in Table 2 (page 54). Tweedy, Browne built that record with very wide diversification. They occasionally bought control of businesses, but the record of the passive investments is equal to the record of the control investments.

Table 3 (page 54) describes the third member of the group who formed Buffett Partnership in 1957. The best thing he did was to quit in 1969. Since then, in a sense, Berkshire Hathaway has been a continuation of the partnership in some respects. There is no single index I can give you that I would feel would be a fair test of investment management at Berkshire. But I think that any way you figure it, it has been satisfactory.

Table 4 (page 54) shows the record of the Sequoia Fund, which is managed by a man whom I met in 1951 in Ben Graham's class, Bill Ruane. After getting out of Harvard Business School, he went to Wall Street. Then he realized that he needed to get a real business education so he came up to take Ben's course at Columbia, where we met in early 1951. Bill's record from 1951 to 1970, working with relatively small sums, was far better than average. When I wound up Buffett Partnership I asked Bill if he would set up a fund to handle all our partners, so he set up the Sequoia Fund. He set it up at a terrible time, just when I was quitting. He went right into the two-tier market and all the difficulties that made for comparative performance for value-oriented investors. I am happy to say that my partners, to an amazing degree, not only stayed with him but added money, with the happy result shown.

There's no hindsight involved here. Bill was the only person I recommended to my partners, and I said at the time that if he achieved a
four-point-per-annum advantage over the Standard & Poor's, that
would be solid performance. Bill has achieved well over that, working
with progressively larger sums of money. That makes things much
more difficult. Size is the anchor of performance. There is no question about it. It doesn't mean you can't do better than average when
you get larger, but the margin shrinks. And if you ever get so you're
managing two trillion dollars, and that happens to be the amount of
the total equity evaluation in the economy, don't think that you'll do
better than average!

I should add that in the records we've looked at so far, throughout
this whole period there was practicallly no duplication in these portfolios. These are men who select securities based on discrepancies
between price and value, but they make their selections very differently. Walter's largest holdings have been such stalwarts as Hudson
Pulp & Paper and Jeddo Highland Coal and New York Trap Rock
Company and all those other names that come instantly to mind to
even a casual reader of the business pages. Tweedy Browne's selections
have sunk even well below that level in terms of name recognition. On
the other hand, Bill has worked with big companies. The overlap
among these portfolios has been very, very low. These records do not
reflect one guy calling the flip and fifty people yelling out the same
thing after him.

Table 5 (page 54) is the record of a friend of mine who is a Harvard
Law graduate, who set up a major law firm. I ran into him in about
1960 and told him that law was fine as a hobby but he could do better.
He set up a partnership quite the opposite of Walter's. His portfolio
was concentrated in very few securities and therefore his record was
much more volatile but it was based on the same discount-from-value

approach. He was willing to accept greater peaks and valleys of performance, and he happens to be a fellow whose whole psyche goes toward concentration, with the results shown. Incidentally, this record belongs to Charlie Munger, my partner for a long time in the operation of Berkshire Hathaway. When he ran his partnership, however, his portfolio holdings were almost completely different from mine and the other fellows mentioned earlier.

Table 6 (page 55) is the record of a fellow who was a pal of Charlie Munger's—another non-business school type—who was a math major at USC. He went to work for IBM after graduation and was an IBM salesman for a while. After I got to Charlie, Charlie got to him. This happens to be the record of Rick Guerin. Rick, from 1965 to 1983, against a compounded gain of 316 percent for the S&P, came off with 22,200 percent, which, probably because he lacks a business school education, he regards as statistically significant.

One sidelight here: it is extraordinary to me that the idea of buying dollar bills for 40 cents takes immediately with people or it doesn't take at all. It's like an inoculation. If it doesn't grab a person right away, I find that you can talk to him for years and show him records, and it doesn't make any difference. They just don't seem able to grasp the concept, simple as it is. A fellow like Rick Guerin, who had no formal education in business, understands immediately the value approach to investing and he's applying it five minutes later. I've never seen anyone who became a gradual convert over a ten-year period to this approach. It doesn't seem to be a matter of IQ or academic training. It's instant recognition, or it is nothing.

Table 7 (page 55) is the record of Stan Perlmeter. Stan was a liberal arts major at the University of Michigan who was a partner in the advertising agency of Bozell & Jacobs. We happened to be in the same building in Omaha. In 1965 he figured out I had a better business than he did, so he left advertising. Again, it took five minutes for Stan to embrace the value approach.

Perlmeter does not own what Walter Schloss owns. He does not own what Bill Ruane owns. These are records made *independently*. But every time Perlmeter buys a stock it's because he's getting more for his money than he's paying. That's the only thing he's thinking about. He's not looking at quarterly earnings projections, he's not looking at next year's earnings, he's not thinking about what day of the week it is, he doesn't care what investment research from any place says, he's not interested in price momentum, volume, or anything. He's simply asking: What is the business worth?

Table 8 (page 55) and Table 9 (page 56) are the records of two pension funds I've been involved in. They are not selected from dozens of pension funds with which I have had involvement; they are the only two I have influenced. In both cases I have steered them toward value-oriented managers. Very, very few pension funds are managed from a value standpoint. Table 8 is the Washington Post Company's Pension Fund. It was with a large bank some years ago, and I suggested that they would do well to select managers who had a value orientation.

As you can see, overall they have been in the top percentile ever since they made the change. The Post told the managers to keep at least 25 percent of these funds in bonds, which would not have been necessarily the choice of these managers. So I've included the bond performance simply to illustrate that this group has no particular expertise about bonds. They wouldn't have said they did. Even with this drag of 25 percent of their fund in an area that was not their game, they were in the top percentile of fund management. The Washington Post experience does not cover a terribly long period but it does represent many investment decisions by three managers who were not identified retroactively.

Table 9 is the record of the FMC Corporation fund. I don't manage a dime of it myself but I did, in 1974, influence their decision to select value-oriented managers. Prior to that time they had selected managers much the same way as most larger companies. They now rank number one in the Becker survey of pension funds for their size over the period of time subsequent to this "conversion" to the value approach. Last year they had eight equity managers of any duration beyond a year. Seven of them had a cumulative record better than the S&P. All eight had a better record last year than the S&P. The net difference now between a median performance and the actual performance of the FMC fund over this period is $243 million. FMC attributes this to the mindset given to them about the selection of managers. Those managers are not the managers I would necessarily select but they have the common denominator of selecting securities based on value.

So these are nine records of "coin-flippers" from Graham-and-Doddsville. I haven't selected them with hindsight from among thousands. It's not like I am reciting to you the names of a bunch of lottery winners—people I had never heard of before they won the lottery. I selected these men years ago based upon their framework for investment decision-making. I knew what they had been taught and additionally I had some personal knowledge of their intellect, character, and temperament. It's very important to understand that this group has assumed far less risk than average; note their record in years when the general market was weak. While they differ greatly in style, these investors are, mentally, always *buying the business, not buying the stock*. A few of them sometimes buy whole businesses. Far more often they simply buy small pieces of businesses. Their attitude, whether buying all or a tiny piece of a business, is the same. Some of them hold portfolios with dozens of stocks; others concentrate on a handful. But all exploit the difference between the market price of a business and its intrinsic value.

I'm convinced that there is much inefficiency in the market. These Graham-and-Doddsville investors have successfully exploited gaps between price and value. When the price of a stock can be influenced by a "herd" on Wall Street with prices set at the margin by the most emotional person, or the greediest person, or the most depressed person, it is hard to argue that the market always prices rationally. In fact, market prices are frequently nonsensical.

I would like to say one important thing about risk and reward. Sometimes risk and reward are correlated in a positive fashion. If someone were to say to me, "I have here a six-shooter and I have slipped one cartridge into it. Why don't you just spin it and pull it once? If you survive, I will give you $1 million." I would decline—perhaps stating that $1 million is not enough. Then he might offer me $5 million to pull the trigger twice—now that would be a positive correlation between risk and reward!

The exact opposite is true with value investing. If you buy a dollar bill for 60 cents, it's riskier than if you buy a dollar bill for 40 cents, but the expectation of reward is greater in the latter case. The greater the potential for reward in the value portfolio, the less risk there is.

One quick example: The Washington Post Company in 1973 was selling for $80 million in the market. At the time, that day, you could have sold the assets to any one of ten buyers for not less than $400 million, probably appreciably more. The company owned the *Post*, *Newsweek*, plus several television stations in major markets. Those same properties are worth $2 billion now, so the person who would have paid $400 million would not have been crazy.

Now, if the stock had declined even further to a price that made the valuation $40 million instead of $80 million, its beta would have been greater. And to people who think beta measures risk, the cheaper price would have made it look riskier. This is truly Alice in Wonderland. I have never been able to figure out why it's riskier to buy $400 million worth of properties for $40 million than $80 million. And, as a matter of fact, if you buy a group of such securities and you know anything at all about business valuation, there is essentially no risk in buying $400 million for $80 million, particularly if you do it by buying ten $40 million piles for $8 million each. Since you don't have your hands on the $400 million, you want to be sure you are in with honest and reasonably competent people, but that's not a difficult job.

You also have to have the knowledge to enable you to make a very general estimate about the value of the underlying businesses. But you do not cut it close. That is what Ben Graham meant by having a margin of safety. You don't try and buy businesses worth $83 million for $80 million. You leave yourself an enormous margin. When you build a bridge, you insist it can carry 30,000 pounds, but you only drive 10,000-pound trucks across it. And that same principle works in investing.

In conclusion, some of the more commercially minded among you may wonder why I am writing this article. Adding many converts to the value approach will perforce narrow the spreads between price and value. I can only tell you that the secret has been out for 50 years, ever since Ben Graham and Dave Dodd wrote *Security Analysis*, yet I have seen no trend toward value investing in the 35 years that I've practiced it. There seems to be some perverse human characteristic that likes to make easy things difficult. The academic world, if anything, has actually backed away from the teaching of value investing over the last 30 years. It's likely to continue that way. Ships will sail around the world but the Flat Earth Society will flourish. There will continue to be wide discrepancies between price and value in the marketplace, and those who read their Graham & Dodd will continue to prosper.

Tables 1–9 follow:

### TABLE 1. WALTER J. SCHLOSS

| | |
|---|---|
| Standard & Poor's 28¼ year compounded gain | 887.2% |
| WJS Limited Partners 28¼ year compounded gain | 6,678.8% |
| WJS Partnership 28¼ year compounded gain | 23,104.7% |
| Standard & Poor's 28¼ year annual compounded rate | 8.4% |
| WJS Limited Partners 28¼ year annual compounded rate | 16.1% |
| WJS Partnership 28¼ year annual compounded rate | 21.3% |

During the history of the Partnership it has owned over 800 issues and, at most times, has had at least 100 positions. Present assets under management approximate $45 million. The difference between returns of the partnership and returns of the limited partners is due to allocations to the general partner for management.

TABLE 2. TWEEDY, BROWNE INC.

|  | Dow Jones* (%) | S & P 500* (%) | TBK Overall (%) | TBK Limited Partners (%) |
|---|---|---|---|---|
| Total Return 15¾ years | 191.8% | 238.5% | 1,661.2% | 936.4% |
| Standard & Poor's 15¾ year annual compounded rate |  |  |  | 7.0% |
| TBK Limited Partners 15¾ year annual compounded rate |  |  |  | 16.0% |
| TBK Overall 15¾ year annual compounded rate |  |  |  | 20.0% |

* *Includes dividends paid for both Standard & Poor's 500 Composite Index and Dow Jones Industrial Average.*

TABLE 3. BUFFETT PARTNERSHIP, LTD.

|  | Overall Results From Dow (%) | Partnership Results (%) | Limited Partners' Results (%) |
|---|---|---|---|
| Annual Compounded Rate | 7.4 | 29.5 | 23.8 |

TABLE 4. SEQUOIA FUND, INC.

|  | Annual Percentage Change** | |
|---|---|---|
|  | Sequoia Fund (%) | S&P 500 Index* (%) |
| Entire Period (July 15, 1970–March 30, 1984) | 775.3% | 270.0% |
| Compound Annual Return | 17.2% | 10.0% |
| Plus 1% Management Fee | 1.0% |  |
| GROSS INVESTMENT RETURN | 18.2% | 10.0% |

* *Includes dividends (and capital gains distributions in the case of Sequoia Fund) treated as though reinvested.*

** *These figures differ slightly from the S&P figures in Table 1 because of a difference in calculation of reinvested dividends.*

TABLE 5. CHARLES MUNGER

|  | Mass. Inv Trust (%) | Investors Stock (%) | Lehman (%) | Tri-Cont. (%) | Dow (%) | Over-all Partnership (%) | Limited Partners (%) |
|---|---|---|---|---|---|---|---|
| Average Annual Compounded Rate | 3.8 | 2.8 | 5.5 | 4.6 | 5.0 | 19.8 | 13.7 |

TABLE 6. PACIFIC PARTNERS, LTD.

| | |
|---|---|
| Standard & Poor's 19 year compounded gain | 316.4% |
| Limited Partners 19 year compounded gain | 5,530.2% |
| Overall Partnership 19 year compounded gain | 22,200.0% |
| Standard & Poor's 19 year annual compounded rate | 7.8% |
| Limited Partners 19 year annual compounded rate | 23.6% |
| Overall Partnership 19 year annual compounded rate | 32.9% |

TABLE 7. PERIMETER INVESTMENTS

| | |
|---|---|
| Total Partnership Percentage Gain 8/1/65 through 10/31/83 | 4277.2% |
| Limited Partners Percentage Gain 8/1/65 through 10/31/83 | 2309.5% |
| Annual Compound Rate of Gain Overall Partnership | 23.0% |
| Annual Compound Rate of Gain Limited Partners | 19.0% |
| Dow Jones Industrial Averages 7/31/65 (Approximate) | 882 |
| Dow Jones Industrial Averages 10/31/83 (Approximate) | 1225 |
| Approximate Compound Rate of Gain of DJI including dividends | 7% |

TABLE 8. THE WASHINGTON POST COMPANY, MASTER TRUST, DECEMBER 31, 1983

| | 5 Years Ended* | |
|---|---|---|
| | % Ret. | Rank |
| All Investments | | |
| Manager A | 20.2 | 3 |
| Manager B | 22.6 | 1 |
| Manager C | — | — |
| Master Trust (All Managers) | 21.8 | 1 |

*Annualized*
*Rank indicates the fund's performance against the A.C. Becker universe.*
*Rank is stated as a percentile: 1 = best performance, 100 = worst.*

TABLE 9. FMC CORPORATION PENSION FUND,
ANNUAL RATE OF RETURN (PERCENT)

| Period ending 1983 | 9 Years |
|---|---|
| FMC (Bonds and Equities Combined) | *17.1 |
| Becker large plan median | 12.6 |
| S&P 500 | 15.6 |

* *18.5 from equities only*

Robert G. Hagstrom, Jr. runs a mutual fund that draws
heavily on Buffett's investment techniques. Hagstrom's
hands-on experience informs his 1994 book about the
Wizard of Omaha. This passage talks about what Buffett
learned from two earlier investment legends: value
investor Benjamin Graham and growth stock investor
Phillip Fisher.

# THE TWO WISE MEN
## by Robert G. Hagstrom, Jr.

### from *The Warren Buffett Way* (1994)

T HE EDUCATION OF Warren Buffett is best understood as a
synthesis of two distinct investment philosophies from the
minds of two legendary figures, Benjamin Graham and
Philip Fisher. "I'm 15 percent Fisher," Buffett said, "and 85 percent
Benjamin Graham." It is not surprising that Graham's influence over
Buffett is broad. Buffett was first an interested reader of Graham, then
student, then employee, then collaborator, and finally his peer. Graham
molded Buffett's untrained mind. However, those who consider Buffett
to be the singular product of Graham's teachings are ignoring the influence of another towering financial mind, Philip Fisher.

After Buffett read Fisher's book, *Common Stocks and Uncommon
Profits* (Harper & Brothers, 1958), he sought out the writer. "When I
met him (Fisher), I was as impressed by the man as by his ideas," said
Buffett. "Much like Ben Graham, Fisher was unassuming, generous in
spirit and an extraordinary teacher." Although Graham's and Fisher's
investment approach differ, Buffett noted, they "parallel in the investment world."

## BENJAMIN GRAHAM

Graham is considered the dean of financial analysis. He was awarded that distinction because "before him there was no (financial analysis) profession and after him they began to call it that." Graham's two most celebrated works are *Security Analysis*, coauthored with David Dodd and originally published in 1934, shortly after the 1929 stock market crash and in the depths of the nation's worst depression; and *The Intelligent Investor*, originally published in 1949. While other academicians sought to explain this economic phenomenon, Graham helped people regain their financial footing and proceed with a profitable course of action.

Graham was born in London on May 9, 1894. His parents moved to New York when he was an infant. Graham's earliest education was at Boy's High in Brooklyn. At age twenty, he received a bachelor of science degree from Columbia University and was elected to Phi Beta Kappa. Graham was fluent in Greek and Latin and held interests in both mathematics and philosophy. Despite his nonbusiness education, he began a career on Wall Street. He started as a messenger at the brokerage firm of Newburger, Henderson & Loeb, posting bond and stock prices on a blackboard for $12 a week. From messenger, he rose to writing research reports and, soon thereafter, was awarded a partnership in the firm. By 1919, he was earning an annual salary of $600,000; he was twenty-five years old. In 1926, Graham formed an investment partnership with Jerome Newman. It was this partnership that hired Buffett some thirty years later. Graham-Newman survived the 1929 crash, the depression, World War II, and the Korean War before it dissolved in 1956.

From 1928 through 1956, while at Graham-Newman, Graham taught night courses in finance at Columbia. Few people know that

Graham was financially ruined by the 1929 crash. For the second time in his life—the first being when his father died, leaving the family financially unprotected—Graham set about to rebuild his fortune. The haven of academia allowed Graham the opportunity for reflection and reevaluation. With the counsel of David Dodd, also a professor at Columbia, Graham produced a complete dissertation on conservative investing.

*Security Analysis* first appeared in 1934. Between them, Graham and Dodd had more than fifteen years of investment experience. It took them four years to complete the book. When *Security Analysis* was first published, Louis Rich of *The New York Times* wrote, "It is a full-bodied mature, meticulous and wholly meritorious outgrowth of scholarly probing and practical sagacity. If this influence should ever exert itself, it will come about by causing the mind of the investor to dwell upon securities rather than upon the market."

In the first edition, Graham and Dodd dedicated significant attention to corporate abuses. Prior to the securities acts of 1933 and 1934, corporate information was misleading and totally inadequate. Most industrial companies refused to divulge sales information, and the valuation of assets was frequently suspicious. Corporate misinformation was used to manipulate the prices of securities, both in initial public offerings and in the aftermarkets. After the securities acts, corporate reforms were slow but deliberate. By the time the third edition of the book appeared in 1951, references to corporate abuses were eliminated, and in its place Graham and Dodd addressed the problems of stockholder-management relations. These problems centered on management's competence and the policy on dividends.

The essence of *Security Analysis* is that a well-chosen, diversified portfolio of common stocks, based on reasonable prices, can be a sound investment. Step by careful step, Graham helped the investor see the logic of his approach.

The first problem that Graham had to contend with was the lack of a single, universal definition for investment. Quoting Justice Brandeis, Graham pointed out that "investment is a word of many meanings." And the issue does not turn on whether the item is a stock (and therefore speculative by definition) or a bond (and therefore an investment). The purchase of a poorly secured bond cannot be considered an investment just because it is a bond. Neither can a stock with a price per share of less than its net current assets be considered a speculation just because it is a stock. The decision to purchase a security with borrowed money in hopes of making a quick profit is speculation, regardless of whether it is a bond or stock. Here, Graham said, intention more than character will determine whether the security is an investment or a speculation.

Considering the complexities of the issue, Graham proposed his own definition. "An investment operation is one which, upon thorough analysis, promises safety of principal and a satisfactory return. Operations not meeting these requirements are speculative." Graham preferred to speak of investment as an operation that precluded the purchase of a single issue. Early on, Graham recommended diversifying investments to reduce risk.

The "thorough analysis" that he insisted upon was explained as "the careful study of available facts with the attempt to draw conclusions therefrom based on established principles and sound logic." Graham went further by describing analysis as a three-step function: descriptive, critical, and selective.

In the descriptive phase, the analyst gathers all the facts outstanding and presents them in an intelligent manner. In the critical phase, the analyst is concerned with the merits of the standards used to communicate information. Ultimately, the analyst is interested in the fair representation of the facts. In the selective phase, the analyst passes judgment on the attractiveness or unattractiveness of the security in question.

For a security to be considered an investment, said Graham, there must be some degree of safety of principal and a satisfactory rate of return. Graham explained that safety is not absolute. Rather, the investment should be considered safe from loss under reasonable conditions. Graham did admit that a most unusual or improbable occurrence can put a safe bond into default. Satisfactory return includes not only income but price appreciation. Graham noted that "satisfactory" is a subjective term. He does say that *return* can be any amount, however low, as long as the investor acts with a degree of intelligence and adheres to the full definition of investment. An individual who conducts a thorough financial analysis based on sound logic, indicating a reasonable rate of return without compromising safety of principal, would be considered, by Graham's definition, an investor, not a speculator.

Had it not been for the bond market's poor performance, Graham's definition of investing might have been overlooked. But when, between 1929 and 1932, the Dow Jones Bond Average declined from 97.70 to 65.78, bonds could not mindlessly be considered pure investments. Like stocks, bonds not only lost considerable value but many issuers went bankrupt. Therefore, what was needed was a process that could distinguish the investment characteristics of both stocks and bonds from their speculative counterparts.

Throughout Graham's life he was disturbed by the issues of investment and speculation. Toward the end of his life, Graham watched with dismay as institutional investors embraced actions that were clearly speculative. Shortly after the 1973–1974 bear market, Graham was invited to attend a conference of money managers hosted by Donaldson, Lufkin, and Jenrette. As Graham sat at the conference roundtable, he was shocked by what was being admitted by his professional peer group. "I could not comprehend," said Graham, "how the management of money by institutions had degenerated from sound investment to this rat race of trying to get the highest possible return in the shortest period."

Graham's second contribution—after distinguishing between investment and speculation—was a methodology whereby the purchase of common stocks would qualify as an investment. Before *Security Analysis*, little had been accomplished using a quantitative approach to selecting stocks. Prior to 1929, listed common stocks were primarily railroads. Industrial and utility companies were a small portion of the overall list of stocks. Banks and insurance companies, the favorites of wealthy speculators, were unlisted stocks. Those companies, primarily railroads, that arguably had investment value traded at a price that was close to their par value. These companies were backed by real capital value.

As the country entered the bull market of the 1920s, the general disposition of all stocks, including industrials, began to improve. Prosperity fueled further investment, most notably in real estate. Despite the short-lived Florida real estate boom in 1925, followed by the Florida real estate bust of 1926, commercial banks and investment banking firms continued to recommend real estate. Real estate investment spurred investment activity and, ultimately, business activity. This link continued to fan the flames of optimism. As Graham noted, uncontrolled optimism can lead to mania, and one of the chief characteristics of mania is its inability to recall the lessons of history.

Looking back, Graham identified three forces that he felt were responsible for the stock market crash. First was the manipulation of stocks by the exchanges and investment firms. Each day, brokers were told which issues to "move" and what to say to generate excitement about the stock. Second was bank policy to lend money for the purpose of buying stocks. Banks loaned money to speculators, who in turn anxiously awaited the latest hot tip from Wall Street. Bank lending for securities purchases rose from $1 billion in 1921 to $8.5 billion in 1929. Since the loans were backed by the value of stocks, when the Crash occurred, like a house of cards, everything tumbled down. Today, there are security laws to protect individuals from brokerage fraud, and the practice of buying securities on margin is greatly curtailed, compared to the 1920s. But the one area that could not be legislated, yet in Graham's mind was just as responsible for the Crash, was excessive optimism—the third force.

The danger of 1929 was not that speculation tried to masquerade as investing but rather that investing fashioned itself into speculation. Graham noted that historical optimism was rampant. Encouraged by the past, investors projected an era of continued growth and prosperity. The buyers of stocks began to lose their sense of proportion about price. Graham said people were paying prices for stocks without any sense of mathematical expectation. Stocks were worth any price that the optimistic market quoted, he said. It was at the height of this insanity that the line between speculation and investment blurred.

When the full impact of the stock market crash was felt, common stocks were once again labeled speculations. As the Depression began, the whole concept of common-stock investing was an anathema. However, noted Graham, investment philosophies change with psychological states. After World War II, confidence in common stocks rose once again. When Graham wrote the third edition of *Security Analysis* between 1949 and 1951, he acknowledged that common stocks had become an instrumental part of an investor's portfolio.

In the twenty years following the stock market crash, numerous academic studies analyzing the different approaches to common stock investing appeared. Graham himself described three approaches: the cross-section approach, the anticipation approach, and the margin of safety approach.

The cross-section approach would be today's equivalent of index investing. As Graham noted, selectivity was exchanged for diversification. An investor would purchase equal amounts of the thirty industrial companies of the Dow Jones Index and benefit equally as well as those selected companies. Graham pointed out that there was no certainty that Wall Street could accomplish results that were better than this index.

The anticipation approach was subdivided into the short-term selectivity and the growth stock approaches. Short-term selectivity is an approach where individuals seek to profit from companies that have the most favorable outlook over the near term, usually six months to a year. Wall Street expends much energy forecasting the economic prospects—including sales volume, costs, and earnings—that a company can expect to achieve. The fallacy of this approach, according to Graham, was that sales and earnings are often volatile and the anticipation of near-term economic prospects could easily be discounted in the stock price. Lastly, and more fundamentally, Graham charged that the value of an investment is not what it will earn this month or next, nor what next quarter's sales volume will be, but what that investment can expect to return to an investor over a long period of time. Decisions based on short-term data are too often superficial and temporary. Not surprising, because of its emphasis on change and transaction, the short-term selectivity approach is the dominant approach on Wall Street.

Growth stocks, simplistically defined, are companies that grow sales and earnings at rates above those of the average business. Graham used the National Investors Corporation definition, which identified growth companies as companies whose earnings move from cycle to cycle. The difficulties of succeeding with the growth-stock approach, explained Graham, centered on the investor's ability to identify growth companies and then to ascertain what degree the current share price already discounted the growth potential of the company.

Each company has what is called a *life cycle* of profits. In the early development stage, a company's revenues accelerate and earnings begin to materialize. During the rapid expansion stage, revenues continue to grow, profit margins expand, and there is a sharp increase in earnings. When a company enters the mature-growth stage, revenues begin to slow, and so do earnings. In the last stage, stabilization-decline, revenues drop, and both profit margins and earnings decline.

Growth investors, according to Graham, face a dilemma. If they select a company that is in the rapid-expansion stage, they may find the success of the company is temporary. Because the company has not endured years of testing, the company's profits may soon evaporate. On the other hand, a company in the mature-growth stage may be in a more advanced stage, soon to enter a stabilization-decline period when earnings begin to shrink. The ability to pinpoint a company on its life cycle has, for decades, perplexed financial analysts.

If we assume that the investor has accurately pinpointed a growth company, what price should the investor pay? Obviously, if it is well known that a company is in a period of prosperity, its share price will be relatively high. Graham asked, How are we to know whether or not the price is too high? The answer is difficult to determine and, furthermore, even if it could be accurately determined, the investor immediately faces a new risk—that the company will grow more slowly than anticipated. If this occurs, the investor would have paid too much and the market likely will then price the shares lower.

If the analyst, in Graham's words, is optimistic about the company's future growth and further believes that the company will be a suitable addition to the portfolio, the analyst has two techniques for purchase: purchase shares of the company when the overall market is trading at a low price (which generally occurs during some type of correction, usually a bear market), or purchase the stock when it trades below its intrinsic value, although the overall market is not substantially cheap. In either technique, Graham said, a "margin of safety" is present in the purchase price.

Buying securities only at market lows leads to some difficulties. First, it entices the investor to develop some formula that indicates at which points the market is expensive and at which points the market is cheap. The investor, Graham explained, becomes hostage to predicting market turns, a process that is far from certain. Second, when the market is fairly valued, investors are unable to profitably purchase common stocks. However, waiting for a market correction before purchasing stocks may become tiring and is, in the end, futile.

Graham suggested that an investor's energies would be better used by identifying undervalued securities, regardless of the overall market price level. For this strategy to work systematically, Graham admitted, investors need a method or technique to identify undervalued stocks. The goal of the analyst is to develop the ability to recommend stocks that are selling below their calculated value. The idea of buying undervalued securities regardless of market levels was a novel idea in the 1930s and 1940s. It was Graham's goal to outline such a strategy.

Graham reduced the concept of sound investing to a motto he called the "margin of safety." This motto sought to unite all securities, stocks, and bonds in a singular approach to investing. If, for example, an analyst reviewed the operating history of a company and discovered that, on average, for the last five years, the company was able to earn annually five times its fixed charges, then a company's bonds, said Graham, possessed a margin of safety. Graham did not expect the investor to accurately determine the company's future income. Instead, he figured that if the margin between earnings and fixed charges was large enough, the investor would be protected from an unexpected decline in the company's income.

Establishing a margin-of-safety concept for bonds was not too difficult. The real test was Graham's ability to adapt the concept for common stocks. Graham reasoned that a margin of safety existed for common stocks if the price of the stock was below its intrinsic value. Obviously, for the concept to work, analysts needed a technique for determining a company's intrinsic value. Graham's definition of intrinsic value, as it appeared in *Security Analysis*, was "that value which is determined by the facts." These facts included a company's assets, its earnings and dividends, and any future definite prospects. Graham admitted that the single most important factor in determining a company's value was its future earnings power. Simplistically, a company's intrinsic value could be found by estimating the earnings of the company and multiplying those by an appropriate capitalization factor. This factor, or multiplier, was influenced by the company's stability of earnings, assets, dividend policy, and financial health.

Using the intrinsic-value approach, Graham said, was limited by an analyst's imprecise calculations for a company's economic future. Graham was concerned that an analyst's projections could be easily negated by a host of potential future factors. Sales volume, pricing, and expenses are difficult to forecast, thus making the application of a multiplier that much more complex. Not to be dissuaded, Graham did suggest that the margin of safety could work successfully in three areas. First, it worked well with stable securities such as bonds and preferred stocks. Second, it could be used in comparative analysis. Third, Graham figured that if the spread between the price of a company and the intrinsic value of a company was large enough, the margin-of-safety concept could be used to select stocks.

Graham asked readers to accept the idea that intrinsic value is an elusive concept. It is distinct from the market's quotation price. Originally, intrinsic value was thought to be the same as a company's book value, or the sum of its real assets minus obligations. This notion led to the early belief that intrinsic value was definite. However, analysts came to know that the value of a company was not only its net real assets but, additionally, the value of the earnings these assets produced. Graham proposed that it was not essential to determine a company's exact intrinsic value but, instead, accept an approximate measure or range of value. To establish a margin of safety, the analyst simply needs an approximate value that is considerably higher or lower than its market price.

Financial analysis is not an exact science, Graham said. There are certain quantitative factors—including balance sheets, income statements, earnings and dividends, assets and liabilities—that do lend themselves to thorough analysis. There are also qualitative factors that are not easily analyzed but are nonetheless essential ingredients in a company's intrinsic value. The two qualitative factors that are customarily addressed are "management capability" and the "nature of the business."

Graham, generally, had misgivings about the emphasis placed on qualitative factors. Opinions about management and the nature of a business are not easily measurable, and that which is difficult to measure, reasoned Graham, could be badly measured. It was not that Graham believed these qualitative factors had no value. Rather, when investors placed too much emphasis on these elusive concepts, the potential for disappointment increased. Optimism over qualitative factors often found its way to a higher multiplier. Graham's experience led him to believe that to the extent investors moved away from hard assets and toward intangibles, such as management capability and the nature of a business, they invited potentially risky ways of thinking.

Make sure of your ground, Graham said. Start with net asset values as the fundamental departure point. If you bought assets, your downside was limited to the liquidation value of those assets. Nobody, reasoned Graham, can bail you out of optimistic growth projections if those projections are unfilled. If a company was perceived to be an attractive business, possessing superb management who predicted high future earnings, it would no doubt attract a growing number of stock buyers. "So they (investors) will buy it," said Graham, "and in doing so they will bid up the price and hence the price to earnings ratio. As more and more investors become enamored with the promised return, the price lifts free from underlying value and floats freely upward, creating a bubble that expands beautifully until finally it must burst."

If the greatest amount of a company's intrinsic value is measured in the quality of management, the nature of the business, and optimistic growth projections, there is little margin of safety, Graham said. If, on the other hand, a greater amount of a company's intrinsic value is the sum of measurable, quantitative factors, Graham figured that the investor's downside was more limited. Fixed assets are measurable. Dividends are measurable. Current earnings as well as historical earnings are measurable. Each of these factors can be demonstrated by figures and become a source of logic referenced by actual experience.

Graham said that having a good memory was his one burden. It was the memory of being financially deprived twice in a lifetime that led him to embrace an investment approach that stressed downside protection versus upside potential. There are two rules of investing, Graham said. The first rule is, Don't lose. The second rule is, Don't forget rule number one. This "don't lose" philosophy steered Graham toward two common stock selection approaches that, when applied, adhered to the margin of safety. The first approach was buying a company for less than two-thirds of its net asset value. The second approach was focusing on low price-to-earnings ratio stocks.

Buying a stock for a price that is less than two-thirds of its net assets fit neatly into Graham's sense of the present and satisfied his desire for some mathematical expectation. Graham gave no weight to a company's plant, property, and equipment. Furthermore, he deducted all of the company's short- and long-term liabilities. What remained was the net current assets. If the stock price was below this per-share value, Graham reasoned that a margin of safety existed. Therefore, a purchase was warranted. Graham considered this to be a foolproof method of investing. He did clarify that the results were based on the probable outcome of a group of stocks (diversification), not on the basis of individual results. Such stocks were pervasive at bear market bottoms and more scarce during bull markets.

Acknowledging that waiting for a market correction before making an investment may be unreasonable, Graham set out to design a second approach to buying stocks. He focused on stocks that were down in price and sold at a low price-to-earnings ratio. Additionally, the company must have some net asset value. In other words, the company must owe less than it is worth. Throughout his career, Graham worked with several variations of this approach. Shortly before his death, Graham was revising the fifth edition of *Security Analysis* with Sidney Cottle. At that time, Graham was analyzing the financial results of stocks that were purchased based on a ten-year, low price-to-earnings multiple, a stock price that was equal to half its previous market high and, of course, a net asset value. Graham tested stocks back to 1961 and found the results very promising.

Both approaches—buying a stock for less than two-thirds of net asset value and buying stocks with low price-to-earnings multiples— had a common occurrence. The stocks that Graham selected, based on these methods, were deeply out of favor with the market. Some macro- or microevent caused the market to price these stocks below their value. Graham felt strongly that these stocks, priced "unjustifiably low," were attractive purchases.

Graham's conviction rested on certain assumptions. First, he believed that the market frequently mispriced stocks. This mispricing was most often caused by the human emotions of fear and greed. At the height of optimism, greed moved stocks beyond their intrinsic value, creating an overpriced market. At other times, fear moved prices below intrinsic value, creating an undervalued market. The second assumption was based on the statistical phenomenon "reversion to the mean," although Graham did not use that term. More eloquently, he quoted Horace who said, "Many shall be restored that now are fallen, and many shall fall that now are in honor." However stated, Graham believed that an investor could profit from the corrective forces of an inefficient market.

## PHILIP FISHER

While Graham was writing *Security Analysis*, Philip Fisher was beginning his career as an investment counselor. After attending the Stanford University Graduate School of Business Administration, Fisher began work as an analyst at the Anglo London & Paris National Bank in San Francisco. In less than two years, he was made head of the bank's statistical department. It was from this perch that he witnessed the 1929 stock market crash. Then, after a brief career with a local brokerage house, Fisher decided to start his own investment counseling firm. On March 1, 1931, Fisher & Company began soliciting clients.

Starting an investment counseling firm in the early 1930s might have appeared unwise. However, Fisher found out, much to his surprise, that he had two advantages. First, every investor with any money after the stock market crash was probably unhappy with his or her present broker. Second, businesspeople, in the midst of the Depression, had plenty of time to sit and talk with Fisher. At Stanford, one of Fisher's business classes had required him to accompany his professor on periodic visits to companies in the San Francisco area. The professor engaged business managers in a series of discussions about their companies. Driving back to Stanford, Fisher and his professor talked endlessly about the companies and managers they visited. "That hour each week, Fisher says, was the most useful training he ever received." It was these experiences, Fisher noted, that led him to believe that superior profits could be made by (1) investing in companies with above average potential and (2) by aligning oneself with

the most capable management. To isolate these exceptional companies, Fisher developed a "point system" that qualified a company by
the characteristics of its business and its management.

The characteristic of a business that most impressed Fisher was a
company's ability to grow sales and profits over the years at rates
greater than the industry average. In order to do so, Fisher believed
that a company needed to possess "products or services with sufficient market potential to make possible a sizable increase in sales
for at least several years." Fisher was not so much concerned with
consistent annual increases in sales. Rather, he judged a company's
success over a period of several years. He was aware that changes in
the business cycle would have a material effect on sales and earnings.
However, Fisher identified companies that, decade by decade, showed
promise of above-average growth. According to Fisher, the two types
of companies that could expect to achieve above-average growth were
companies that, were (1) "fortunate and able" and were (2) "fortunate
because they are able."

Aluminum Company of America was an example, Fisher said, of a
company that was "fortunate and able." The company was "able"
because the founders of the company were people of great ability.
Alcoa's management foresaw the commercial uses for their product
and worked aggressively to capitalize the aluminum market to
increase sales. The company was also "fortunate," Fisher said, because
events outside management's immediate control were having a positive impact on the company and its market. The swift development of
airborne transportation was rapidly increasing sales of aluminum.
Because of the aviation industry, Alcoa was benefiting far more than
management originally envisioned.

Du Pont was a company, according to Fisher, that was "fortunate because it was able." If Du Pont had stayed with its original product, blasting powder, the company would have fared as well as most typical mining companies. But because management capitalized on the knowledge it had gained through the manufacturing of gunpowder, Du Pont was able to launch new products, including nylon, cellophane, and Lucite. These products created their own markets, producing billions of dollars in sales for Du Pont.

A company's research and development efforts, Fisher noted, contribute mightily to the sustainability of the company's above-average growth in sales. Obviously, Fisher explained, neither Du Pont nor Alcoa would have succeeded over the long term without a significant commitment to research and development. Even nontechnical businesses, he noted, need a dedicated research effort to produce better products and more efficient services.

In addition to research and development, Fisher also examined a company's sales organization. According to him, a company could develop outstanding products and services, but unless they were "expertly merchandised," the research and development effort would never translate into revenues. It is the responsibility of the sales organization to help customers understand the benefits of a company's products and services. A sales organization, Fisher explained, should also monitor its customer's buying habits and be able to spot changes in a customer's needs. The sales organization, according to Fisher, becomes the invaluable link between the marketplace and the research and development unit.

However, market potential alone is insufficient. Fisher believed that, even though capable of producing above-average sales growth, a company was an inappropriate investment if it was unable to generate profits for shareholders. "All the sales growth in the world won't produce the right type of investment vehicle if, over the years, profits do not grow correspondingly," he said. Accordingly, Fisher examined a company's profit margins, its dedication to maintaining and improving profit margins, and, finally, its cost analysis and accounting controls.

Fisher believed that superior investment returns were never obtained by investing in marginal companies. Those companies often produce adequate profits during expansion periods but see their profits decline rapidly during difficult economic times. For this reason, Fisher sought companies that were not only the lowest-cost producer of products or services but were dedicated to remaining so. A company with a low breakeven point, or a correspondingly high profit margin, is better able to withstand depressed economic environments. Ultimately it can drive out weaker competitors thereby strengthening its own market position. No company, Fisher said, will be able to sustain its profitability unless it is able to break down the costs of doing business while simultaneously understanding the cost of each step in the manufacturing process. In order to do so, he explained, a company must instill adequate accounting controls and cost analysis. This cost information, Fisher noted, enables a company to direct its resources to those products or services with the highest economic potential. Furthermore, accounting controls will help identify snags in a company's operations. These snags, or inefficiencies, act as an early warning device aimed at protecting the company's overall profitability.

Fisher's sensitivity about a company's profitability was linked with another concern, which he identified as the ability of a company to grow in the future without requiring equity financing. If a company is only able to grow by issuing equity, he said, the larger number of shares outstanding will cancel out any benefit that stockholders might realize from the company's growth. A company with high profit margins, he explained, is better able to generate funds internally. These funds can be used to sustain its growth without diluting existing shareholder's ownership, a situation caused by equity financing. In addition, a company that is able to maintain adequate cost controls over its fixed assets and working capital needs is better able to manage its cash needs and avoid equity financing.

Fisher was aware that superior companies possess not only above-average business characteristics but, equally as important, are directed by individuals who possess above-average management capabilities. These managers, he said, are determined to develop new products and services that will continue to spur sales growth long after current products or services are largely exploited. Many companies, Fisher noted, have adequate growth prospects from existing lines of products and services that will sustain these companies for several years, but few have policies in place to ensure consistent gains for ten to twenty years. "Management must have a viable policy," he said, "for attaining these ends with all the willingness to subordinate immediate profits for the greater long-range gains that this concept requires." Subordinating immediate profits, he explained, should not be confused with sacrificing immediate profits. The above-average manager simultaneously has the ability to implement the company's long-range plans while focusing on the daily operations of the company.

In addition to this ability, Fisher asked, does the business have a management of unquestionable integrity and honesty? Do the managers behave as if they are trustees for the stockholders, or does it appear as if management is only concerned with its own well-being? One way to determine management's intention, Fisher confided, is to observe how management communicates with its shareholders. All businesses, good and bad, will experience a period of unexpected difficulties. Commonly, when business is good, management talks freely; but when business declines, does management talk openly about the company's difficulties or does it clam up? How management responds to business difficulties, Fisher noted, tells a lot about itself.

For a business to be successful, he argued, management must develop good working relations with all of its employees. Employees, he explained, should genuinely feel that their company is a good place to work. Blue-collar employees should feel that they are treated with respect and decency. Executive employees should feel that promotion is based on ability, not favoritism. Also, Fisher asked, what is the depth of management? Has the chief executive officer a talented team, and is he able to delegate authority to run parts of the business?

Finally, Fisher examined the peculiarity of a company, that is, its business and management aspects plus how it compares to other businesses in the same industry. In this search, Fisher tried to uncover clues that might lead him to understand the superiority of a company in relation to its competitors. Fisher argued that reading only the financial reports of a company is not enough to justify an investment. The essential step in prudent investing is to uncover as much about a company as possible from those individuals who are familiar with the company. Admittedly, Fisher was attempting a catch-all inquiry. He called this random inquiry "scuttlebutt." Today we might call it the business grapevine. If handled properly, Fisher claimed, scuttlebutt will provide substantial clues that will enable the investor to identify outstanding investments.

Fisher's scuttlebutt investigation led him to interview customers and vendors. He sought out former employees as well as consultants who had worked for the company. Fisher contacted research scientists in universities, government employees, and trade association executives. He also interviewed competitors. Although executives may sometimes hesitate to disclose too much about their own company, Fisher noted, they never lack an opinion about their competitors. "It is amazing," Fisher said, "what an accurate picture of the relative points of strength and weaknesses of each company in an industry can be obtained from a representative cross section of the opinions of those who in one way or another are concerned with any particular company."

Most investors are unwilling to commit the time and energy Fisher required to understand a company. Developing a scuttlebutt network and arranging interviews is time consuming; replicating the scuttlebutt process for each company can be exhausting. Fisher reduced his workload by reducing the number of companies he owned. According to Fisher, he would rather own a few outstanding companies than a larger number of average businesses. Generally, his portfolios included fewer than ten companies, and often three to four companies represented 75 percent of his equity portfolio.

Fisher believed that to be successful, investors needed to do but a few things well. This included investing in companies that were within the investor's circle of competence. Fisher said earlier mistakes were "to project my skill beyond the limits of experience. I began investing outside the industries which I believed I thoroughly understood, in completely different spheres of activity; situations where I did not have comparable background knowledge."

IN COMPARISON

The differences between Graham and Fisher are apparent. Graham, the quantitative analyst, emphasized only those factors that could be measured: fixed assets, current earnings, and dividends. Graham's investigative research included only corporate filings and annual reports. Unlike Fisher, Graham did no interviewing of customers, competitors, or managers. He was only interested in developing an investment approach that could easily and safely be adapted by the average investor. In order to limit risk, Graham counseled investors to fully diversify their portfolio holdings.

Fisher's approach to investing can be viewed as the antithesis of Graham. Fisher, the qualitative analyst, emphasized those factors that he believed increased the value of a company: future prospects and management capability. Whereas Graham was interested in purchasing only cheap stocks, Fisher was interested in purchasing companies that had the potential to increase their intrinsic value over the long term. Unlike Graham, Fisher would go to great lengths, including conducting extensive interviews, to uncover bits of information that might improve his selection process. Finally, in contrast to Graham, Fisher preferred to concentrate his portfolio holdings and include only a few stocks.

Warren Buffett believes that these two different doctrines "parallel in the investment world." His investment approach has been to combine a qualitative understanding of the business and its management, taught by Fisher, with a quantitative understanding of price and value, taught by Graham.

## SYNTHESIS

Shortly after Graham's death in 1976, Buffett became the designated steward of Graham's value approach to investing. Indeed, Buffett's name became synonymous with value investing. This appointment appeared logical. He was the most famous of Graham's dedicated students, and Buffett himself never missed an opportunity to acknowledge the intellectual debt he owed to Graham. Even today, Buffett considers Graham to be the one individual, after his father, who had the most influence on his investment life. How, then, does Buffett reconcile his intellectual indebtedness to Graham with stock purchases such as American Express (1964), The Washington Post Company (1973), GEICO (1978), Capital Cities/ABC (1986), The Coca-Cola Company (1988), and Wells Fargo & Company (1990)? None of these companies passed Graham's strict financial test for purchase, yet Buffett made significant investments in all of them.

In his earlier purchases, Buffett exhibited unquestioning dedication to Graham's approach. Searching for companies that were selling for less than their net working capital, Buffett bought an anthracite company, a street railway company, and a windmill company. Soon Buffett began to realize that a few stocks he had purchased using Graham's strict quantitative guidelines were becoming unprofitable investments. While he was working at Graham-Newman, Buffett's research led him to dig deeper into a company's financial reports in hopes of understanding what was causing a company's stock price to languish. What Buffett learned was that several companies that he had bought at a cheap price (hence they met Graham's test for purchase) were cheap because their underlying businesses were suffering.

As early as 1965, Buffett was becoming aware that Graham's strategy of buying cheap stocks was not ideal. According to Buffett, Graham's value approach was to buy a stock so low in price that some "hiccup" in the company's business would allow investors to sell their shares at higher prices. Buffett called this strategy the "cigar butt" approach to investing. Walking down the street, an investor eyes a cigar butt lying on the ground and picks it up for one last puff.

Although it's a lousy smoke, its bargain price makes the puff all the more worthwhile. For Graham's strategy to consistently work, Buffett argued, someone must play the role of liquidator. If not a liquidator, then some other investor must be willing to purchase shares of your company, forcing the price of the stock upward.

As Buffett explained, if you paid $8 million for a company whose assets are worth $10 million, you will profit handsomely if the assets are sold on a timely basis. However, if the underlying economics of the business are poor and it takes ten years to sell the business, your total return is likely to be below average. "Time is the friend of the wonderful business," Buffett learned, "the enemy of mediocre." Unless he could facilitate the liquidation of his poorly performing companies and profit from the difference between his purchase price and the market value of the assets of a company, his performance would replicate the poor economics of the underlying business.

From his earliest investment mistakes, Buffett began moving away from Graham's strict teachings. "I evolved," he admitted, but "I didn't go from ape to human or human to ape in a nice even manner." He was beginning to appreciate the qualitative nature of certain companies, compared to the quantitative aspects of others, but he still found himself searching for bargains. "My punishment," he confessed, "was an education in the economics of short-line farm implementation manufacturers (Dempster Mill Manufacturing), third-place department stores (Hochschild-Kohn), and New England textile manufacturers (Berkshire Hathaway)." Buffett, attempting to explain his dilemma, quoted Keynes: "The difficulty lies not in the new ideas but in escaping from the old ones." Buffett's evolution was delayed, he admitted, because what Graham taught him was so valuable to him.

Even today, Buffett continues to embrace Graham's primary idea, the theory of the margin of safety. "Forty-two years after reading that," Buffett noted, "I still think those are the right three words." What Buffett learned from Graham was that successful investing involved the purchase of stocks when the market price of those stocks was at a significant discount to the underlying business value.

In 1984, speaking before students at Columbia University to mark the fiftieth anniversary celebration of *Security Analysis*, Buffett explained that there is a group of successful investors who acknowledge Ben Graham as their common intellectual patriarch. Graham provided the theory of margin of safety, but each student, noted Buffett, has developed different ways to apply this theory to determine a company's business value. However, the common theme is that they are all searching for some discrepancy between the value of a business and the price of the securities of that business. Individuals who are confused by Buffett's recent purchases fail to separate theory and methodology. Buffett clearly embraces Graham's margin of safety theory, but he has steadfastly moved away from Graham's methodology. According to Buffett, the last time it was easy to profit from Graham's methodology was in 1973–1974.

As early as 1969, Buffett was studying Fisher's writings. But it was Charlie Munger who was most responsible for moving Buffett toward Fisher's thinking. Charlie, in a sense, was the embodiment of Fisher's qualitative theories. Charlie had a keen appreciation of the value of a better business. Both See's Candy Shops and Buffalo News were tangible examples of good businesses available at reasonable prices. Charlie educated Buffett about the wisdom of paying up for a good business.

Ben Graham, the East Coast academician, represents the low-risk quantitative approach to investing. Fisher, the West Coast entrepreneur, represents a higher-risk qualitative approach to investing. It is interesting that Buffett, who has combined the quantitative attributes of Graham with the qualitative attributes of Fisher, has settled in Nebraska, midway between the coasts.

From Fisher, Buffett learned that the type of business purchased matters a lot. He also learned that management can affect the value of the underlying business, hence management's attributes needed to be studied as well. Fisher counseled that in order to become fully informed about a business, an investor had to investigate all aspects of the company and its competitors. From Fisher, Buffett learned the value of scuttlebutt. Throughout the years, Buffett has developed an extensive network of contacts who assist him in evaluating different businesses.

Finally, Fisher taught Buffett not to overstress diversification. According to Fisher, investors have been misled, believing that putting their eggs in several baskets reduces risk. The disadvantage of purchasing too many stocks is that it becomes impossible to watch all the eggs in all the different baskets. Investors run the risk of putting too little in a company that they are more familiar with and too much in a company that they are unfamiliar with. According to Fisher, buying a company without a thorough understanding of the business may be more risky than having limited diversification.

Graham did not think about businesses. Nor did he ponder the capabilities of management. He limited his research investigation to corporate filings and annual reports. If there was a mathematical probability of making money because the share price was less than the assets of the company, Graham purchased the company, regardless of its business or its management. In order to increase the probability of success, Graham chose to purchase as many of these statistical equations as possible. This thinking is the polar opposite of Fisher's. If Graham's teachings were limited to these precepts, Buffett would have little regard for him. But the margin of safety theory that Graham emphasized is so important to Buffett that all other current weaknesses of Graham's methodology can be overlooked.

In addition to the margin of safety theory, which became the intellectual framework for Buffett's thinking, Graham helped Buffett appreciate the folly of following stock market fluctuations. Stocks have an investment characteristic and a speculative characteristic, Graham taught Buffett. The margin of safety helps explain a stock's investment characteristic. The speculative characteristics of a stock are a consequence of people's fear and greed. These emotions, present in most investors, cause stock prices to gyrate far above and below a company's intrinsic value. Graham taught Buffett that if he could insulate himself from the emotional whirlwinds of the stock market, he had the opportunity to exploit the irrational behavior of other investors, who purchased stocks based on emotion, not logic. Buffett learned from Graham how to think independently. If you have reached a logical conclusion based on sound judgment, Graham counseled Buffett, do not be dissuaded just because others may disagree. "You are neither right nor wrong because the crowd disagrees with you," wrote Graham. "You are right because your data and reasoning are right."

Buffett's dedication to both Graham and Fisher is understandable. Graham gave Buffett the intellectual basis for investing, the margin of safety, and helped Buffett learn to master his emotions in order to take advantage of market fluctuations. Fisher gave Buffett an updated, workable methodology that enabled him to identify good long-term investments. The frequent confusion surrounding Buffett's investment actions is easily understood when people acknowledge that Buffett is the synthesis of both Graham's and Fisher's philosophy.

"It is not enough to have good intelligence," wrote Descartes, "the principle thing is to apply it well." It is the application that separates Buffett from other investment managers. A number of his peers are highly intelligent, disciplined, and dedicated. Buffett stands above them all because of his formidable ability to implement his strategies.

An investor who put $10,000 to work in **Peter Lynch**'s
Fidelity Magellan Fund in 1977 would have accumulated
$280,000 by 1990. Lynch's 1989 book, written with **John
Rothchild**, included this passage defining the perfect
stock.

# THE PERFECT STOCK, WHAT A DEAL!
by Peter Lynch with John Rothchild

from *One Up on Wall Street* (1989)

G ETTING THE STORY on a company is a lot easier if you
understand the basic business. That's why I'd rather invest
in panty hose than in communications satellites, or in
motel chains than in fiber optics. The simpler it is, the better I like it.
When somebody says, "Any idiot could run this joint," that's a plus as
far as I'm concerned, because sooner or later any idiot probably is
going to be running it.

If it's a choice between owning stock in a fine company with excellent management in a highly competitive and complex industry, or a
humdrum company with mediocre management in a simpleminded
industry with no competition, I'd take the latter. For one thing, it's
easier to follow. During a lifetime of eating donuts or buying tires,
I've developed a feel for the product line that I'll never have with laser
beams or microprocessors.

"Any idiot can run this business" is one characteristic of the perfect
company, the kind of stock I dream about. You never find the perfect
company, but if you can imagine it, then you'll know how to recognize
favorable attributes, the most important thirteen of which are as follows:

## (1) IT SOUNDS DULL—OR, EVEN BETTER, RIDICULOUS

The perfect stock would be attached to the perfect company, and the perfect company has to be engaged in a perfectly simple business, and the perfectly simple business ought to have a perfectly boring name. The more boring it is, the better. Automatic Data Processing is a good start.

But Automatic Data Processing isn't as boring as Bob Evans Farms. What could be duller than a stock named Bob Evans? It puts you to sleep just thinking about it, which is one reason it's been such a great prospect. But even Bob Evans Farms won't win the prize for the best name you could give to a stock, and neither will Shoney's or Crown, Cork, and Seal. None of these has a chance against Pep Boys— Manny, Moe, & Jack.

Pep Boys—Manny, Moe, and Jack is the most promising name I've ever heard. It's better than dull, it's ridiculous. Who wants to put money into a company that sounds like the Three Stooges? What Wall Street analyst or portfolio manager in his right mind would recommend a stock called Pep Boys—Manny, Moe, and Jack—unless of course the Street already realizes how profitable it is, and by then it's up tenfold already.

Blurting out that you own Pep Boys won't get you much of an audience at a cocktail party, but whisper "GeneSplice International" and everybody listens. Meanwhile, GeneSplice International is going nowhere but down, while Pep Boys—Manny, Moe, and Jack just keeps going higher.

If you discover an opportunity early enough, you probably get a few dollars off the price just for the dull or odd name, which is why I'm always on the lookout for the Pep Boys or the Bob Evanses, or the occasional Consolidated Rock. Too bad that wonderful aggregate company changed its name to Conrock and then the trendier Calmat. As long as it was Consolidated Rock, nobody paid attention to it.

## (2) IT DOES SOMETHING DULL

I get even more excited when a company with a boring name also does something boring. Crown, Cork, and Seal makes cans and bottle caps. What could be duller than that? You won't see an interview with the CEO of Crown, Cork, and Seal in *Time* magazine alongside an interview with Lee Iacocca, but that's a plus. There's nothing boring about what's happened to the shares of Crown, Cork, and Seal.

I already mentioned Seven Oaks International, the company that processes the coupons that you hand in at the grocery store. There's another tale that's guaranteed to shut your eyes—as the stock sneaks up from $4 to $33. Seven Oaks International and Crown, Cork, and Seal make IBM seem like a Las Vegas revue, and how about Agency Rent-A-Car? That's the glamorous outfit that provides the car the insurance company lets you drive while yours is being repaired. Agency Rent-A-Car came public at $4 a share and Wall Street hardly noticed. What self-respecting tycoon would want to think about what people drive while their cars are in the shop? The Agency Rent-A-Car prospectus could have been marketed as an anesthetic, but the last time I looked, the stock was $16.

A company that does boring things is almost as good as a company that has a boring name, and both together is terrific. Both together is guaranteed to keep the oxymorons away until finally the good news compels them to buy in, thus sending the stock price even higher. If a company with terrific earnings and a strong balance sheet also does dull things, it gives you a lot of time to purchase the stock at a discount.

Then when it becomes trendy and overpriced, you can sell your shares to the trend-followers.

## (3) IT DOES SOMETHING DISAGREEABLE

Better than boring alone is a stock that's boring and disgusting at the same time. Something that makes people shrug, retch, or turn away in disgust is ideal. Take Safety-Kleen. That's a name with promise to begin with—any company that uses a *k* where there ought to be a *c* is worth investigating. The fact that Safety-Kleen was once related to Chicago Rawhide is also favorable (see "It's a Spinoff" later in this chapter).

Safety-Kleen goes around to all the gas stations and provides them with a machine that washes greasy auto parts. This saves auto mechanics the time and trouble of scrubbing the parts by hand in a pail of gasoline, and gas stations gladly pay for the service. Periodically the Safety-Kleen people come around to remove the dirty sludge and oil from the machine, and they carry the sludge back to the refinery to be recycled. This goes on and on, and you'll never see a miniseries about it on network TV.

Safety-Kleen hasn't rested on the spoils of greasy auto parts. It has since branched out into restaurant grease traps and other sorts of messes. What analyst would want to write about this, and what portfolio manager would want to have Safety-Kleen on his buy list? There aren't many, which is precisely what's endearing about Safety-Kleen. Like Automatic Data Processing, this company has had an unbroken run of increased earnings. Profits have gone up every quarter, and so has the stock.

Or how about Envirodyne? This one was pointed out to me a few years ago by Thomas Sweeney, then Fidelity's forest products analyst and now the manager of Fidelity Capital Appreciation Fund. Envirodyne passes the odd name test: it sounds like something you could bounce off the ozone layer, when actually it has to do with lunch. One of its subsidiaries, Clear Shield, makes plastic forks and straws, the perfect business that any idiot could run, but in reality it has topflight management with a large personal stake in the company.

Envirodyne is number two in plastic cutlery and number three in plastic straws, and being the lowest-cost producer gives it a big advantage in the industry.

In 1985, Envirodyne started negotiating to buy Viskase, a leading producer of intestinal byproducts, particularly the casings surrounding hot dogs and sausages. They got Viskase from Union Carbide at a bargain price. Then in 1986 they bought Filmco, the leading producer of the PVC film that's used to wrap leftover food items. Plastic forks, hot-dog casings, plastic wrap—pretty soon they'll take over the family picnic.

Largely as a result of these acquisitions, the earnings increased from 34 cents a share in 1985 to $2 a share in 1987—and should top $2.50 in 1988. The company has used its substantial cash flow to pay down its debt on the various acquisitions. I bought it for $3 a share in September, 1985. At the high in 1988 it sold for $36⅞.

## (4) It's a Spinoff

Spinoffs of divisions or parts of companies into separate, freestanding entities—such as Safety-Kleen out of Chicago Rawhide or Toys "R" Us out of Interstate Department Stores—often result in astoundingly lucrative investments. Dart & Kraft, which merged years ago, eventually separated so that Kraft could become a pure food company again. Dart (which owns Tupperware) was spun off as Premark International and has been a great investment on its own. So has Kraft, which was bought out by Philip Morris in 1988.

Large parent companies do not want to spin off divisions and then see those spinoffs get into trouble, because that would bring embarrassing publicity that would reflect back on the parents. Therefore, the spinoffs normally have strong balance sheets and are well-prepared to succeed as independent entities. And once these companies are granted their independence, the new management, free to run its own show, can cut costs and take creative measures that improve the near-term and long-term earnings.

Here is a list of some recent spinoffs that have done well, and a couple that haven't done so well:

| | | STRONG PERFORMERS | | | |
|---|---|---|---|---|---|
| Parent | Spinoff | Approx. First Trade | Low | High | October 31, 1988 |
| Teledyne | Argonaut* | $18 | $15 | $52 1/8 | 43 1/4 |
| | Amer. Ecology | 4 | 2 3/4 | 50 1/4 | 12 3/4 |
| US Gypsum | AP Green | 11 | 11 | 26 | 26 3/4 |
| IU Intl. | Gotaas Larsen | 6 | 2 5/8 | 36 1/4 | 47 3/4 |
| Masco Corp. | Masco Ind. | 2 | 1 1/2 | 18 3/4 | 11 3/8 |
| Kraft | Premark Intl. | 19 | 17 1/2 | 36 1/4 | 29 7/8 |
| Tandy | Intertan | 10 | 10 | 31 1/4 | 35 1/4 |
| Singer | SSMC | 13 | 11 1/2 | 31 3/8 | 23 |
| Natomas | Amer. President | 16 | 13 7/8 | 51 | 32 3/8 |
| Interlake | Acme Steel | 8 | 7 5/8 | 24 1/2 | 23 1/2 |
| Transamer. | Imo Delaval | 8 | 6 3/4 | 23 | 18 1/2 |
| Transunion | Intl. Shiphold. | 2 | 2 3/8 | 20 | 17 |
| Gen. Mills | Kenner Parker | 16 | 13 7/8 | 51 1/2 | —** |

WEAKER PERFORMERS

| Parent | Spinoff | Approx. First Trade | Low | High | October 31, 1988 |
|---|---|---|---|---|---|
| Borg Warner | York Int. | $14 | $13 1/2 | $59 3/4 | $51 5/8 |
| Time Inc. | Temple Inland | 34 | 20 1/2 | 68 1/2 | 50 3/4 |
| Penn Cent. | Sprague Tech. | 15 | 7 1/8 | 20 | 12 1/8 |
| John Blair | Advo Systems | 6 | 4 | 12 3/4 | 3 7/8 |
| Datapoint | Intelogic Trace*** | 8 | 2 1/2 | 18 1/8 | 3 3/4 |
| Coca-Cola | Coca-Cola Ent. | 15 1/2 | 10 1/2 | 21 1/4 | 14 1/2 |

* Both Argonaut and American Ecology were spun out of Teledyne, which is one of the great all-time stocks in its own right.
** Acquired by Tonka in Oct. 1987 for $49.50 a share
*** Troubled company during spinoff

The literature sent to shareholders explaining the spinoff is usually hastily prepared, blasé, and understated, which makes it even better than the regular annual reports. Spinoff companies are often misunderstood and get little attention from Wall Street. Investors often are sent shares in the newly created company as a bonus or a dividend for owning the parent company, and institutions, especially, tend to dismiss these shares as pocket change or found money. These are favorable omens for the spinoff stocks.

This is a fertile area for the amateur shareholder, especially in the recent frenzy of mergers and acquisitions. Companies that are targets of hostile takeovers frequently fight off raiders by selling or spinning off divisions that then become publicly traded issues on their own. When a company is taken over, the parts are often sold off for cash, and they, too, become separate entities in which to invest. If you hear about a spinoff, or if you're sent a few fractions of shares in some newly created company, begin an immediate investigation into buying more. A month or two after the spinoff is completed, you can check to see if there is heavy insider buying among the new officers and directors. This will confirm that they, too, believe in the company's prospects.

The greatest spinoffs of all were the "Baby Bell" companies that were created in the breakup of ATT: Ameritech, Bell Atlantic, Bell South, Nynex, Pacific Telesis, Southwestern Bell, and US West. While the parent has been an uninspiring performer, the average gain from stock in the seven newly created companies was 114 percent from November, 1983, to October, 1988. Add in the dividends and the total return is more like 170 percent. This beats the market twice around, and it beats the majority of all known mutual funds, including the one run by yours truly.

Once liberated, the seven regional companies were able to increase earnings, cut costs, and enjoy higher profits. They got all the local and regional telephone business, the yellow pages, along with 50 cents for every $1 of long-distance business generated by ATT. It was a great niche. They had already gone through an earlier period of heavy spending on modern equipment, so they didn't have to dilute shareholders' equity by selling extra stock. And human nature being what it is, the seven Baby Bells set up a healthy competition amongst themselves, and also between themselves and their proud parent, Ma Bell. Ma, meanwhile, was losing its stranglehold on its highly profitable leased equipment business, and facing new competitors such as Sprint and MCI, and sustaining heavy losses in its computer operations.

Investors who owned the old ATT stock had eighteen months to decide what to do. They could sell ATT and be done with the whole complicated mess, they could keep ATT plus the shares and fractions of shares in the new Baby Bells that they received, or they could sell the parent and keep the Baby Bells. If they did their homework, they sold ATT, kept the Baby Bells, and added to their position with as many more shares as they could afford.

Pounds of material were sent out to the 2.96 million ATT shareholders explaining the Baby Bells' plans. The new companies laid out exactly what they were going to do. A million employees of ATT and countless suppliers could have seen what was going on. So much for the amateur's edge being restricted to a lucky few. For that matter, anyone who had a phone knew that there were big changes going on. I participated in the rally, but only in a modest way—I never dreamed that conservative companies such as these could do so well so quickly.

## (5) THE INSTITUTIONS DON'T OWN IT, AND THE ANALYSTS DON'T FOLLOW IT

If you find a stock with little or no institutional ownership, you've found a potential winner. Find a company that no analyst has ever visited, or that no analyst would admit to knowing about, and you've got a double winner. When I talk to a company that tells me the last analyst showed up three years ago, I can hardly contain my enthusiasm. It frequently happens with banks, savings-and-loans, and insurance companies, since there are thousands of these and Wall Street only keeps up with fifty to one hundred.

I'm equally enthusiastic about once-popular stocks the professionals have abandoned, as many abandoned Chrysler at the bottom and Exxon at the bottom, just before both began to rebound.

Data on institutional ownership are available from the following sources: *Vicker's Institutional Holdings Guide, Nelson's Directory of Investment Research*, and the *Spectrum Surveys*, a publication of CDA Investment Technologies. Although these publications are not always easy to find, you can get similar information from the *Value Line Investment Survey* and from the S&P stock sheets, also called tear sheets. Both are routinely provided by regular stockbrokers.

## (6) THE RUMORS ABOUND: IT'S INVOLVED WITH TOXIC WASTE AND/OR THE MAFIA

It's hard to think of a more perfect industry than waste management. If there's anything that disturbs people more than animal casings, grease, and dirty oil, it's sewage and toxic waste dumps. That's why I got very excited one day when the solid waste executives showed up in my office. They had come to town for a solid waste convention complete with booths and slides—imagine how attractive that must have been. Anyway, instead of the usual blue cotton button-down shirts that I see day after day, they were wearing polo shirts that said "Solid Waste." Who would put on shirts like that, unless it was the Solid Waste bowling team? These are the kind of executives you dream about.

As you already know if you were fortunate enough to have bought some, Waste Management, Inc. is up about a hundredfold.

Waste Management is a better prospect even than Safety-Kleen because it has two unthinkables going for it: toxic waste itself, and also the Mafia. Everyone who fantasizes that the Mafia runs all the Italian restaurants, the newsstands, the dry cleaners, the construction sites, and the olive presses also probably thinks that the Mafia controls the garbage business. This fantastic assertion was a great advantage to the earliest buyers of shares in Waste Management, which as usual were underpriced relative to the actual opportunity.

Maybe the rumors of the Mafia in waste management kept away the same investors who worried about the Mafia in hotel/casino management. Remember the dreaded casino stocks that are now on everybody's buy list? Respectable investors weren't supposed to touch them because the casinos allegedly were all Mafia. Then the earnings exploded and the profits exploded, and the Mafia faded into the background. When Holiday Inn and Hilton got into the casino business, it suddenly was all right to own casino stocks.

## (7) There's Something Depressing about It

In this category my favorite all-time pick is Service Corporation International (SCI), which also has a boring name. I got this pick from George Vanderheiden, the onetime Fidelity electronics analyst who's done a great job running the Fidelity Destiny Fund.

Now, if there's anything Wall Street would rather ignore besides toxic waste, it's mortality. And SCI does burials.

For several years this Houston-based enterprise has been going around the country buying up local funeral homes from the mom-and-pop owners, just as Gannett did with the small-town newspapers. SCI has become a sort of McBurial. It has picked up the active funeral parlors that bury a dozen or more people a week, ignoring the smaller one- or two-burial parlors.

At last count the company owned 461 funeral parlors, 121 cemeteries, 76 flower shops, 21 funeral product-and-supply manufacturing centers, and 3 casket distribution centers, so they're vertically integrated. They broke into the big-time when they buried Howard Hughes.

They also pioneered the pre-need policy, a layaway plan that's been very popular. It enables you to pay off your funeral service and your casket right now while you can still afford it, so your family won't have to pay for it later. Even if the cost has tripled by the time you require a funeral service, you're locked in at the old prices. This is a great deal for the family of the deceased, and an even greater deal for the company.

SCI gets the money from its pre-need sales right away, and the cash just keeps on compounding. If they sell $50 million worth of these policies each year, it will add up to billions by the time they've had all the funerals. Lately they've gone beyond their own operations to offer the pre-need policies to other funeral homes. Over the past five years the sales of pre-arranged funerals have been climbing at 40 percent a year.

Once in a while a positive story is topped off by an extraordinary kicker, an unexpected valuable card that turns up. In SCI's case it happened when the company struck a very lucrative bargain with another company (American General) that wanted to buy the real estate under one of SCI's Houston locations. In return for the rights to this land, American General, which owned 20 percent of SCI's stock, gave all their stock back to SCI. Not only did SCI retrieve 20 percent of its shares at no cost, but it was allowed to continue to operate the funeral home at the old location for two years, until it could open a new home at a different site in Houston.

The best thing about this company is that it was shunned by most professional investors for years. Despite an incredible record, the SCI executives had to go out on cavalcades to beg people to listen to their story. That meant that amateurs in the know could buy stock in a proven winner with a record of solid growth in earnings, and at much lower prices than they'd have to pay for a hot stock in a popular industry. Here was the perfect opportunity—everything was working, you could see it happening, the earnings kept increasing, there was rapid growth with almost no debt—and Wall Street turned the other way.

Only in 1986 did SCI develop a big following among the institutions, who now own over 50 percent of the shares, and more analysts started covering the company. Predictably the stock was a twenty-bagger before SCI got Wall Street's full attention, but since then it has greatly underperformed the market. In addition to the burdens of high institutional ownership and broad coverage by brokers, the company has been hurt in the last few years by entering the casket business through two acquisitions that have not contributed to profits. Also, the price of buying quality funeral homes and cemeteries has risen sharply, and the growth in pre-need insurance has been less than expected.

### (8) IT'S A NO-GROWTH INDUSTRY

Many people prefer to invest in a high-growth industry, where there's a lot of sound and fury. Not me. I prefer to invest in a low-growth industry like plastic knives and forks, but only if I can't find a no-growth industry like funerals. That's where the biggest winners are developed.

There's nothing thrilling about a thrilling high-growth industry, except watching the stocks go down. Carpets in the 1950s, electronics in the 1960s, computers in the 1980s, were all exciting high-growth industries, in which numerous major and minor companies unerringly failed to prosper for long. That's because for every single product in a hot industry, there are a thousand MIT graduates trying to figure out how to make it cheaper in Taiwan. As soon as a computer company designs the best word-processor in the world, ten other competitors are spending $100 million to design a better one, and it will be on the market in eight months. This doesn't happen with bottle caps, coupon-clipping services, oil-drum retrieval, or motel chains.

SCI was helped by the fact that there's almost no growth in the funeral industry. Growth in the burial business in this country limps along at one percent a year, too slow for the action-seekers who've gone into computers. But it's a steady business with as reliable a customer base as you could ever find.

In a no-growth industry, especially one that's boring and upsets people, there's no problem with competition. You don't have to protect your flanks from potential rivals because nobody else is going to be interested. This gives you the leeway to continue to grow, to gain market share, as SCI has done with burials. SCI already owns 5 percent of the nation's funeral homes, and there's nothing stopping them from owning 10 percent or 15 percent. The graduating class of Wharton isn't going to want to challenge SCI, and you can't tell your friends in the investment banking firms that you've decided to specialize in picking up dirty oil from the gas stations.

### (9) IT'S GOT A NICHE

I'd much rather own a local rock pit than own Twentieth Century-Fox, because a movie company competes with other movie companies, and the rock pit has a niche. Twentieth Century-Fox understood that when it bought up Pebble Beach, and the rock pit with it.

Certainly, owning a rock pit is safer than owning a jewelry business. If you're in the jewelry business, you're competing with other jewelers from across town, across the state, and even abroad, since vacationers can buy jewelry anywhere and bring it home. But if you've got the only gravel pit in Brooklyn, you've got a virtual monopoly, plus the added protection of the unpopularity of rock pits.

The insiders call this the "aggregate" business, but even the exalted name doesn't alter the fact that rocks, sand, and gravel are as close to inherently worthless as you can get. That's the paradox: mixed together, the stuff probably sells for $3 a ton. For the price of a glass of orange juice, you can purchase a half ton of aggregate, which, if you've got a truck, you can take home and dump on your lawn.

What makes a rock pit valuable is that nobody else can compete with it. The nearest rival owner from two towns over isn't going to haul his rocks into your territory because the trucking bills would eat up all his profit. No matter how good the rocks are in Chicago, no Chicago rock-pit owner can ever invade your territory in Brooklyn or Detroit. Due to the weight of rocks, aggregates are an exclusive franchise. You don't have to pay a dozen lawyers to protect it.

There's no way to overstate the value of exclusive franchises to a company or its shareholders. INCO is the world's great producer of nickel today, and it will be the world's great producer in fifty years. Once I was standing at the edge of the Bingham Pit copper mine in Utah, and looking down into that impressive cavern, it occurred to me that nobody in Japan or Korea can invent a Bingham pit.

Once you've got an exclusive franchise in anything, you can raise prices. In the case of rock pits you can raise prices to just below the point that the owner of the next rock pit might begin to think about competing with you. He's figuring his prices via the same method.

To top it off, you get big tax breaks from depreciating your earth movers and rock crushers, plus you get a mineral depletion allowance, the same as Exxon and Atlantic Richfield get for their own oil and gas deposits. I can't imagine anyone's going bankrupt over a rock pit. So if you can't run your own rock pit, the next best thing is buying shares in aggregate-producing companies such as Vulcan Materials, Calmat, Boston Sand & Gravel, Dravo, and Florida Rock. When larger companies such as Martin-Marietta, General Dynamics, or Ashland sell off various parts of their businesses, they always keep the rock pits.

I always look for niches. The perfect company would have to have one. Warren Buffett started out by acquiring a textile mill in New Bedford, Massachusetts, which he quickly realized was not a niche business. He did poorly in textiles but went on to make billions for his shareholders by investing in niches. He was one of the first to see the value in newspapers and TV stations that dominated major markets, beginning with the *Washington Post*. Thinking along the same lines, I bought as much stock as I could in Affiliated Publications, which owns the local *Boston Globe*. Since the *Globe* gets over 90 percent of the print ad revenues in Boston, how could the *Globe* lose?

The *Globe* has a niche, and the Times Mirror Company has several, including the *Los Angeles Times*, *Newsday*, the *Hartford Courant*, and the *Baltimore Sun*. Gannett owns 90 daily newspapers, and most of them are the only major dailies in town. Investors who discovered the advantages of exclusive newspaper and cable franchises in the early 1970s were rewarded with a number of ten-baggers as the cable stocks and media stocks got popular on Wall Street.

Any reporter, ad executive, or editor who worked at the *Washington Post* could have seen the profits and the earnings and understood the value of the niche. A newspaper company is a great business for a variety of reasons as well.

Drug companies and chemical companies have niches—products that no one else is allowed to make. It took years for SmithKline to get the patent for Tagamet. Once a patent is approved, all the rival companies with their billions in research dollars can't invade the territory. They have to invent a different drug, prove it is different, and then go through three years of clinical trials before the government will let them sell it. They have to prove that it doesn't kill rats, and most drugs, it seems, do kill rats.

Or perhaps rats aren't as healthy as they used to be. Come to think of it, I once made money on a rat stock—Charles River Breeding Labs. There's a business that turns people off.

Chemical companies have niches in pesticides and herbicides. It's not any easier to get a poison approved than it is to get a cure approved. Once you have a patent and the federal go-ahead on a pesticide or a herbicide, you've got a money machine. Monsanto has several today.

Brand names such as Robitussin or Tylenol, Coca-Cola or Marlboro, are almost as good as niches. It costs a fortune to develop public confidence in a soft drink or a cough medicine. The whole process takes years.

### (10) PEOPLE HAVE TO KEEP BUYING IT

I'd rather invest in a company that makes drugs, soft drinks, razor blades, or cigarettes than in a company that makes toys. In the toy industry somebody can make a wonderful doll that every child has to have, but every child gets only one each. Eight months later that product is taken off the shelves to make room for the newest doll the children have to have—manufactured by somebody else.

Why take chances on fickle purchases when there's so much steady business around?

### (11) IT'S A USER OF TECHNOLOGY

Instead of investing in computer companies that struggle to survive in an endless price war, why not invest in a company that benefits from the price war—such as Automatic Data Processing? As computers get cheaper, Automatic Data can do its job cheaper and thus increase its own profits. Or instead of investing in a company that makes automatic scanners, why not invest in the supermarkets that install the scanners? If a scanner helps a supermarket company cut costs just three percent, that alone might double the company's earnings.

## (12) THE INSIDERS ARE BUYERS

There's no better tip-off to the probable success of a stock than that people in the company are putting their own money into it. In general, corporate insiders are net sellers, and they normally sell 2.3 shares to every one share that they buy. After the 1,000-point drop from August to October, 1987, it was reassuring to discover that there were four shares bought to every one share sold by insiders across the board. At least they hadn't lost their faith.

When insiders are buying like crazy, you can be certain that, at a minimum, the company will not go bankrupt in the next six months. When insiders are buying, I'd bet there aren't three companies in history that have gone bankrupt near term.

Long term, there's another important benefit. When management owns stock, then rewarding the shareholders becomes a first priority, whereas when management simply collects a paycheck, then increasing salaries becomes a first priority. Since bigger companies tend to pay bigger salaries to executives, there's a natural tendency for corporate wage-earners to expand the business at any cost, often to the detriment of shareholders. This happens less often when management is heavily invested in shares.

Although it's a nice gesture for the CEO or the corporate president with the million-dollar salary to buy a few thousand shares of the company stock, it's more significant when employees at the lower echelons add to their positions. If you see someone with a $45,000 annual salary buying $10,000 worth of stock, you can be sure it's a meaningful vote of confidence. That's why I'd rather find seven vice presidents buying 1,000 shares apiece than the president buying 5,000.

If the stock price drops after the insiders have bought, so that you have a chance to buy it cheaper than they did, so much the better for you.

It's simple to keep track of insider purchases. Every time an officer or a director buys or sells shares, he or she has to declare it on Form 4 and send the form to the Securities and Exchange Commission advising them of the fact. Several newsletter services, including *Vicker's Weekly Insider Report* and *The Insiders*, keep track of these filings. *Barron's*, *The Wall Street Journal*, and *Investor's Daily* also carry the information. Many local business newspapers report on insider trading on local companies—I know the *Boston Business Journal* has such a column. Your broker may also be able to provide the information, or you may find that your local library subscribes to the newsletters. There's also a tabulation of insider buying and selling in the *Value Line* publication.

(Insider selling usually means nothing, and it's silly to react to it. If a stock had gone from $3 to $12 and nine officers were selling, I'd take notice, particularly if they were selling a majority of their shares. But in normal situations insider selling is not an automatic sign of trouble within a company. There are many reasons that officers might sell. They may need the money to pay their children's tuition or to buy a new house or to satisfy a debt. They may have decided to diversify into other stocks. But there's only one reason that insiders buy: They think the stock price is undervalued and will eventually go up.)

## (13) THE COMPANY IS BUYING BACK SHARES

Buying back shares is the simplest and best way a company can reward its investors. If a company has faith in its own future, then why shouldn't it invest in itself, just as the shareholders do? The announcement of massive share buybacks by company after company broke on October 20, 1987 the fall of many stocks, and stabilized the market at the height of its panic. Long term, these buybacks can't help but reward investors.

When stock is bought in by the company, it is taken out of circulation, therefore shrinking the number of outstanding shares. This can have a magical effect on earnings per share, which in turn has a magical effect on the stock price. If a company buys back half its shares and its overall earnings stay the same, the earnings per share have just doubled. Few companies could get that kind of result by cutting costs or selling more widgets.

Exxon has been buying in shares because it's cheaper than drilling for oil. It might cost Exxon $6 a barrel to find new oil, but if each of its shares represents $3 a barrel in oil assets, then retiring shares has the same effect as discovering $3 oil on the floor of the New York Stock Exchange.

This sensible practice was almost unheard of until quite recently. Back in the 1960s, International Dairy Queen was one of the pioneers in share buybacks, but there were few others who followed suit. At the delightful Crown, Cork, and Seal they've bought back shares every year for the last twenty. They never pay a dividend, and they never make unprofitable acquisitions, but by shrinking shares they've gotten the maximum impact from the earnings. If this keeps up, someday there will be a thousand shares of Crown, Cork, and Seal—worth $10 million apiece.

At Teledyne, chairman Henry E. Singleton periodically offers to buy in the stock at a much higher price than is bid on the stock exchange. When Teledyne was selling for $5, he might have paid $7, and when the stock was at $10, then he was paying $14, and so on. All along he's given shareholders a chance to get out at a fancy premium. This practical demonstration of Teledyne's belief in itself is more convincing than the adjectives in the annual report.

The common alternatives to buying back shares are (1) raising the dividend, (2) developing new products, (3) starting new operations, and (4) making acquisitions. Gillette tried to do all four, with emphasis on the final three. Gillette has a spectacularly profitable razor business, which it gradually reduced in relative size as it acquired less profitable operations. If the company had regularly bought back its shares and raised its dividend instead of diverting its capital to cosmetics, toiletries, ballpoint pens, cigarette lighters, curlers, blenders, office products, toothbrushes, hair care, digital watches, and lots of other diversions, the stock might well be worth over $100 instead of the current $35. In the last five years, Gillette has gotten back on track by eliminating losing operations and emphasizing its core shaving business, where it dominates the market.

The reverse of buying back shares is adding more shares, also called diluting. International Harvester, now Navistar, sold millions of additional shares to raise cash to help it survive a financial crisis brought about by the collapse of the farm-equipment business. Chrysler, remember, did just the opposite—buying back stock and stock warrants and shrinking the number of outstanding shares as the business improved. Navistar is once again a profitable company, but because of the extraordinary dilution, the earnings have a minimal impact, and shareholders have yet to benefit from the recovery to any significant degree.

## THE GREATEST COMPANY OF ALL

If I could dream up a single glorious enterprise that combines all of the worst elements of Waste Management, Pep Boys, Safety-Kleen, rock pits, and bottle caps, it would have to be Cajun Cleansers. Cajun Cleansers is engaged in the boring business of removing mildew stains from furniture, rare books, and draperies that are victims of subtropical humidity. It's a recent spinoff from Louisiana BayouFeedback.

Its headquarters are located in the bayous of Louisiana, and to get there you have to change planes twice, then hire a pickup truck to take you from the airport. Not one analyst from New York or Boston ever visited Cajun Cleansers, nor has any institution bought a solitary share.

Mention Cajun Cleansers at a cocktail party and soon you'll be talking to yourself. It sounds ridiculous to everyone within earshot.

While expanding quickly through the bayous and the Ozarks, Cajun Cleansers has had incredible sales. These sales will soon accelerate because the company just received a patent on a new gel that removes all sorts of stains from clothes, furniture, carpets, bathroom tiles, and even aluminum siding. The patent gives Cajun the niche it's been looking for.

The company is also planning to offer lifetime prestain insurance to millions of Americans, who can pay in advance for a guaranteed removal of all the future stain accidents they ever cause. A fortune in off-balance-sheet revenue will soon be pouring in.

No popular magazines except the ones that think Elvis is alive have mentioned Cajun and its new patent. The stock opened at $8 in a public offering seven years ago and soon rose to $10. At that price the important corporate directors bought as many shares as they could afford.

I hear about Cajun from a distant relative who swears it's the only way to get mildew off leather jackets left too long in dank closets. I do some research and discover that Cajun has had a 20 percent growth rate in earnings for the past four years, it's never had a down quarter, there's no debt on the balance sheet, and it did well in the last recession. I visit the company and find out that any trained crustacean could oversee the making of the gel.

The day before I decide to buy Cajun Cleansers, the noted economist Henry Kaufman has predicted that interest rates are going up, and then the head of the Federal Reserve slips on the lane at a bowling alley and injures his back, both of which combine to send the market down 15 percent, and Cajun Cleansers with it. I get in at $7.50, which is $2.50 less than the directors paid.

That's the situation at Cajun Cleansers. Don't pinch me. I'm dreaming.

Kirk Kazanjian's 2002 interview with fund manager William Miller addresses several questions: How does Miller's Legg Mason Value Trust so consistently beat the S&P 500? Is Miller a value investor? What is a value investor, anyway?

# WILLIAM MILLER
# BY KIRK KAZANJIAN

from *Value Investing with the Masters* (2002)

ILL MILLER IS arguably the most intriguing and controversial value manager in the business today. This Baltimore-based investment pro has gained fame for beating the S&P 500 each and every year since 1991 as skipper of the Legg Mason Value Trust. That even eclipses Peter Lynch's legendary record. Miller also manages the newer and much smaller Legg Mason Opportunity Trust.

Miller's approach has been criticized by some, who claim he's not really a value manager. After all, the 51-year-old owns such stocks as AOL Time Warner, Dell Computer, and Amazon.com, which are normally found in growth portfolios. These names sit next to more traditional value stocks such as Waste Management and Fannie Mae. How do such companies qualify as value stocks? According to Miller, it's because they were selling at a discount to business value when he bought them. He believes simple benchmarks such as price-to-earnings ratios are insufficient when it comes to valuing complex business entities.

A former philosophy student and longtime market observer, Miller joined Legg Mason as director of research in 1981. He co-managed Value Trust from its inception in 1982 and has run it solo since 1990. Miller still studies the great philosophers and finds that many of their teachings apply to his work as an investor.

I previously interviewed Miller for my book *Wizards of Wall Street*. Given the vast changes in the markets since that book was published, I thought it would be interesting to get an update.

**Kazanjian:** You started off as a philosophy student, but one of your former professors says he used to find you in the library reading *The Wall Street Journal* instead of the world's greatest philosophers.

**Miller:** I was always interested in things financial. When I was 9 or 10 years old, I was watching my father read the financial pages of the newspaper, which had a different visual aspect from the sports pages. I asked him what *that* was. He said those were stocks and stocks' prices. I then asked what that meant. He pointed to one name and said, "If you look here, you'll see it says +¼. If you owned one share of that company, you would have 25 cents more today than you had yesterday." I said, "What do you have to do to get that 25 cents?" He said, "Nothing. It does it by itself." It was that conversation that got me interested in the markets. I thought, Wow! You can make money without doing any work. That's the business I want to be in.

I probably had come in from mowing the grass for 25 cents for two hours, so stocks sounded like a pretty good deal. It was much later that I realized only the market rate of return took no work. Getting an excess rate of return was a different matter.

Then, as an undergraduate in college, I majored in economics and European intellectual history.

**Kazanjian:** How did you wind up studying for a Ph.D. in philosophy?

**Miller:** The decision to go to graduate school was driven by the lack of finding anything else that was terribly interesting. Economics, both 30 years ago and today, is highly stylized and basically a mathematical exercise. When I looked at other alternatives, law school seemed to be a huge waste of time, since you spent three years trying to figure out where to put commas in documents. Business school would have been more interesting, but I had an Army obligation. While I was in the Army, a friend was at the Harvard Business School, and I was stationed for a short time near Boston. I visited him and saw he was spending two years studying cases that seemed to be very commonsensical. At the end of the day, I had to determine what I found most interesting. I thought philosophy was intellectually interesting, so I studied that.

**Kazanjian:** I understand that your father actually discouraged you from getting into the investment field despite your early interest in stocks.

**Miller:** It was the worst advice I ever received. When I got out of the Army in 1975, the market had just finished its worst period since the Great Depression. It wasn't the kind of field people recommended as a profession that was full of opportunity.

**Kazanjian:** You left the Ph.D. program before getting your degree. What happened after that?

**Miller:** In 1977, I went to work in Pennsylvania for a company called J. E. Baker. As assistant to the CEO, I was a jack of all trades, doing whatever he asked. Initially, it was a lot of number crunching on acquisitions. He was looking for somebody who had a conceptual grounding in economics.

**Kazanjian:** When did you join Legg Mason?

**Miller:** In 1981, as director of research.

**Kazanjian:** How did you make that transition?

**Miller:** It was fairly seamless in that my wife was a broker at Legg Mason. She had joined the firm in 1975 to help put me through graduate school, and I knew Legg Mason's principals. It was, and still is, a fairly small firm based in Baltimore. They talked to me about joining the research effort, which didn't interest me much. Then they talked about diversifying into money management. I found that much more appealing. By that time I was treasurer at J. E. Baker and enjoyed overseeing the company's investment portfolios. Chip Mason, Legg Mason's CEO, planned to start a fund that would reflect the firm's research ideas. I joined in October of 1981, and we started Value Trust in March or April of 1982. My predecessor as director of research, Ernie Kiehne, and I co-managed the fund. He was the senior manager. Our initial portfolio consisted mostly of stocks Ernie had followed for a long time.

**Kazanjian:** Had you ever invested in the stock market at that point?

**Miller:** Yes. When I was in graduate school, some friends sent me money, saying, "You always talk about the stock market, and you think you can invest in it. Here's some of our money. See what you can do with it." We formed a little investment partnership, and I invested for them in the early and mid-1970s, before joining Legg Mason.

**Kazanjian:** When you joined the firm in 1981, what was your investment philosophy?

**Miller:** The same as it is now: value. However, it's much more sophisticated now than it was then.

**Kazanjian:** Where did that value orientation come from?

**Miller:** From my reading. I've read everything I could about investing for as far back as I can remember. I've always thought the right way to do something is to determine who's best at it and see what he or she does. It seemed fairly clear to me that Ben Graham was the intellectual leader of the security analysis field. Then, reading about Warren Buffett and seeing how he had survived and prospered during the difficult period from the late 1960s to the early 1970s was a real eye-opener. It also always made intuitive sense to me to try to buy things at the best possible price in relation to underlying value. I remember talking to [fellow value manager] Bob Torray over 10 years ago. He believed that if you explained value investing to people, either they got it or they didn't. You couldn't convince somebody it was a good way to invest if they didn't instantaneously see that. Most people, for whatever reason, seem more psychologically attuned to buying companies that are growing, have great prospects, or for whatever reason have something people can get excited about. Valuation tends to be a much less important factor for most people than it is for me.

**Kazanjian:** I want to dig deeper into your investment approach in a moment, but given the kinds of companies you own, one might wonder whether you still follow the rules of Graham and Buffett.

**Miller:** We are absolutely valuation purists. But we are not valuation simpletons. Many people have taken what Graham said in interviews or wrote in *The Intelligent Investor* and extracted only the simplest possible rules from them. But, if you actually get into Graham's *Security Analysis* or some of the interviews he gave late in life, you see there's much more to it. I was going through some of Graham's later interviews and saw one where he was asked before a congressional committee whether stock prices were too high and what stock prices depended on. His comment was that they depended on earnings and, most importantly, on future prospects and to a minor extent on current asset values. Most people believe that if you talked to Graham, he would be most focused on current asset values and least on future prospects. But that's not what he said.

As to Buffett, if you read his work closely, you find that our methodologies are virtually identical. Buffett says he tries to buy businesses at the cheapest price relative to future cash flows. He doesn't precisely calculate the cash flows. As he says, he would rather be vaguely right than precisely wrong. We do a more extensive and detailed analysis, but it's the same approach.

**Kazanjian:** Are you saying people have misinterpreted Graham's teaching?

**Miller:** No, I don't think they have misinterpreted it. They just take too narrow a view. Graham believed in low PE ratios and low price-to-book-value. All of that is correct. It's just not the full story. It would be like asking Michael Jordan how much money he makes. If he said he made $200,000 a year, that would be true. But he also makes a whole lot more than that. That's the same thing with Graham. It's true that he was a low-PE guy, but he was a lot more than that.

**Kazanjian:** How do you define value investing today?

**Miller:** I take it right out of the textbooks. If you go to any finance or investment textbook and look up value or valuation, it will say the value of any investment is the present value of the future free cash flows of that investment. I can't find any textbook that defines value differently. They all get it from John Burr Williams, whose Ph.D. dissertation in the 1930s later became the book *The Theory of Investment Value*. He called it the "rule of present worth." The only way you can compare two distinct investments, such as aluminum and computer companies, is to look at them on a comparable basis. The only reasonable comparison is between the returns you expect to earn from them. That's what I'm trying to do. Investing, as Buffett said, is putting money out today with the expectation of getting more back tomorrow. The question is how you do that. We believe the best way to determine the most reasonable expectation of what we're going to get back from an investment is to think about how our view of future cash flows differs from that of the market.

**Kazanjian:** Where do you find your ideas initially?

**Miller:** They come from all different sources. Many come from the new-low list. We look at anything that looks cheap statistically and do a lot of computer screening. That's a starting point for many value investors, but some of my peers put a lot more weight on the statistics coming out of computer screens than we do. We just use them to get a universe of names to investigate more deeply. We get ideas from spectacular blowups in the market— Waste Management or McKesson/HBOC in 1999 are good examples—or from companies that are perceived to have lost out in some competitive battle, such as Toys 'R' Us. Also, people who know our style are always serving up investment ideas. Ninety-nine percent of them aren't interesting, but occasionally we find one that's worth doing some work on.

**Kazanjian:** Stocks on the new-low list are obviously companies no one wants right now. They have problems. What makes you decide it's okay to buy? Are you hoping for a turnaround?

**Miller:** We do a lot of turnarounds, but we tell our analysts to avoid the word *hope* in their research and instead use *believe* or *expect*. Normally, companies that are perceived right out of the box as terrific companies with strong competitive advantages will not make it into our portfolio because they never hit one of our valuation metrics and therefore don't come to our attention. As a result, we've missed many great companies that it turns out were undervalued—Microsoft and Charles Schwab being prime examples. They are stocks that always looked expensive, so we never took an opportunity to analyze them in depth. If you think about it, the only way you can earn an excess return by owning a particular company is if the market hasn't valued it properly. If the market has it properly valued, you will earn the market rate of return or the rate of return of the underlying company, whichever is lower. The market has to be systematically wrong about the prospects of a particular business for you to earn an excess return over any extended period of time. When growth investors do really well, they do so because the companies grew faster and longer than the market believed. To most value investors, a company is undervalued because the market has overly discounted some negative event or is too pessimistic about something that's weighing on the stock price.

**Kazanjian:** How do you know that it's just an overreaction and not something more serious?

**Miller:** You analyze the business. You have to get into actually figuring out what the company does and what its competitive advantage is. Most important, you must understand the long-term economic model of the business. How much capital does it require to operate? What returns are normal in that industry? Where is the company positioned in the industry? How can its management execute in a way to deliver the business model?

**Kazanjian:** Let's talk about some of the holdings in your portfolio. You own a lot of names that you would not normally find in a value fund, such as AOL Time Warner, Dell Computer, and Amazon.com. Tell me how those stocks justifiably fit into a value portfolio and how you came to find them originally.

**Miller:** The important thing to understand is that when we say we are value investors, both of those words are important to us: *value* and *investing*. First, we believe that many people who call themselves value investors often don't do very sophisticated valuation work. Second, and more important, they don't invest. They trade. They buy stocks and flip them out if they go up 50 or 100 percent or trade up to some historical valuation metric. What captures people's attention when they look at our portfolio are names such as Dell, AOL Time Warner, United Healthcare, and more recently, Amazon.com—stocks that are being bought mostly by growth investors. We bought these companies when they were really cheap. We've made 30 to 40 times our money in both Dell and AOL. Most investors rarely hold companies long enough to make 30 to 40 times their money. They're lucky if they make 50, 100, or 200 percent. You get those returns only if you actually invest in companies as opposed to trading them and trying to guess when the stock is going to pull back. We don't spend time trying to guess stock price action. We spend our time trying to value businesses.

When we analyzed Dell, for example, in February 1996, that was a period when everybody thought we were going to have a recession. Investors had sold tech stocks down to levels that looked to us to offer an opportunity. Most value people at the time were buying paper, steel, and aluminum, which also were in the dumps. When we did all the valuation work on those companies, we concluded that they were not terribly attractive or mispriced by the market. Their business fundamentals were poor and were likely to remain so. On the other hand, when we looked at Dell, trading at the time around $1–2 on a split-adjusted basis, we saw a company that had a superior business model and excellent competitive advantages and was growing at 25 to 30 percent a year, earning 30 percent on invested capital, and trading at five times earnings. Why would we ever buy a paper company at five times what they hope to earn if paper prices rise when instead we can buy a terrific company at five times today's earnings? When we got further into the detail of the business, it looked to us like the market had systematically misunderstood the potential of the company. Historically, PC companies traded between 6 and 12 times earnings. Even when value investors were buying PC companies, they would buy at 5 to 6 times and sell at 12 times earnings because that was the peak multiple these companies historically had attained. When we analyzed Dell, we concluded it was worth at least 25 times earnings as a business. If you were to buy the whole company, you would pay up to 25 times earnings, whereas the market had peaked valuation out historically at around 12 times. So we thought it was worth about 5 times what the market thought it was worth. It's highly unusual to find companies that appear to be so mispriced, and we loaded up on it. As it turned out, we were right. We actually underestimated the ability of management to execute what turned out to be a superior business model.

Fortunately, because what we do is dynamic valuation, our models are updated every quarter or more often as we get more fundamental data. We're always trying to figure out the underlying business value and the intrinsic value of the company. Earlier in 1999, Dell reached a level where we thought it was moderately overpriced, so we sold a fairly significant portion of it.

**Kazanjian:** Was it a similar story with AOL?

**Miller:** AOL was much more controversial when we bought it in the fall of 1996. People thought AOL was going bankrupt, and the stock had lost three-quarters of its value from May to November. Our analysis was that the company was worth roughly double what we were paying for it. We do scenario analyses of the companies, since we don't have any idea of what the future is actually going to look like. We try to map out the possible futures, assign probability weightings to them, and figure out which one appears to be most likely. Then we determine the value under that scenario. Under one scenario, we figured AOL could be worth multiples of the central value we had calculated.

**Kazanjian:** That was when AOL was having significant capacity problems and people couldn't log on. Scenario one must have been that everybody would switch from AOL to other carriers, which is what a lot of Wall Street was thinking.

**Miller:** That was certainly a scenario, but when AOL was being sued by the state attorneys general and there were stories in the news every day about how people couldn't log on, we found it fascinating that it wasn't losing subscribers. The value proposition was very powerful. Ordinarily, if you buy a product or service that you pay for up front and then can't use, you ask for your money back and switch to somebody else. But AOL's customer base continued to grow. That told us there was a very different value proposition going on there. It's like when Coca-Cola changed the Coke formula. People wanted old Coke back. They didn't want the new Coke. Here, people didn't want CompuServe or the Microsoft Network. They wanted AOL. When we analyzed traffic patterns, we found that 80 percent of the customers of the Microsoft Network used it just as a portal to the Internet, whereas 80 percent of AOL's customers stayed on the proprietary service and did not pass through to the Internet. This again supported the view that there was tremendous value in the service. We knew people wouldn't stay with the company forever if they couldn't log on. So we analyzed how long it would take AOL to solve this problem. There were two different issues. One was technological. Could they deploy enough technology over the requisite time horizon to solve the problem? We believed the answer was yes. Second, could they finance it, since it required a lot of upfront capital and they didn't have a lot of money? Would it put too much strain on their financial condition? Our answer, after analyzing the situation, was that adequate financing would be available. We made a big bet on AOL, and fortunately we turned out to be right.

**Kazanjian:** Since you bought both Dell and AOL, they're up 20 to 40 times your original cost. Without these two stocks, your fund would clearly not be where it is today.

**Miller:** There's no question that without our two largest holdings [Dell and AOL were Miller's top holdings in the late 1990s] going up the most, we would not have done as well. Back when I was director of research, we used to put together a Thanksgiving list—12 stock picks for the forthcoming year. It had a really good record of beating the market. In fact, *The Wall Street Journal* began to pick it up in the early 1980s. They published our Thanksgiving list on Thanksgiving Day. A reporter called me once and said, "I went back and analyzed all your lists. They did beat the market, but there are 12 stocks on each list." I said, "Yeah, I know, one for every month." He said, "If you throw out last year's two best performers, you wouldn't have beaten the market. The year before that, the only reason you beat it was because you had a big takeover." I replied, "If the assumption is we don't own the things that enable us to beat the market, then it follows that we won't beat the market. But we do own them." It's like AOL and Dell. We do own them. Part of the process that has enabled us to beat the market is selecting and then holding these businesses. The other thing people misunderstand about our success is that we've owned Dell and AOL only since 1996. But we've outperformed every year since 1991, long before we owned Dell and AOL. We've also outperformed the S&P 500 over the entire history of the fund.

**Kazanjian:** In 2000, Value Trust was down 7.1 percent, even though you still beat the S&P 500. What's interesting is that many value funds did well that year. What happened?

**Miller:** First of all, we have a big fund. Counting all the different share classes and assets that shadow the fund, it's a $20 billion-plus portfolio. Unlike many value portfolios, it's also highly focused. The average value fund owns about 100 names and turns the portfolio over between 80 and 90 percent a year. We own 35 names and we turn the portfolio over every 5 to 10 years. Part of the reason we did so well relative to other value funds in the late 1990s was that we correctly identified in 1995–96 that the best values in the market were in technology. By 2000, the market had repriced technology to a level that fully reflected the value. We began selling those tech stocks in the first quarter of 2000. But because we have a large amount of assets, it took us most of the year to get the portfolio to where it currently is, which is underweight in technology. Even though we were behind the market in the first quarter of 2000, we beat the market in the second half of the year, and therefore pulled ahead of it. By contrast, most value people hadn't changed their port-folios in years. They underperformed the market for a long time, many since 1994. They were up in 2000, but had really dreadful absolute and relative results for years, whereas we were able to beat the market handily throughout the 1990s.

**Kazanjian:** It sounds like the stocks that helped to fuel your performance during the period when value was out of favor dragged you down in 2000 because you couldn't sell them fast enough before they got clobbered.

**Miller:** Yes. We sold tons of stocks that had done really well for us. We still have some AOL, but we sold a mountain of it in 2000. We sold all of our Nokia and most of our Nextel and Dell. You just can't sell millions of shares in a short period of time.

**Kazanjian:** You are back in Dell now. What made you return?

**Miller:** We sold almost all of our Dell in the first quarter of 2000. By the fourth quarter, Dell had retreated all the way back to levels we thought were attractive, so we bought a lot, and it's worked out well.

**Kazanjian:** You've been buying some controversial tech and telecom names.

**Miller:** In the first quarter of 2001, we bought a ton of Amazon.com and Nextel.

**Kazanjian:** Let's talk about Amazon. That's obviously a name few consider to be a value stock. Take me through how you valued that company and why you consider it to be a bargain.

**Miller:** First of all, let me clarify a term here. I don't believe there's such a thing as a "value stock" or a "growth stock." I don't think *value* and *growth* describe companies. They describe styles of investing. It's bizarre when people categorize companies as value or growth. From a pure financial theory standpoint, growth is an input to the calculation of value. It's part of the exercise of figuring out what the intrinsic value of something is. In addition, if you decide that the world falls into growth and value categories on the basis of price-to-book-value, companies such as General Motors that write off a large portion of their book value as they did in the early 90s suddenly get transformed into growth stocks. If companies such as JDS Uniphase make idiotic acquisitions at very high valuations by issuing stock and then capitalizing it as goodwill, they become value stocks. AOL is 50 times above what we paid for it, yet it's now in the value index because its price-to-book-value has magically kicked it into that category due to the acquisition of Time Warner for stock.

Value and growth do describe styles of investing. There are growth investors and there are value investors. For growth investors, growth is the driving force of their investment process. They are looking for growth. Growth to them is a marker of what will lead to good returns. They like growing revenues, growing earnings, perhaps a growing return on capital. For value investors, valuation is the driving force of the process. Some value investors want growth and others are more like we are, which is agnostic about whether something is growing or not. We're trying to buy things at the largest discount to intrinsic business value.

**Kazanjian:** How did you determine Amazon's intrinsic value?

**Miller:** Intrinsic business value is the present value of the future free cash flows that an investment will generate over its lifetime. The way we valued Amazon is we built a model of the company, projected its free cash flows, and discounted those back in. Because we don't have any idea—nor does anyone else—about what the actual cash flows of Amazon will be, we projected a wide variety of cash flows based on various scenarios. We believe that if you take Amazon's last-quarter revenues and losses, guidance for the year, and the consensus of analysts' expectations, you get a value of about $30. If we run a variety of scenarios, including one where you give it 15 years of revenue growth, you get a wild valuation in the $100-plus range. We don't believe Amazon is currently worth $100, but we do believe it's worth $30. If you go out a year and Amazon hits its numbers, the company's value will probably rise by 30 percent a year.

**Kazanjian:** You're about the only value investor I know saying this about Amazon. Most of your value peers contend the stock is grossly overvalued.

**Miller:** First, I don't know of any other value investor who has actually tried to value Amazon by analyzing its business model and projecting its cash flow. What they are doing is looking at the history of Amazon and saying this company is losing a lot of money, is generating negative cash flow, and yet has an equity market value of $3 billion, and therefore is overpriced. Everybody we've talked to who claims the stock is overpriced either is plugging in the wrong numbers or is assuming things that aren't visible and for which there is no evidence—namely, that

Amazon's creditors will cut it off. We're trying to make our projections tie in with what is actually occurring. You'll also note that Moody's has put Amazon on credit watch for an upgrade. They have obviously been able to gain confidence that Amazon is actually making its numbers, which gives us confidence that our models are roughly correct. One last comment: The Internet was obviously a huge bubble and many stocks have collapsed to pennies on the dollar. At the same time, Amazon is going up in a down market. Amazon has beaten the market every single year it's been public except for 2000. Why? Maybe something is going on at the company that's different from what the general perception is.

**Kazanjian:** Are you the largest shareholder of Amazon's common stock?

**Miller:** Jeff Bezos, the founder, is the largest shareholder, but we're the largest institutional shareholder, right behind Jeff.

**Kazanjian:** Do you look at Amazon the same way you did AOL when you first bought it in 1996?

**Miller:** Amazon is similar to AOL in some ways and dissimilar in others. One similarity is that Amazon has a large and loyal customer base. That ultimately is going to drive Amazon's long-term value. The dissimilarity is that Amazon's total value is multiples of what AOL was selling for in 1996. So AOL's theoretical value and economics in 1996 were better than Amazon's. The market has discounted a bit more improvement in Amazon than it did at the time for AOL. From a timing standpoint it's very similar to AOL in 1996. AOL in 1996 was losing gobs of money. People thought it was going bankrupt and were very skeptical of the business model. That's exactly what's going on with Amazon today. We believe that before the end of 2002, Amazon will turn from cash-negative to cash-positive. That's what enabled AOL to get its first big valuation upgrade, and I expect the same thing will happen with Amazon.

**Kazanjian:** You also own Amazon convertibles in the Opportunity Trust, along with bonds in distressed companies, such as Exodus Communications. Why buy debt over equities?

**Miller:** It has to do with the relative risk and return. The great thing about financial theory is that it provides a way to value any asset. If we buy a bond, it's an asset. How do we value it? By taking the present value of the future free cash flows. If we take a business such as Exodus, we come up with a value for the company. The value of the business is independent of how it is financed. But how it is financed determines who has access to that value. If a company is worth $1 billion and doesn't have any debt, that $1 billion all accrues to the equity holders. If a company is worth $1 billion and has $1 billion of debt, the equity holders don't have an asset that's worth anything. In the case of Exodus, the debt is trading at 15 cents on the dollar subsequent to its bankruptcy filing and default. The current value of the senior debt is around $300 million. We value the company at about $1 billion, so we believe we'll make several times our money through the bankruptcy reorganization.

**Kazanjian:** I want to return to a point you made a minute ago about value investors not even looking at Amazon. Do you think a lot of value investors just unintentionally overlook stocks conventionally viewed as being overpriced when, in fact, they represent good values after all?

**Miller:** We've certainly overlooked a lot of great ideas and probably still do. If you think about it, Microsoft was a great value 10 years ago. So was Cisco. These companies went up hundreds of times. Even after its severe correction, Cisco is valued at around $120 billion. It was valued at around $1 billion 10 years ago. There are a lot of companies that turn out to be great values that value investors don't look at because they seem expensive at the time. Another good example is Wal-Mart. In the early 1970s, when the stock market was trading at seven times earnings, Wal-Mart traded at 24 times earnings. Had you bought it then and held on, you would have creamed the market over that entire period because Wal-Mart was significantly undervalued.

One thing we've learned over the years is that simple-minded computer screens—such as screens for low-PE or low-price-to-book or low-price-to-cash-flow stocks—do not tell you much about value. They can leave out many great companies that look expensive but are actually worth a lot more than they're trading for. The problem is it's very difficult for a value investor, ourselves included, to actually figure out how to search for stocks that look statistically expensive yet are actually cheap. Looking expensive isn't the same as being expensive, and looking cheap isn't the same as being cheap.

**Kazanjian:** Besides valuation, what are the reasons you would sell a stock?

**Miller:** We have a threefold sell discipline. The first one is if the company's fairly priced. Second, we will sell if we find a better bargain. We try to remain fully invested. If we find something that's more undervalued on a tax-adjusted basis than what we already own, we'll sell the least attractive thing in the portfolio.

**Kazanjian:** What's the third reason?

**Miller:** If the investment case changes. Perhaps the government comes in and says it's going to change the reimbursement rates for nursing homes. Guess what? All your cash flows are going to change. Since the terrorists attacked the World Trade Center, the investment opportunities in defense stocks changed.

**Kazanjian:** Do you pay much attention to the market, interest rates, and so on?

**Miller:** We pay a lot of attention to them. The justifiable valuation of a market with 7 percent inflation is radically different from the valuation of a market with 2 percent inflation. We pay attention, we just don't forecast it.

**Kazanjian:** How patient are you with companies that don't move up in price for months or years?

**Miller:** We will own a company as long as we're confident of the business value and in management's ability to execute those values. As long as we trust management and believe it's dealing with us in a fair way, we will hold the stock.

**Kazanjian:** Tell me more about the additional analysis you do on companies before buying.

**Miller:** We do virtually anything we can to help us add value. We talk to management, suppliers, competitors, and analysts. Because we are long-term owners of these companies and don't blow out of the stock because it misses a quarter or underperforms for X periods of time, our discussions with managements center on long-term issues that short-term investors don't care about as much.

**Kazanjian:** What are the characteristics of the most successful companies you've ever owned?

**Miller:** They tend to have low valuations and are trading way down from their prior highs because of some problem, perceived or real. They are leaders in their industries, have managements who actually care about shareholder value, and, most important, have a fundamental economic model where they can earn above their cost of capital.

**Kazanjian:** Value Trust is the only fund to have outperformed the S&P 500 every year since 1991. There are thousands of stock funds out there. Why do you think you're the only manager who has been able to accomplish this feat?

**Miller:** I think there are several reasons. Most important, in my opinion, is that most managers do not really invest long term. Their turnover rate is way too high. They trade stocks too much and are not really thinking about what the long-term rate of return is on the asset they're buying. I'd say most managers fail to really understand and correctly value the assets they're buying. One of the points Warren Buffett so correctly makes is that stocks represent ownership interest in businesses. If you understand the value of the business, over time that will help you understand the value of the stock. I think most money managers are focused too much on the stock and the stock price, and not on the value of the business. Furthermore, people tend to get caught up in style boxes and strategy, instead of considering whether those styles and strategies are effective or not. People tend to be too dogmatic. They confuse their objective with their strategy. The objective for an active money manager is to add value over the benchmark. After all, the client can get the market rate of return tax efficiently at an extremely low cost. The only reason to pay for an active manager is because that manager does better than the index. People have confused the objective, which is to do better than the index, with the strategy—for example, to invest using growth or value. What happens is that people get caught up in trying to continue to do what they used to do in the past, apart from whether it worked or not, because they see their job as buying growth or value, as opposed to beating the market. My view is that my job is to beat the market, and the way I do that is by having a valuation-driven strategy.

It's certainly a strategy that has worked for Miller, even during periods when value has been deeply out of favor. By being more flexible than many of his value peers, and keeping his eye on outperforming the market, he has been able to stand far above the crowd.

Going forward, Miller continues to believe that stocks will shower investors with greater returns than any other major asset class, although he's only expecting average annual returns of around 8 percent. He contends that his forecast is bullish, even though it calls for much more moderate expectations than investors became accustomed to in the recent past.

Behavioral scientists have discovered a variety of common and sometimes self-destructive mental short-cuts that seem wired into our brains. **Gary Belsky** and **Thomas Gilovich** in their fascinating 1999 book discussed how such short-cuts can affect financial decisions.

# THE EGO TRAP
## by Gary Belsky and Thomas Gilovich

from *Why Smart People Make Big Money Mistakes*
*—and How to Correct Them* (1999)

*Quick! How do you pronounce the capital of Kentucky: "Loo-ee-ville" or "Loo-iss-ville"? Now, how much money would you bet that you know the correct answer to the question: $5, $50, $500?*

THIS IS PROBABLY the most challenging chapter in this book for us to write—not because the subject is complicated, but because the message we want to send might seem to fly in the face of our book's overriding premise. That premise, of course, is that individuals like you can learn from your mistakes. By identifying and understanding your behavioral-economic shortcomings, you can correct them and enjoy more financial freedom. This chapter, however, is a cautionary tale, like the yellow flag that's waved to warn race car drivers that conditions are a bit treacherous.

The core idea of this chapter is not particularly uplifting: You're probably not as smart as you think you are. That's okay; neither are we. Few people are. Indeed, for almost as long as psychologists have been exploring human nature, they have been amassing evidence that people tend to overestimate their own abilities, knowledge, and skills. In a favorable light this might be called optimism, and it's a propelling force in human achievement. It's also a bracing, cheerful way to go through life. After all, who wants to read their children a bedtime story whose main character is a train that says, "I doubt I can, I doubt I can"?

In a harsher light, though, such optimism might be called overconfidence, and in financial matters the tendency to place too much stock in what you know, or what you think you know, can cost you dearly. In fact, depending on how much you would have wagered that you knew how to pronounce the capital of Kentucky, you might already be $500 in the hole. You see, we constructed the problem at the top of this chapter to play on people's tendency toward overconfidence. Here's how: Because people are sure they know the "s" in Louisville is silent (which it is), they're confident that such knowledge is all they need to win the proffered bet. In fact, what they really need is the knowledge that the capital of Kentucky is Frankfort.

No fair? All right, we tricked you (or at least tried to). Guilty as charged. But our point is no less valid. Overconfidence is pervasive, even among people who presumably have good reason to think highly of themselves. Numerous studies over the years have demonstrated significant overconfidence in the judgments of doctors, lawyers, engineers, psychologists, and securities analysts. For example, 68 percent of lawyers involved in civil cases believe that their side will prevail, but—of course—only 50 percent can. Perhaps more important, even when people know as much as they think they know, it's often not as much as they need to know. In this chapter we will examine the pervasiveness of overconfidence, its psychological roots, and the ways it can adversely affect financial decisions. We'll also explain why it's one of the most difficult behavioral-economic traits to overcome, and we'll offer suggestions about how you might nonetheless do just that.

### CONFIDENCE GAME

*Give high and low estimates for the average weight of an empty Boeing 747 aircraft. Choose numbers far enough apart to be 90 percent certain that the true answer lies somewhere in between.*

*Now give high and low estimates for the diameter of the earth's moon in miles. Again, choose numbers far enough apart to be 90 percent certain that the true answer lies somewhere in between.*

There is one other barrier we must overcome if this chapter is to be successful. Even if we can sell you on the notion that overconfidence is common and troublesome, there's a strong chance that you'll think it's not really a problem for *you*. The very tendency we're writing about could, ironically, make you overly confident that overconfidence is not one of your issues. First, overconfidence is not always arrogance. So even if you already think you're a lousy shopper, you might be worse than you think. Second, overconfidence often appears in the form of unrealistically high appraisals of one's own qualities versus those of others.

The classic example of this tendency is a 1981 survey of automobile drivers in Sweden, in which 90 percent of them described themselves as above average drivers. Clearly a large number of the respondents were giving themselves the benefit of what should have been a very large doubt. You might think you are immune to this "Lake Wobegon effect," so named after Garrison Keillor's fictional community where "all the women are strong, all the men are good-looking, and all the children are above average." But try this one: What is your usual reaction when you meet a person whom someone has said looks "just like you"? If you are like most people, your reaction is typically one of alarm, even horror: "You're kidding! Is *that* what I look like?" What this means, of course, is that the picture we carry around of ourselves in our heads is a bit more favorable than the image others have of us.

Among people who study such things, the ubiquity of overconfidence is hardly in dispute. And if you stop to think about it, signs of overconfidence are rampant in all walks of life, particularly when it comes to money. If people were not overconfident, for example, significantly fewer people would ever start a new business: most entrepreneurs know the odds of success are against them, yet they try anyway. That their optimism is misplaced—that they are overconfident—is evidenced by the fact that more than two-thirds of small businesses fail within four years of inception. Put another way, most small-business owners believe that they have what it takes to overcome the obstacles to success, but most of them are wrong.

At this juncture we should probably clarify what we mean by overconfidence. We're not talking specifically about conscious arrogance, although overconfidence might certainly manifest itself in such out-and-out hubris. It's not so much that some folks think they are especially gifted and some folks do not, although that is certainly true. Rather, what research psychologists have discovered about overconfidence is that most people—those with healthy egos and those in the basement of self-esteem—consistently overrate their abilities, knowledge, and skill, at whatever level they might place them. Over the years researchers have demonstrated the pervasiveness of this phenomenon in myriad ways. One of the more famous efforts was a series of studies in the 1970s conducted by Sarah Lichtenstein, Baruch Fischhoff, and

Lawrence Phillips. Participants in these studies were first required to answer a few simple factual questions (for example, "Is Quito the capital of Ecuador?) and then to estimate the probability that their answers were correct (for instance, "I'm 60 percent sure that Quito is Ecuador's capital"). Consistently, participants overestimated the true probability; however high or low they placed the odds that their answers were correct, they were too confident with their estimates. Even for questions in which they were 100 percent certain that their answer was correct, they were right only 80 percent of the time.

You might resist the significance of these findings on the grounds that they involve only people's responses to trivia questions. "Who can get too worked up about one's knowledge of foreign capitals?" "I bet it would be different if people were asked things they care about and had more opportunities to learn." Well, in fact, researchers have done just that, by asking people questions about the one topic they care more about and know more about than anything—themselves! Psychologist Lee Ross and his Stanford colleagues Bob Vallone, Dale Griffin, and Sabrina Lin asked Stanford undergraduates at the beginning of the year whether they thought they would drop a course, join a fraternity or sorority, become homesick, and so on. On average the students expressed 84 percent confidence in their answers. But follow-up information obtained later in the year revealed that they were right only 70 percent of the time. Indeed, even when they were 100 percent certain of their predictions, their predictions were confirmed only 85 percent of the time.

A helpful way to understand overconfidence—and how it can sneak up on you—is to take another look at the questions posed at the beginning of this section. If you haven't already, make a serious effort to choose pairs of numbers that would give you that 90 percent level of certainty. In other words, come up with answers for which you'd be comfortable betting $9 against the prospect of winning just $1 that the real answers are within your chosen ranges. Go ahead, try.

Okay, we won't keep you in suspense. An empty 747 weighs approximately 390,000 pounds, and the diameter of the moon is roughly 2,160 miles. Chances are these answers don't fall within your high and low estimates for each question. Indeed, when Cornell's Russo, along with fellow psychologist Paul J. H. Shoemaker of the University of Chicago, offered these and eight other similar questions to more than one thousand U.S. and European business executives, the majority missed four to seven of them. How is this evidence of overconfidence? Because most people who attempt to answer these questions don't recognize how little they really know about the subjects or how difficult it is to bracket high and low estimates so that there's a sufficiently strong chance that the real answer will fall somewhere in between. As a result, most people fail to spread their estimates far enough apart to account for their ignorance.

If you had said to yourself something like this—"I really have no idea how much a 747 weighs, so I better err on the side of shooting too high and too low"—then you might have spread your guesses wide enough apart. Instead what people typically do is come up with their best estimate of the plane's actual weight and the moon's actual diameter and then move up and down from those figures to arrive at their high and low estimates. Quite frankly, though, unless you work for Boeing or NASA, your initial estimates are likely to be wildly off the mark, so the adjustments up and down need to be much bolder. Sticking close to an initial, uninformed estimate reeks of overconfidence.

Yet another way to think about overconfidence and its causes is to examine what behavioral economists call the "planning fallacy."

Essentially, this is the phenomenon responsible for one of the most common human foibles: the inability to complete tasks on schedule. We may not need to prove to you that such a fallacy exists, presuming as we do that your life (like ours) is filled with projects that take much longer to complete than you expected. In one interesting study, published in 1994 in the *Journal of Personality and Social Psychology*, a group of psychology students was asked to estimate as accurately as possible how long it would take to complete their honors thesis.

The study's authors—Roger Buehler of Simon Fraser University in Barnaby, British Columbia; and Dale Griffin and Michael Ross of the University of Waterloo in Ontario—also asked the students to estimate how long it would take to complete the thesis "if everything went as well as it possibly could" and "if everything went as poorly as it possibly could." Here are the results: Their best guess averaged out to 33.9 days; that's how long the typical student thought it would take him or her to finish a thesis. Assuming everything went perfectly, the average estimate for completion was 27.4 days, whereas the average estimate if things went poorly was 48.6 days. As it turns out, the average time it actually took the students to complete their thesis was a whopping 55.5 days. Depending on which estimate you use—the best, worst, or most likely case—the students were on average anywhere from 14 percent to 102 percent more confident than they should have been about the time it would take them to complete their thesis. Sound familiar?

The planning fallacy, by the way, also explains why so many public works projects take so long to complete and go so disastrously over budget. When government officials in Sydney, Australia, for example, decided in 1957 to build an opera house, they estimated that it would be completed in 1963 at a cost of $7 million. A scaled-back version finally opened in 1973 and cost $102 million. Similarly, when the city of Montreal was selected to host the 1976 Summer Olympics, the mayor announced that the entire Olympiad would cost $120 million and that the track and field events would take place in a stadium with a first-of-its-kind retractable roof. The games went off as planned, of course, but the stadium did not get its roof until 1989. And oh yes: the roof ended up costing $120 million, or almost as much as was budgeted for the entire Olympics. (Why "almost as much," even though it was the same amount? Because we didn't succumb to the money illusion that leads people to ignore the effects of inflation.)

## SHOW ME THE MONEY

At this point you might be wondering how overconfidence affects financial decisions. Sure, people don't know how little they know about world capitals or plane weights—or how long it will take them to complete a college paper or to build a screened-in porch. And yes, government projects sometimes consume more tax dollars than anyone was able to forecast in advance. Folks underestimate. But what does any of this have to do with finances? As it happens, a lot. One impact is profoundly practical. Because people are over-confident, they're likely to think they are in better financial shape than they are. Consider the results of a 1996 survey of American parents by the International Association of Financial Planning. Some 83 percent of respondents with children under the age of eighteen said that they have a financial plan, while three-quarters of them expressed confidence about their long-term financial well-being. Yet less than half of respondents said they were saving for their children's education, and less than 10 percent described their financial plan as addressing basic issues such as investments budgeting, insurance, savings, wills, and estates. Is their confidence justified? Perhaps, but we doubt it.

That's one financial consequence of overconfidence: underpreparedness. Another is the willingness with which most people spend large amounts of money for products and services about which they know very little. Oftentimes, certainly, this is the result of nothing more than laziness and resignation: you realize that you know nothing about, say, washing machines, but you really don't care. You've heard of Maytag, you love those Maytag repairman commercials, so a Maytag it is. Alas, we can't help you much there. Where we can help is to point out that many people make spending decisions that they think are informed but that are in fact not very informed at all.

One of our favorite stories about this happened a little while back, when a friend Gary knows was shopping for treadmills. A few weeks earlier Gary had skimmed an article that evaluated more than a dozen brands of treadmills. Gary suggested that his friend read the article. The friend, however, thought that was unnecessary; he believed that he had learned all he needed to know about treadmills in discussions with several trainers at his health club. Gary's friend bought Brand X, Brand X fell apart three weeks after the warranty expired, Gary's friend was out $1,100. After that happened, Gary's friend went back and read the treadmill article. Sure enough, Brand X had received a subpar rating, in part because the treadmill testers found that it didn't stand up to prolonged heavy pounding. Bad news for a treadmill, really, but even worse news for Gary's friend.

Our point in telling this story is to show how a little knowledge can lead to a lot of overconfidence. Remember, Gary's friend wasn't arrogant, he didn't assume that he had some innate knowledge about treadmills. He actually spent some time researching the subject, shopping at different stores, and buttonholing the trainers at his gym. That's a lot more than many people would do in that situation. No, his problem wasn't hubris—he didn't think he was a treadmill expert—his problem was overconfidence. He thought he knew enough about treadmills to make an informed decision. He overestimated his abilities.

## THE FIZZBO FALLACY

Yet another area in which overconfidence seems to thrive is residential real estate, where the acronym FSBO—or "Fizzbo" in industry jargon—stands for "For Sale By Owner." It's the term used to describe the roughly 20 percent of homeowners each year who try to sell their house without aid of a real estate agent, in the hopes of saving the 6 percent broker's commission. But Fizzbo might just as easily stand for "For Sale By Overconfident." That's because most homeowners who try to sell their house on their own underestimate the complexity of the task and overestimate their ability to handle it. Indeed, according to the nonprofit United Homeowners Association, the majority of all Fizzbos each year end up being sold through a traditional broker. More important, even those Fizzbos that are successfully completed may not be the money savers people think they are. Many times Fizzbos end up costing their owners large sums of money. It's true they save 6 percent, but because of a lack of experience the house sells for a lower price, actually costing the owner money. In other words, even though you don't have to pay a commission, you may still end up getting less than you would have had you hired a broker—perhaps as much as 10 percent less (although accurate statistics are not easily available).

There are several reasons for this. For example, some Fizzbo sellers price their home too low, and miss out on thousands of dollars of potential gain. More likely, many homeowners overestimate the value of their home—an example of the endowment effect we talked about earlier—and as a result their property takes longer to sell. The longer your home stays on the market, the more potential buyers wonder what's wrong with it and the lower the bids you'll get. A good real estate broker, moreover, has the knowledge and skills to market your home in the best possible way, and crucially, he or she is likely to generate a far greater number of interested buyers than you can, which will increase the likelihood that you'll enjoy the luxury of competing and escalating bids. This is because 85 percent of home buyers still use a broker to find homes. Finally, buyers these days know what you're up to when you try a Fizzbo: They know you're saving the broker's commission, and they will expect you to share those savings by accepting a below market bid.

## UNFAIR TRADE

To be sure, none of the above necessarily means that you won't save a bundle if you sell your house on your own—or that every real estate broker is worth the commission. It's just a reminder that overconfidence can be your undoing in a variety of ways. Which brings us to the real meat of this chapter, a point that if made successfully will cause us to consider this whole enterprise a success. Our point has to do with investing, and it is bound to be seen by some as the most controversial statement in this book, the one most sure to raise eyebrows among readers. Here it is: Any individual who is not professionally occupied in the financial services industry (and even most of those who are) and who in any way attempts to actively manage an investment portfolio is probably suffering from overconfidence. That is, anyone who has confidence enough in his or her abilities and knowl-edge to invest in a particular stock or bond (or actively managed mutual fund or real estate investment trust or limited partnership) is most likely fooling himself.

In fact, most such people—probably you—have no business at all trying to pick investments, except perhaps as sport. Such people—again, probably you—should simply divide their money among sev-eral index mutual funds and turn off CNBC. The best that such people—yes, you—should hope for is to match the average perform-ance of the stock and bond markets over the course of their investing life. Such a result ain't too bad.

Okay, now that we've insulted you sufficiently, let's go over our case, which at its essence is that most individual investors have no business thinking they can pick stocks or bonds with any more suc-cess than Tom and Gary would enjoy playing doubles at Wimbledon. Consider the following for a moment: As we saw earlier, the typical mutual fund manager—someone who spends every day in pursuit of brilliant investment ideas—will over the course of time be quite lucky if he or she manages simply to match the overall performance of the stock market. In fact, in most years the majority of these *pro-fessional* money managers actually performs worse than stocks in gen-eral. Indeed, over periods of a decade or more, roughly 75 percent of all stock funds underperform the market. Yes, a handful of fund managers consistently outperform the market over time, and yes, a small group of investors have become famous over the years for exceptional stock picking. But the operative words here are "handful" and "small." The fact of the matter is that most people have no reason to think they can be more successful identifying worthy investments or timing the ups and downs of the stock and bond markets than they would be if they made their decisions by throwing darts at the financial pages.

That fact was emphasized in a 1998 study by Terrance Odean and Brad M. Barber of the University of California–Davis. Odean, you might recall, has spent a great deal of time in recent years analyzing the trading records of tens of thousands of individual investors at a large national discount brokerage firm. One of his conclusions, which we discussed earlier, was that individual investors routinely sold winning stocks and held on to losers. In his most recent work, Odean (and Barber) turned up an equally important find: that individuals who trade stocks most frequently post exceptionally poor investment results. Using account data for more than sixty thousand households, Odean and Barber analyzed the common stock investment performance of individual investors from February 1991 through December 1996. During that time, the average household earned an annualized average return of 17.7 percent—a result that itself was hardly better than the relevant benchmark index, which returned an annualized 17.1 percent during the period. More important, the 20 percent of households that traded the most—turning over roughly 10 percent of their portfolio each month, vs. 6.6 percent for all households—earned an average annual return of just 10 percent.

Think about this for a minute. It's no stretch to assume that the people who traded the most did so because they believed their stock-picking skills to be superior to those of the average investor. Yet their results were actually far inferior to those of the average investor. If that's not a sign of overconfidence, we'd be hard-pressed to explain what it might be. To quote Odean and Barber: "We argue that the well-documented tendency for human beings to be over-confident can best explain the high trading levels and the resulting poor performance of individual investors. Our central message is that trading is hazardous to your wealth."

That's one of our central messages, too, and it further applies to those of you who have sense enough to stay away from individual stock picking but nonetheless believe you have the skill to identify those few mutual fund managers among thousands who can beat the market over time. As far as we know, there has not yet been created a reliable way to evaluate individual mutual funds with any greater degree of accuracy than there is to evaluate individual stocks or bonds. As you'll soon see, the average individual investor in mutual funds consistently fares worse than the average mutual fund, as hard as that may be to believe. Several traits contribute to this startling fact, but it is our belief that a major reason most individual investors underperform the benchmark investment averages over time is that most individual investors think they know more about investing than they actually do.

## I, ME, MINE

Why is this so? Why do so many people try to time the stock market or believe they can find the next Microsoft or Home Depot? Why do so many people think so highly of their investing acumen? To some extent the phenomenon is a function of the prosperous times in which we live. At this writing, the stock market has been booming for longer than fifteen years. On Wall Street they have a phrase—"a rising tide lifts all boats"—that means that even some bad stocks go up in price when the market in general is rising. We might just as easily coin another phrase—"a rising market lifts all egos"—that means that many people inflate the effect of their own decisions and underestimate how much of their recent investment performance is due simply to the fact that the U.S. economy and stock market have been on a roll and that they're just along for the ride. By way of analogy, if Tom and Gary had managed to sneak their way onto the roster of the Green Bay Packers in 1996, the team probably still would have won the Super Bowl that season. But that doesn't mean Tom and Gary can block or tackle or do much more to help a football team than start the "wave."

## OLD DOGS, OLD TRICKS

But maybe a better question about overconfidence—financial and otherwise—is not why people are overconfident to begin with, but why they stay overconfident. You see, the problem with overconfidence is not the innate bias toward optimism that most people seem to possess. That's a good thing; it keeps the world moving forward. The problem is the inability to temper optimism as a result of prior experience. Frankly, we don't learn well enough from our mistakes. Consider: If overconfidence is as big a problem as we say it is, it should be a short-term problem at worst. The learning process would ideally go something like this: We think highly of ourselves, the world and events show us who is boss, and we become less confident and more realistic about our knowledge and skills. Yet in the main, this doesn't happen. In their analysis of the planning fallacy, Buehler, Griffin, and Ross discussed several reasons people consistently fall prey to that type of optimism and overconfidence. One reason was a persistent habit of focusing on future plans rather than past experiences. We can always envision specific reasons why *this* project will get done on time. But the best laid plans are typically done in by elements we cannot anticipate. What a focus on the specifics of a particular project does, then, is force us into an "inside" view of the problem that distracts us from thinking about how infrequently we get things done as quickly as we initially expected. In our experiences, a similar phenomenon happens to investors, the result of this and several habits that we suspect you'll find very familiar.

## HEADS I WIN, TAILS IT'S CHANCE

The average reader might have a ready explanation for the dogged persistence of overconfidence, an explanation that goes something like this: "People stay overconfident because they conveniently remember their successes but repress or forget their failures." That's not far off: there are psychological forces at work that can indeed make our triumphs more memorable than our defeats. But as is so often the case in psychology, the true story is a bit more complicated. Sometimes our *failures* are the most vivid memories of all. If you were ever one word away from winning a spelling contest, for example, it's a lock that you'll carry the memory of the word that eliminated you to the grave.

But here's how overconfidence is preserved: Even when you remember your defeats, you may remember them in a way that alters their perceived implications for the future. Harvard psychologist Eileen Langer describes this phenomenon as "heads I win, tails it's chance. The idea here is that when things happen that confirm the correctness of your actions or beliefs, you attribute the events to your own high ability. Conversely, when things happen that prove your actions or beliefs to have been mistaken or wrong-headed, you attribute those disconfirming events to some other cause over which you had no control. The net result is that you emerge from a checkered history of success and failure with a robust optimism about your prospects for the future. A little better luck, or a little fine tuning, and the outcome will be much better the next time.

Case in point: A fellow Gary knows invested in Applied Materials in 1996 because the company was the dominant supplier of the machines that computer makers use to make their chips. And he took full credit when the stock raged over the next year. He proudly explained that he understood better than most how ubiquitous computer chips were becoming and how changing technology required manufacturers to constantly update their equipment. His confidence in his ability to pick winners soared. On the other hand, when economic problems in Asia pulverized the share prices of all semiconductor equipment makers in 1997, his confidence in his investing acumen was not shaken. After all, how could he know that Asia's woes would hurt Applied Materials' profits? Well, one answer is that he might have known had he bothered to learn that 50 percent of semiconductor equipment purchases at the time originated in Asia. The better answer is that Gary's friend, who is not in the semiconductor business, might not be the best person to evaluate the future of the companies that manufacture chip-making equipment.

But what if Gary's friend worked in the computer industry? What if he did understand the vagaries of the chip-making cycle? Wouldn't that qualify him to invest in high-tech companies? Before you answer, take a look at the next section.

## ALL TOO FAMILIAR

The last contributor to investor overconfidence that we want to mention is a hybrid of sorts. In many ways it's a variation of the endowment effect we explained earlier, whereby people tend to place an inordinately high value on what is theirs, relative to the value they would otherwise place on such things. But this principle applies not only to concrete items, but to ideas as well. Essentially, we place too much value on what we know from our own personal experience simply because it is from our own personal experience. To illustrate, we'll turn to a 1997 study by Gur Huberman, a finance professor at Columbia University in New York City. Huberman was intrigued by the fact that throughout the world, most investors own more stock of companies in their own country than of those in foreign countries.

To some extent, certainly, this reflects the ease of investing domestically; you don't have to worry about another country's laws or currency exchange rates. But Huberman thought that another factor might be at work, a psychological need on the part of investors to feel comfortable about their investments, with that comfort coming from familiarity. This may seem perfectly reasonable, but it may also be another example of overconfidence, inasmuch as investors might overestimate their knowledge about companies and stocks simply because they are more familiar with them.

To test his theory, Huberman examined the stock ownership records of (what were then) seven U.S. "Baby Bells," the regional phone companies created by the government breakup of AT&T in the 1980s. His research showed that in all but one state (Montana), more people held more shares of their local phone companies than any other Baby Bell. Again, this may make perfect sense to you: if a person thought regional phone companies were a good investment, why not invest in the one with which they are most familiar? Well, one reason might be that their phone company wasn't the best of the seven Baby Bells. On average, in fact, the odds were six to one against. And since we're pretty sure that most of the investors in question didn't conduct research that showed their Baby Bell to be superior, the only conclusion to be reached is that investors had a "good feeling" about their phone company relative to the others simply because it was their phone company.

This idea—invest in what you know—has become increasingly popular in recent years, associated with such investing legends as Peter Lynch, manager of the highly successful Fidelity Magellan mutual fund for thirteen years, and Warren Buffett, longtime chairman of the even more successful Berkshire Hathaway holding company. Indeed, it is often recounted how Lynch loved the coffee at Dunkin' Donuts and made a fortune investing in the company's stock or how Buffett's addiction to Cherry Coke was a key component in his decision to invest in Coca-Cola shares before the company's stock exploded.

Similarly, the "invest in what you know" approach is at least partly responsible for the fact that employees typically allocate more than a third of their retirement account assets to the stock of the company for which they work, despite the risks of such a strategy: your biggest investment—your job—is already tied to the fortunes of your workplace, so by stashing retirement assets in your company stock, you're putting too many eggs in one basket. That's why most financial planning pros recommend you keep no more than 10 percent of your 401(k) assets in your own company's shares.

In any event, the problem with all of this is that people overconfidently confuse familiarity with knowledge. For every example of a person who made money on an investment because she used a company's product or understood its strategy, we can give you five instances where such knowledge was insufficient to justify the investment. A classic example is Apple Computer. Without debating the merits of the PC versus the Macintosh, it's safe to say that many Mac users were convinced the company's technology was superior to that of its competitors, and as a result, many of them invested in Apple's shares with exceeding confidence. What these investors couldn't foresee was that Apple's strategy to forgo licensing its technology to clone makers would leave the door wide open for PC manufacturers to pounce. As a result, the only thing that seems to have shrunk faster than Apple's share of the personal computer market is its stock price. Because this entire book was written on Macintosh machines, we're hoping that Apple makes a comeback, but so much for investing in what you know.

## HOW TO THINK AND WHAT TO DO

### WARNING SIGNS

Overconfidence may cost you money if . . .

- you make large spending decisions without much research.
- you take heart from winning investments but "explain away" poor ones.
- you think you are "beating the market" consistently.
- you make frequent trades, especially with a discount or online brokerage.
- you think selling your home without a broker is smart and easy.
- you don't know the rate of return on your investments.
- you believe that investing in what you know is a guarantee of success.

Although you might not have guessed it, it was not our goal in this chapter to beat all remnants of self-confidence out of your system. Some of you may be every bit as smart as you think you are, and far be it from us to keep the next Peter Lynch or Warren Buffett from making his or her mark on the investment world. Our goal, rather, was twofold. First, we'd like to convince most of you to cast the bulk of your investment lot with the overall market by investing almost exclusively in index mutual funds. Because we make the case for this approach elsewhere in the book, we won't belabor the point here. But the plain truth is that most investors miss out on potential profits because they believe they can outthink the market when all evidence says they can't.

Our second goal is based to some extent on the belief that we won't easily achieve our first. Most of you will continue to pick individual stocks, bonds, funds, and the like in part because you think you have the skill and in part because it's fun. That's okay—it is fun. What we hope to have accomplished in this chapter is to convince you that you are likely overestimating your abilities and thus need to reevaluate the effort you put into investment decisions (and spending decisions, too). We don't want to abuse you, just humble you, so that you'll be less likely to make mistakes that cause you to lose money or miss out on gains.

**Investor, know thyself.** Maybe you *are* as good an investor as you think. But experience tells us that many people overestimate their hit-to-miss ratio, either because they conveniently ignore or explain away their failures or because they don't do a full accounting when calculating their performance records. In other words, your market-beating 15 percent average annual gains might really be a solid 10 percent or an anemic 5 percent if you count the commissions you paid and the taxes you incurred. This is especially true for active traders who buy and sell stocks on a daily, weekly, or monthly basis. We're against such an approach, but if that's your passion, it is essential that you review your investment records carefully, keeping these costs in mind. Because the math required for this effort can often be quite complicated, we suggest you avail yourself of any number of fine computer software programs oriented toward investment record keeping. Or you might simply go to the bookstore and pick up any number of investment books that offer worksheets to figure this out. Be warned, though: What you discover may be a blow to your ego.

If you are a person who's prone to kicking yourself for investment opportunities that you missed, we suggest you undertake the following exercise. For at least a month, write down every investment idea that you have, then tuck that paper away in a drawer somewhere. In about a year take it out and see how all your picks have done. We suspect that while several will have outperformed the market, an equal or greater number won't. Again, this is a useful and interesting way to avoid succumbing to fond memories.

**Take 25 percent off the top (and add 25 percent to the bottom).** Unfortunately there's no hard and fast rule for quantifying how big a problem overconfidence and optimism may be for you or anyone else. Nonetheless, a helpful way to deal with overconfidence is to incorporate an "overconfidence discount" into your projections, both on the upside and on the downside. This notion, as it happens, is already a common rule of thumb in some areas of life. For example, most experts counsel homeowners to add 10 percent to contractors' remodeling estimates, in terms of both cost and completion time. Our experience suggests 25 percent may be a better figure, but you can choose whatever number you're comfortable with. The key is to apply the discount on both sides of the transaction. For example, if you're thinking about investing in a stock, force yourself to come up with a realistic performance appraisal over your intended holding period, as well as the potential downside if things go wrong for the company. Then subtract

25 percent from your optimistic forecast and add 25 percent to your doomsday scenario. If the trade-off between potential risk and reward still seems worth it, go ahead. If not, you might want to walk away. In either case, though, the exercise is almost certain to make you consider aspects of the investment that you had otherwise ignored or forgotten.

**Get a second opinion.** This advice, about as commonsensical as we can get, is a great tonic for people who tend to think too highly of their own experiences. But what we're suggesting may not be what you're thinking. Yes, it's always a fine idea to ask your friends and other knowledgeable people what they think about an investment or purchase you're considering. But what if they are as overconfident or uninformed as you are? For example, what good did it do for Gary's friend to have asked his trainer about treadmills? Our idea is slightly different. We're suggesting that when you make important financial decisions you should ask trusted friends or experts what they think of your decision-making *process.* In other words, don't ask if they agree with your decision, ask if they think the way you went about reaching your decision was wise and thorough. Had Gary's friend asked him that question, Gary might have said that he thought it unwise to ignore the opinions of the professionals at the ratings magazine whose job it is to evaluate products.

But even as we recommend you seek counsel from others, we must once again throw up a yellow flag of caution. People often rely *too* heavily on the opinions and actions of others. You may not be as smart as you think you are, but you may still be smarter than many other folks.

Charles Mackay's 1841 book is on just about
everyone's list of investment classics, even though it's
not really an investment book. Mackay recounts centuries' worth of witch hunts, alchemist dreams, super-
stitious ravings and speculative frenzies, including the
tulip boom of 1634.

# TULIPOMANIA
by Charles Mackay

from *Extraordinary Popular Delusions and
the Madness of Crowds* (1841)

THE TULIP—SO named, it is said, from a Turkish word, sig-
nifying a turban—was introduced into western Europe
about the middle of the sixteenth century. Conrad Gesner,
who claims the merit of having brought it into repute,—little
dreaming of the commotion it was shortly afterwards to make in the
world—says that he first saw it in the year 1559, in a garden at
Augsburg, belonging to the learned Counsellor Herwart, a man very
famous in his day for his collection of rare exotics. The bulbs were
sent to this gentleman by a friend at Constantinople, where the
flower had long been a favourite. In the course of ten or eleven
years after this period, tulips were much sought after by the wealthy,
especially in Holland and Germany. Rich people at Amsterdam sent
for the bulbs direct to Constantinople, and paid the most extrava-
gant prices for them. The first roots planted in England were
brought from Vienna in 1600. Until the year 1634 the tulip annually increased in reputation, until it was deemed a proof of bad taste

in any man of fortune to be without a collection of them. Many learned men, including Pompeius de Angelis, and the celebrated Lipsius of Leyden, the author of the treatise "De Constantia," were passionately fond of tulips. The rage for possessing them soon caught the middle classes of society, and merchants and shopkeepers, even of moderate means, began to vie with each other in the rarity of these flowers and the preposterous prices they paid for them. A trader at Harlaem was known to pay one-half of his fortune for a single root, not with the design of selling it again at a profit, but to keep in his own conservatory for the admiration of his acquaintance.

One would suppose that there must have been some great virtue in this flower to have made it so valuable in the eyes of so prudent a people as the Dutch; but it has neither the beauty nor the perfume of the rose—hardly the beauty of the "sweet, sweet-pea;" neither is it as enduring as either. Cowley, it is true, is loud in its praise. He says—

> "The tulip next appeared, all over gay,
> But wanton, full of pride, and full of play;
> The world can't show a dye but here has place;
> Nay, by new mixtures, she can change her face;
> Purple and gold are both beneath her care,
> The richest needlework she loves to wear;
> Her only study is to please the eye,
> And to outshine the rest in finery."

This, though not very poetical, is the description of a poet. Beckmann, in his *History of Inventions*, paints it with more fidelity, and in prose more pleasing than Cowley's poetry. He says, "There are few plants which acquire, through accident, weakness, or disease, so many variegations as the tulip. When uncultivated, and in its natural state, it is almost of one colour, has large leaves, and an extraordinarily long stem. When it has been weakened by cultivation, it becomes more agreeable in the eyes of the florist. The petals are then paler, smaller, and more diversified in hue; and the leaves acquire a softer green colour. Thus this masterpiece of culture, the more beautiful it turns, grows so much the weaker, so that, with the greatest skill and most careful attention, it can scarcely be transplanted, or even kept alive."

Many persons grow insensibly attached to that which gives them a great deal of trouble, as a mother often loves her sick and ever-ailing child better than her more healthy offspring. Upon the same principle we must account for the unmerited encomia lavished upon these fragile blossoms. In 1634, the rage among the Dutch to possess them was so great that the ordinary industry of the country was neglected, and the population, even to its lowest dregs, embarked in the tulip trade. As the mania increased, prices augmented, until, in the year 1635, many persons were known to invest a fortune of 100,000 florins in the purchase of forty roots. It then became necessary to sell them by their weight in *perits*, a small weight less than a grain. A tulip of the species called *Admiral Liefken*, weighing 400 *perits*, was worth 4400 florins; an *Admiral Van der Eyck*, weighing 446 *perits*, was worth 1260 florins; a *Childer* of 106 *perits* was worth 1615 florins; a *Viceroy* of 400 *perits*, 3000 florins; and, most precious of all, a *Semper Augustus*, weighing 200 *perits*, was thought to be very cheap at 5500 florins. The latter was much sought after, and even an inferior bulb might command a price of 2000 florins. It is related that, at one time, early in 1636, there were only two roots of this description to be had in all Holland, and those not of the best. One was in the possession of a dealer in Amsterdam, and the other in Harlaem. So anxious were the speculators to obtain them, that one person offered the fee-simple of twelve acres of building-ground for the Harlaem tulip. That of Amsterdam was bought for 4600 florins, a new carriage, two grey horses, and a complete set of harness. Munting, an industrious author of that day, who wrote a folio volume of one thousand pages upon the tulipomania, has preserved the following list of the various articles, and their value, which were delivered for one single root of the rare species called the *Viceroy*:

|  |  | florins |
|---|---|---|
| Two lasts of wheat | | 448 |
| Four lasts of rye | | 558 |
| Four fat oxen | | 480 |
| Eight fat swine | | 240 |
| Twelve fat sheep | | 120 |
| Two Hogsheads of wine | | 70 |
| Four tuns of beer | | 32 |
| Two tuns of butter | | 192 |
| One thousand lbs. of cheese | | 120 |
| A complete bed | | 100 |
| A suit of clothes | | 80 |
| A silver drinking-cup | | 60 |
| | | 2500 |

People who had been absent from Holland, and whose chance it was to return when this folly was at its maximum, were sometimes led into awkward dilemmas by their ignorance. There is an amusing instance of the kind related in Blainville's *Travels*. A wealthy merchant, who prided himself not a little on his rare tulips, received upon one occasion a very valuable consignment of merchandise from the Levant. Intelligence of its arrival was brought him by a sailor, who presented himself for that purpose at the counting-house, among bales of goods of every description. The merchant, to reward him for his news, munificently made him a present of a fine red herring for his breakfast. The sailor had, it appears, a great partiality for onions, and seeing a bulb very like an onion lying upon the counter of this liberal trader, and thinking it, no doubt, very much out of its place among silks and velvets, he slily seized an opportunity and slipped it into his pocket, as a relish for his herring. He got clear off with his prize, and proceeded to the quay to eat his breakfast. Hardly was his back turned when the merchant missed his valuable *Semper Augustus*, worth three thousand florins, or about 280*l.* sterling. The whole establishment was instantly in an uproar; search was everywhere made for the precious root, but it was not to be found. Great was the merchant's distress of mind. The search was renewed, but again without success. At last some one thought of the sailor.

The unhappy merchant sprang into the street at the bare suggestion. His alarmed household followed him. The sailor, simple soul! had not thought of concealment. He was found quietly sitting on a coil of ropes, masticating the last morsel of his *"onion."* Little did he dream that he had been eating a breakfast whose cost might have regaled a whole ship's crew for a twelvemonth; or, as the plundered merchant himself expressed it, "might have sumptuously feasted the Prince of Orange and the whole court of the Stadtholder." Anthony caused pearls to be dissolved in wine to drink the health of Cleopatra; Sir Richard Whittington was as foolishly magnificent in an entertainment to King Henry V.; and Sir Thomas Gresham drank a diamond dissolved in wine to the health of Queen Elizabeth, when she opened the Royal Exchange; but the breakfast of this roguish Dutchman was as splendid as either. He had an advantage, too, over his wasteful predecessors: *their* gems did not improve the taste or the wholesomeness of *their* wine, while *his* tulip was quite delicious with his red herring. The most unfortunate part of the business for him was, that he remained in prison for some months on a charge of felony preferred against him by the merchant.

Another story is told of an English traveller, which is scarcely less ludicrous. This gentleman, an amateur botanist, happened to see a tulip-root lying in the conservatory of a wealthy Dutchman. Being ignorant of its quality, he took out his penknife, and peeled off its coats, with the view of making experiments upon it. When it was by this means reduced to half its size, he cut it into two equal sections, making all the time many learned remarks on the singular appearances of the unknown bulb. Suddenly the owner pounced upon him, and, with fury in his eyes, asked him if he knew what he had been doing? "Peeling a most extraordinary onion," replied the philosopher. "*Hundert tausend duyvel!*" said the Dutchman; "it's an *Admiral van der Eyck.*" "Thank you," replied the traveller, taking out his note-book to make a memorandum of the same; "are these admirals common in your country?" "Death and the Devil!" said the Dutchman, seizing the astonished man of science by the collar; "come before the syndic, and you shall see." In spite of his remonstrances, the traveller was led through the streets followed by a mob of persons. When brought into the presence of the magistrate, he learned, to his consternation, that the root upon which he had been experimentalising was worth four thousand florins; and, notwithstanding all he could urge in extenuation, he was lodged in prison until he found securities for the payment of this sum.

The demand for tulips of a rare species increased so much in the year 1636, that regular marts for their sale were established on the Stock Exchange of Amsterdam, in Rotterdam, Harlaem, Leyden, Alkmar, Hoorn, and other towns. Symptoms of gambling now became, for the first time, apparent. The stock-jobbers, ever on the alert for a new speculation, dealt largely in tulips, making use of all the means they so well knew how to employ to cause fluctuations in prices. At first, as in all these gambling mania, confidence was at its height, and every body gained. The tulip-jobbers speculated in the rise and fall of the tulip stocks, and made large profits by buying when prices fell, and selling out when they rose. Many individuals grew suddenly rich. A golden bait hung temptingly out before the people, and one after the other, they rushed to the tulip-marts, like flies around a honey-pot. Every one imagined that the passion for tulips would last for ever, and that the wealthy from every part of the world would send to Holland, and pay whatever prices were asked for them. The riches of Europe would be concentrated on the shores of the Zuyder Zee, and poverty banished from the favoured clime of Holland. Nobles, citizens, farmers, mechanics, sea-men, footmen, maid-servants, even chimney-sweeps and old clotheswomen, dabbled in tulips. People of all grades converted their property into cash, and invested it in flowers. Houses and lands were offered for sale at ruinously low prices, or assigned in payment of bargains made at the tulip-mart. Foreigners became smitten with the same frenzy, and money poured into Holland from all directions. The prices of the necessaries of life rose again by degrees: houses and lands, horses and carriages, and luxuries of every sort, rose in value with them, and for some months Holland seemed the very antechamber of Plutus. The operations of the trade became so extensive and so intricate, that it was found necessary to draw up a code of laws for the guidance of the dealers. Notaries and clerks were also appointed, who devoted themselves exclusively to the interests of the trade. The designation of public notary was hardly known in some towns, that of tulip-notary usurping its place. In the smaller towns, where there was no exchange, the principal tavern was usually selected as the "show-place," where high and low traded in tulips, and confirmed their bargains over sumptuous entertainments. These dinners were sometimes attended by two or three hundred persons, and large vases of tulips, in full bloom, were placed at regular intervals upon the tables and sideboards for their gratification during the repast.

At last, however, the more prudent began to see that this folly could not last for ever. Rich people no longer bought the flowers to keep them in their gardens, but to sell them again at cent per cent profit. It was seen that somebody must lose fearfully in the end. As this conviction spread, prices fell, and never rose again. Confidence was destroyed, and a universal panic seized upon the dealers. *A* had agreed to purchase ten *Semper Augustines* from *B*, at four thousand florins each, at six weeks after the signing of the contract. *B* was ready with the flowers at the appointed time; but the price had fallen to three or four hundred florins, and *A* refused either to pay the difference or receive the tulips. Defaulters were announced day after day in all the towns of Holland. Hundreds who, a few months previously, had begun to doubt that there was such a thing as poverty in the land suddenly found themselves the possessors of a few bulbs, which nobody would buy, even though they offered them at one quarter of the sums they had paid for them. The cry of distress resounded every where, and each man accused his neighbour. The few who had contrived to enrich themselves hid their wealth from the knowledge of their fellow-citizens, and invested it in the English or other funds. Many who, for a brief season, had emerged from the humbler walks of life, were cast back into their original obscurity. Substantial merchants were reduced almost to beggary, and many a representative of a noble line saw the fortunes of his house ruined beyond redemption.

When the first alarm subsided, the tulip-holders in the several towns held public meetings to devise what measures were best to be taken to restore public credit. It was generally agreed that deputies should be sent from all parts to Amsterdam, to consult with the government upon some remedy for the evil. The government at first refused to interfere, but advised the tulip-holders to agree to some plan among themselves. Several meetings were held for this purpose; but no measure could be devised likely to give satisfaction to the deluded people, or repair even a slight portion of the mischief that had been done. The language of complaint and reproach was in every body's mouth, and all the meetings were of the most stormy character. At last, however, after much bickering and ill-will, it was agreed, at Amsterdam, by the assembled deputies, that all contracts made in the height of the mania, or prior to the month of November, 1636, should be declared null and void, and that, in those made after that date, purchasers should be freed from their engagements, on paying ten per cent to the vendor. This decision gave no satisfaction. The vendors who had their tulips on hand were, of course, discontented, and those who had pledged themselves to purchase, thought themselves hardly treated. Tulips which had, at one time, been worth six thousand florins, were not to be procured for five hundred; so that the composition of ten per cent was one hundred florins more than the actual value. Actions for breach of contract were threatened in all the courts of the country; but the latter refused to take cognisance of gambling transactions.

The matter was finally referred to the Provincial Council at the Hague, and it was confidently expected that the wisdom of this body would invent some measure by which credit should be restored. Expectation was on the stretch for its decision, but it never came. The members continued to deliberate week after week, and at last, after thinking about it for three months, declared that they could offer no final decision until they had more information. They advised, however, that, in the meantime, every vendor should, in the presence of witnesses, offer the tulips *in natura* to the purchaser for the sums agreed upon. If the latter refused to take them, they might be put up for sale by public auction, and the original contractor held responsible for the difference the actual and the stipulated price. This was exactly the plan recommended by the deputies, and which was already shown to be of no avail. There was no court in Holland which could enforce payment. The question was raised in Amsterdam, but the judges unanimously refused to interfere, on the ground that debts contracted in gambling were no debts in law.

Thus the matter rested. To find a remedy was beyond the power of the government. Those who were unlucky enough to have had stores of tulips on hand at the time of the sudden reaction were left to bear their ruin as philosophically as they could; those who had made profits were allowed to keep them; but the commerce of the country suffered a severe shock, from which it was many years ere it recovered.

The example of the Dutch was imitated to some extent in England. In the year 1636 tulips were publicly sold in the Exchange of London, and the jobbers exerted themselves to the utmost to raise them to the fictitious value they had acquired in Amsterdam. In Paris also the jobbers strove to create a tulipomania. In both cities they only partially succeeded. However, the force of example brought the flowers into great favour, and amongst a certain class of people tulips have ever since been prized more highly than any other flowers of the field. The Dutch are still notorious for their partiality to them, and continue to pay higher prices for them than any other people. As the rich Englishman boasts of his fine race-horses or his old pictures, so does the wealthy Dutchman vaunt him of his tulips.

In England, in our day, strange as it may appear, a tulip will produce more money than an oak. If one could be found, *rara in terris*, and black as the black swan of Juvenal, its price would equal that of a dozen acres of standing corn. In Scotland, towards the close of the seventeenth century, the highest price for tulips, according to the authority of a writer in the supplement to the third edition of the *Encyclopedia Britannica*, was ten guineas. Their value appears to have diminished from that time till the year 1769, when the two most valuable species in England were the *Don Quevedo* and the *Valentinier*, the former of which was worth two guineas and the latter two guineas and a half. These prices appear to have been the minimum. In the year 1800, a common price was fifteen guineas for a single bulb. In 1835, a bulb of the species called the Miss Fanny Kemble was sold by public auction in London for seventy-five pounds. Still more remarkable was the price of a tulip in the possession of a gardener in the King's Road, Chelsea;—in his catalogues it was labelled at two hundred guineas.

# MISTAKES OF THE FIRST
# TWENTY-FIVE YEARS
# (A CONDENSED VERSION)
## by Warren E. Buffett

from *Berkshire Hathaway 1989 Annual Report*

To quote Robert Benchley, "Having a dog teaches a boy fidelity, perseverance, and to turn around three times before lying down." Such are the shortcomings of experience. Nevertheless, it's a good idea to review past mistakes before committing new ones. So let's take a quick look at the last 25 years.

• My first mistake, of course, was in buying control of Berkshire. Though I knew its business—textile manufacturing—to be unpromising, I was enticed to buy because the price looked cheap. Stock purchases of that kind had proved reasonably rewarding in my early years, though by the time Berkshire came along in 1965 I was becoming aware that the strategy was not ideal.

If you buy a stock at a sufficiently low price, there will usually be some hiccup in the fortunes of the business that gives you a chance to unload at a decent profit, even though the long-term performance of the business may be terrible. I call this the "cigar butt" approach to investing. A cigar butt found on the street that has only one puff left in it may not offer much of a smoke, but the "bargain purchase" will make that puff all profit.

Unless you are a liquidator, that kind of approach to buying businesses is foolish. First, the original "bargain" price probably will not turn out to be such a steal after all. In a difficult business, no sooner is one problem solved than another surfaces—never is there just one cockroach in the kitchen. Second, any initial advantage you secure will be quickly eroded by the low return that the business earns. For example, if you buy a business for $8 million that can be sold or liquidated for $10 million and promptly take either course, you can realize a high return. But the investment will disappoint if the business is sold for $10 million in ten years and in the interim has annually earned and distributed only a few percent on cost. Time is the friend of the wonderful business, the enemy of the mediocre.

You might think this principle is obvious, but I had to learn it the hard way—in fact, I had to learn it several times over. Shortly after purchasing Berkshire, I acquired a Baltimore department store, Hochschild, Kohn, buying through a company called Diversified Retailing that later merged with Berkshire. I bought at a substantial discount from book value, the people were first-class, and the deal included some extras—unrecorded real estate values and a significant LIFO inventory cushion. How could I miss? So-o-o—three years later I was lucky to sell the business for about what I had paid. After ending our corporate marriage to Hochschild, Kohn, I had memories like those of the husband in the country song, "My Wife Ran Away With My Best Friend and I Still Miss Him a Lot."

I could give you other personal examples of "bargain-purchase" folly but I'm sure you get the picture: It's far better to buy a wonderful company at a fair price than a fair company at a wonderful price. . . . I was a slow learner. But now, when buying companies or common stocks, we look for first-class businesses accompanied by first-class managements.

• That leads right into a related lesson: Good jockeys will do well on good horses, but not on broken-down nags. Both Berkshire's textile business and Hochschild, Kohn had able and honest people running them. The same managers employed in a business with good economic characteristics would have achieved fine records. But they were never going to make any progress while running in quicksand.

I've said many times that when a management with a reputation for brilliance tackles a business with a reputation for bad economics, it is the reputation of the business that remains intact. I just wish I hadn't been so energetic in creating examples. My behavior has matched that admitted by Mae West: "I was Snow White, but I drifted."

• A further related lesson: Easy does it. After 25 years of buying and supervising a great variety of businesses, . . . I have *not* learned how to solve difficult business problems. What we have learned is to avoid them. To the extent we have been successful, it is because we concentrated on identifying one-foot hurdles that we could step over rather than because we acquired any ability to clear seven-footers.

The finding may seem unfair, but in both business and investments it is usually far more profitable to simply stick with the easy and obvious than it is to resolve the difficult. On occasion, tough problems must be tackled as was the case when we started our Sunday paper in Buffalo. In other instances, a great investment opportunity occurs when a marvelous business encounters a one-time huge, but solvable, problem as was the case many years back at both American Express and GEICO. Overall, however, we've done better by avoiding dragons than by slaying them.

• My most surprising discovery: the overwhelming importance in business of an unseen force that we might call "the institutional imperative." In business school, I was given no hint of the imperative's existence and I did not intuitively understand it when I entered the business world. I thought then that decent, intelligent, and experienced managers would automatically make rational business decisions. But I learned over time that isn't so. Instead, rationality frequently wilts when the institutional imperative comes into play.

For example: (1) As if governed by Newton's First Law of Motion, an institution will resist any change in its current direction; (2) Just as work expands to fill available time, corporate projects or acquisitions will materialize to soak up available funds; (3) Any business craving of the leader, however foolish, will be quickly supported by detailed rate-of-return and strategic studies prepared by his troops; and (4) The behavior of peer companies, whether they are expanding, acquiring, setting executive compensation or whatever, will be mindlessly imitated.

Institutional dynamics, not venality or stupidity, set businesses on these courses, which are too often misguided. After making some expensive mistakes because I ignored the power of the imperative, I have tried to organize and manage Berkshire in ways that minimize its influence . . .

• After some other mistakes, I learned to go into business only with people whom I like, trust, and admire. As I noted before, this policy of itself will not ensure success: A second-class textile or department-store company won't prosper simply because its managers are men that you would be pleased to see your daughter marry. However, an owner—or investor—can accomplish wonders if he manages to associate himself with such people in businesses that possess decent economic characteristics. Conversely, we do not wish to join with managers who lack admirable qualities, no matter how attractive the prospects of their business. We've never succeeded in making a good deal with a bad person.

• Some of my worst mistakes were not publicly visible. These were stock and business purchases whose virtues I understood and yet didn't make. It's no sin to miss a great opportunity outside one's area of competence. But I have passed on a couple of really big purchases that were served up to me on a platter and that I was fully capable of understanding. For Berkshire's shareholders, myself included, the cost of this thumbsucking has been huge.

• Our consistently-conservative financial policies may appear to have been a mistake, but in my view were not. In retrospect, it is clear that significantly higher, though still conventional, leverage ratios at Berkshire would have produced considerably better returns on equity than the 23.8% we have actually averaged. Even in 1965, perhaps we could have judged there to be a 99% probability that higher leverage would lead to nothing but good. Correspondingly, we might have seen only a 1% chance that some shock factor, external or internal, would cause a conventional debt ratio to produce a result falling somewhere between temporary anguish and default.

We wouldn't have liked those 99:1 odds—and never will. A small chance of distress or disgrace cannot, in our view, be offset by a large chance of extra returns. If your actions are sensible, you are certain to get good results; in most such cases, leverage just moves things along faster.... I have never been in a big hurry: We enjoy the process far more than the proceeds—though we have learned to live with those also.

We hope in another 25 years to report on the mistakes of the first 50. If we are around in 2015 to do that, you can count on this section occupying many more pages than it does here.

Benjamin Graham as a teacher, writer and investor helped define the role of the securities analyst. He also helped to launch the careers of several now-legendary investors, including Warren Buffett. **Charles Ellis** wrote this appreciation for the *Financial Analysts Journal* in 1982.

# BEN GRAHAM:
# IDEAS AS MEMENTOS
by Charles D. Ellis

Ben Graham developed the idea of our profession just as surely as Sir Robert Peel created the idea of an effective policeman, and just as certainly as the London constables are still called Bobbies in respect for Sir Robert's conceptualization of their mission and qualifications, those of us who serve in the profession as financial analysts are living out Ben's idea of what we might be able to do. We are, at least we aspire to be, adherents to the mission he originated.

My own acquaintance with Ben was all too brief: In his late 70s, he joined in a series of seminars I was leading for Donaldson, Lufkin & Jenrette, to which were invited in groups of 20 the leading investment managers of the day. By common consent, Ben was the best informed, the most inquisitive, the most delighted with ideas and differences of view in the group. And, of course, he charmed us all by his grace and wit and appreciation.

Sometimes, the incidental imperfection serves to illuminate the excellence of the man. For me, there is still special pleasure in the impossibility of sorting out one trivial misunderstanding. Ben was very pleased with Jacob Bronowski's television series on *The Ascent of Man*, watched every program, and was reading the book of the program's transcripts. Naturally Ben was delighted with Bronowski's research and ideas: They were the twin dimensions of Ben's work. But Ben was even more enchanted by Bronowski's extraordinary ability, as Ben saw it, to "get every word in every sentence in every performance exactly right—exactly the way it was in the book!" It never occurred to Ben that the book was made *after* the television program, and that it was the book that was accurately repeating Bronowski. Twice I tried to help Ben "get the cart before the horse," to no avail, and then realized he liked it the way he had it, and would rather get on with the serious discussion of ideas.

Here, then, are a few excerpts from a dozen articles Ben wrote for the *Financial Analysts Journal* over 30 years.

### The Campaign for Professionalism

Ben was an early advocate of what we now call Chartered Financial Analysts and the extensive examination and education program that is conducted through the CFA Institute. His campaign for this professionalism was evident in a 1945 *FAJ* article where he posed the rhetorical question: Should security analysts have a professional rating? For a mind as quick to isolate the central argument, the analysis was not difficult. First,

The crux of the question is whether security analysis as a calling has enough of the professional attribute to justify the requirement that its practitioners present to the public evidence of fitness for their work.

Second,

The right of every individual to practice his chosen trade is

subject to the higher right of society to impose standards of fitness where these are advisable.

Third,

It would seem to follow, almost as an axiom, that security analysts would welcome a rating of quasi-professional character, and
will work hard to develop this rating into a universally accepted
warranty of good character and sound competence.[*]

The elegance of Ben's thinking was complemented by a plain way
with words—and dress. He wore dark suits of a durable fabric that
would last and last, and he described his work as "stock market operations." In a similar vein, his term for the reorganized professional was
simply Qualified Security Analyst.

In the course of a 1946 article, written as "Cogitator," Ben admonished his colleagues, saying that a professional analyst was "right"
in recommending purchase of a security only when the stock appreciated in price for the reasons identified by the analyst. You should
be right for the right reason—the one you identified when making
your recommendation:

Recommendations to buy a stock for the main reason that next
year's earnings are going to be higher . . . are among the most
common in Wall Street. They have the advantage of being subject to rather simple tests. Such a recommendation will be right
if both (a) the earnings increase and (b) the price advances—say,
at least 10 per cent—within the next 12 months.

---

[*] "Should Security Analysts Have a Professional Rating?" January 1945.

The objection to this type of recommendation is a practical one. It is naive to believe that in the typical case the market is unaware of the prospects for improved earnings next year. If this is so, the favorable factor is likely to be discounted, and the batting average of recommendations based on this simple approach can scarcely be very impressive.*

Evident in this brief excerpt is Ben's respect for the other investors working in the market. In later years, after many more smart people had come into the market, he would doubt the ability of any large institutional investor to outperform the market *and* the competition.

ORGANIZED KNOWLEDGE

Ben enjoyed throughout his life that open-minded thirst for understanding and information that we admire in the term "childlike." At 80, he was working out a new formulation—and testing it against actual market results. In 1946, at the time of the announcement of a new Awards Committee on Corporate Disclosure, Ben addressed the need for organized knowledge in a profession:

It is amazing to reflect how little systematic knowledge Wall Street has to draw upon as regards the historical behavior of securities with defined characteristics. We do, of course, have charts showing the long-term price movements of stock groups and of individual stocks. But there is no real classification here, except by type of business. (An exception is Barron's index of Low Priced Stocks.) Where is the continuous, ever growing body of knowledge and technique handed down by the analysts of the

---

* "On Being Right in Security Analysis," First Quarter 1946 (as "Cogitator").

past to those of the present and the future? When we contrast the annals of medicine with those of finance, the paucity of our recorded and digested experience becomes a reproach.

There are explanations and answers in rebuttal. Security analysis is a fledgling science; give it (and *The Analysts Journal*) time to spread its wings. Contrariwise, many of us believe, perhaps unconsciously rather than consciously, that there is not enough permanence in the behavior of security patterns to justify a laborious accumulation of case histories. If physicians and research men keep on investigating cancer, they will probably end by understanding and controlling it—because the nature of cancer does not change during the years it is being studied. But the factors underlying security values and the price behavior of given types of securities do suffer alteration through the years. By the time we have completed the cumbersome processes of inductive study, by the time our tentative conclusions have been checked and counterchecked through a succession of market cycles, the chances are that new economic factors will have supervened—and thus our hard won technique becomes obsolete before it is ever used.

That is what we may think, but how do we know whether, or to what extent, it is so? We lack the codified experience which will tell us whether codified experience is valuable or valueless. In the years to come we analysts must go to school to the older established disciplines. We must study their ways of amassing and scrutinizing facts and from this study develop methods of research suited to the peculiarities of our own field of work.

To what extent do we address ourselves to the 'classification and methodical exploitation . . . of the salient and recurrent phenomena'? Of this we have as yet only the rudiments. Very little effort has been made to construct systematic inductive studies of our experience with various types of securities, or security situations. The experience we draw upon in forming our judgments is largely a matter of rule-of-thumb, of vague impressions or even prejudices, rather than the resultant of many recorded and carefully studied case histories.[*]

## INTRINSIC VALUE

Ben was clearly identified in his investing with "intrinsic value," but not with "growth stocks." The reason for his preference was the confidence he could have in his own work when the analysis focused on present assets and liabilities rather than depending upon estimates of future values. Ben would have, of course, been comfortable with Baron Rothschild's summary of a lifetime's learning: "Buy assets; sell earnings."

Here is Ben's logic from a 1957 article:

Of the various basic approaches to common-stock valuation, the most widely accepted is that which estimates the average earnings and dividends for a period of years in the future and capitalizes these elements at an appropriate rate. This statement is reasonably definite in form, but its application permits of the widest range of techniques and assumptions, including plain guesswork. The analyst has first a broad choice as to the future period he will consider; then the earnings and dividends for the period must be estimated, and finally a capitalization rate selected in accordance with his judgment or his prejudices. We may observe here that since there is no *a priori* rule governing the number of years to which the valuer should look forward in the future, it is

---

[*] "The Hippocratic Method in Security Analysis," Second Quarter 1946 (as "Cogitator").

almost inevitable that in bull markets investors and analysts will tend to see far and hopefully ahead, whereas at other times they will not be so disposed to 'heed the rumble of a distant drum.' Hence arises a high degree of built-in instability in the market valuation of growth stocks, so much so that one might assert with some justice that the more dynamic the company the more inherently speculative and fluctuating may be the market history of its shares. (On this point the philosophically inclined are referred to the recent article of David Durand on 'Growth Stocks and the Petersburg Paradox,' in the September 1957 issue of the *Journal of Finance*. His conclusion is 'that the growth— stock problem offers no great hope of satisfactory solution.')

When it comes to estimating future earnings few analysts are willing to venture forth, Columbus-like, on completely uncharted seas. They prefer to start with known quantities—e.g., current or past earnings—and process these in some fashion to reach an esti- mate for the future. As a consequence, in security analysis the past is always being thrown out of the window of theory and coming in again through the back door of practice. It would be a sorry joke on our profession if all the elaborate data on past operations, so industriously collected and so minutely analyzed, should prove in the end to be quite unrelated to the real determinants of the value—the earnings and dividends of the future.[*]

## THE PSYCHOLOGY OF THE STOCK MARKET

In 1958, Ben was Visiting Professor of Finance At UCLA, and gave a long talk on what he perceived to be speculation in common stock:

---

[*] "Two Illustrative Approaches to Formula Valuations of Common Stocks," November 1957.

Let me start with a summary of my thesis. In the past the speculative elements of the common stock resided almost exclusively
in the company itself; they were due to uncertainties, or fluctuating elements, or downright weaknesses in the industry, or the
corporation's individual set-up. These elements of speculation
still exist, of course; but it may be said that they have been sen-
sibly diminished by a number of long-term developments to
which I shall refer. But in revenge a new and major element of
speculation has been introduced into the common-stock arena
from outside the companies. It comes from the attitude and
viewpoint of the stock-buying public and their advisers—chiefly
us security analysts. This attitude may be described in a phrase:
primary emphasis upon future expectations.

Ben developed his thesis, to the pleasure of his audience, with a bit
of personal history:

In 1912 I had left college for a term to take charge of a research
project for U.S. Express Co. We set out to find the effect on revenues of a proposed revolutionary new system of computing
express rates. For this purpose we used the so-called Hollerith
machines, leased out by the then Computing-Tabulating-
Recording Co. They comprised card-punches, card-sorters, and
tabulators—tools almost unknown to businessmen, then, and
having their chief application in the Census Bureau. I entered Wall
Street in 1914, and the next year the bonds and common stock of
C.-T.-R. Co. were listed on the New York Exchange. Well, I had
a kind of sentimental interest in that enterprise, and besides I considered myself a sort of technological expert on their products,
being one of the few financial people who had seen and used them.

So early in 1916 I went to the head of my firm, known as Mr. A. N., and pointed out to him the C.-T.-R. stock was selling in the middle 40s . . . ; that it had earnings of $6.50 in 1915; that its book value—including, to be sure, some non-segregated intangibles—was $130; that it had started a $3 dividend; and that I thought rather highly of the company's products and prospects. Mr. A. N. looked at me pityingly. 'Ben,' said he, 'Do not mention that company to me again. I would not touch it with a ten-foot pole. (His favorite expression.) Its 6% bonds are selling in the low 80s and they are no good. So how can the stock be any good? Everybody knows there is nothing behind it but water.' (Glossary: In those days that was the ultimate of condemnation. It meant that the asset-account on the balance sheet was fictitious. Many industrial companies—notably U.S. Steel—despite their $100 par, represented nothing but water, concealed in a written-up plant account. Since they had 'nothing' to back them but earning power and future prospects, no self-respecting investor would give them a second thought.)

I returned to my statistician's cubby-hole, a chastened young man. Mr. A. N. was not only experienced and successful, but extremely shrewd as well. So much was I impressed by his sweeping condemnation of Computing-Tabulating-Recording that I never bought a share of it in my life, not even after its name was changed to IBM in 1926. . . .

Always seeking *lessons* to be drawn from experiences, Ben summarized this lesson:

It seems a truism to say that the old-time common-stock investor was not much interested in capital gains. He bought almost entirely for safety and income, and let the speculator concern himself with price appreciation. Today we are likely to say that the more experienced and shrewd the investor, the less attention he pays to dividend returns, and the more heavily his interest centers on long-term appreciation. Yet one might argue, perversely, that precisely because the old-time investor did not concentrate on future capital appreciation he was virtually guaranteeing to himself that he would have it, at least in the field of industrial stocks. And, conversely, today's investor is so concerned with anticipating the future that he is already paying handsomely for it in advance. Thus what he has projected with so much study and care may actually happen and still not bring him any profit. If it should fail to materialize to the degree expected he may in fact be faced with a serious temporary and perhaps even permanent loss.[*]

ON PRICE-EARNINGS RATIOS

Observing how markets change and reverse apparent certainties, Ben gently admonished,

It casts some little doubt in my mind as to the complete dependability of the popular belief among analysts that prominent and promising companies will now always sell at high price-earnings ratios; that this is a fundamental fact of life for investors and they may as well accept and like it. I have no desire at all to be dogmatic on this point. All I can say is that it is not settled in my mind, and each of you must seek to settle it for yourself.

[*] "The New Speculation in Common Stocks," June 1958.

His conclusion draws upon his beloved classics:

When Phaethon insisted on driving the chariot of the Sun, his father, the experienced operator, gave the neophyte some advice which the latter failed to follow—to his cost. Ovid summed up Phoebus Apollo's counsel in three words:

> *Medius tutissimus ibis*
> *You will go safest in the middle course*

I think this principle holds good for investors and their security-analyst advisers.[*]

## BEATING THE MARKET

In 1963, Ben wrote about the future of financial analysis, in the course of which he mused about technical analysis:

My views on the validity of stock-market forecasting have been unfavorable for about half a century. This may entitle me to a high mark for consistency, but it hardly qualifies me as an impartial student of the subject . . . .[**]

## JUDGMENT AND EFFICIENT MARKETS

Despite his doubts about the ability of large institutions to beat the market regularly, Ben was confident that analysts could be "right" and that markets could be "wrong":

---

[*] Ibid.

[**] "The Future of Financial Analysis," May/June 1963.

In its extreme form the hypothesis of the efficient market makes two declarations: (1) The price of nearly every stock at nearly all times reflects whatever is knowable about the company's affairs; hence no consistent profits can be made by seeking out and using additional information, including that held by 'insiders.' (2) Because the market has complete or at least adequate information about each issue, the prices it registers are therefore 'correct,' 'reasonable' or 'appropriate.' This would imply that it is fruitless, or at least insufficiently rewarding, for security analysts to look for discrepancies between price and value.

I have no particular quarrel with declaration one, though assuredly there are times when a researcher may unearth significant information about a stock, not generally known and reflected in the price. But I deny emphatically that because the market has all the information it needs to establish a correct price the prices it actually registers are in fact correct. Take as my example a fine company such as Avon Products. How can it make sense to say that its price of 140 was 'correct' in 1973 and that its price of 32 was also 'correct' in 1974? Could anything have happened—outside of stock-market psychology—to reduce the value of that enterprise by 77 per cent or nearly six billion dollars? The market may have had all the information it needed about Avon; what it lacked is the right kind of judgment in evaluating its knowledge.

Descartes summed up the matter more than three centuries ago, when he wrote in his 'Discours de la Methode': 'Ce n'est pas assez d'avoir l'esprit bon, mais le principal est de l'appiquer bien.' In English: 'It is not enough to have a good intelligence'—and I add, 'enough information'—'the principal thing is to apply it well.'

I can assure the reader that among the 500-odd NYSE issues selling below the seven times earnings today, there are plenty to be found for which the prices are not 'correct' ones, in any meaningful sense of the term. They are clearly worth more than their current selling prices, and any security analyst worth his salt should be able to make up an attractive portfolio out of this 'universe.'*

The pioneer of fundamental research in the 1930s, Ben felt the world of investors had changed—surely more as a result of his work than any ten others—and could say in 1976:

I am no longer an advocate of elaborate techniques of security analysis in order to find superior value opportunities. This was a rewarding activity, say, 40 years ago, when our textbook 'Graham and Dodd' was first published; but the situation has changed a good deal since then. In the old days any well-trained security analyst could do a good professional job of selecting undervalued issues through detailed studies; but in the light of the enormous amount of research now being carried on, I doubt whether in most cases such extensive efforts will generate sufficiently superior selections to justify their cost. To that very limited extent I'm on the side of the 'efficient market' school of thought now generally accepted by the professors.**

Later that year, Warren Buffett wrote in his FAJ tribute to Ben:

A remarkable aspect of Ben's dominance of his professional field was that he achieved it without that narrowness of mental

---

* "The Future of Common Stocks," September/October 1974.

** "A Conversation with Benjamin Graham," September/October 1976.

activity that concentrates all effort on a single end. It was, rather, the incidental by-product of an intellect whose breadth almost exceeded definition. Virtually total recall, unending fascination with new knowledge and an ability to recast it in a form applicable to seemingly unrelated problems made exposure to his thinking in any field a delight. There was an absolutely open-ended, no-scores-kept generosity of ideas, time and spirit. If clarity of thinking was required, there was no better place to go. And if encouragement or counsel was needed, Ben was there.[*]

He still is for those who enjoyed even briefly the pleasure of his company.

---

[*] Warren E. Buffett, "Benjamin Graham (1894–1976)," November/December 1976.

John Bogle in 1974 founded the Vanguard Group, which has since become the world's second-largest fund family. He is a tower of integrity in the fund industry and a strong campaigner for the rights of fund investors.

# ON SIMPLICITY
## BY JOHN C. BOGLE

from *Common Sense on Mutual Funds* (1999)

W̲E LIVE IN a world where a seemingly infinite amount of information is available to just about everyone. Financial facts, figures, and theories once available only to investment professionals are now at the fingertips of individual investors. No longer must the investor depend on the services of an investment professional. Buy and sell to your heart's content over the World Wide Web. The information age has truly transformed the world of investing.

Today, investors are bombarded on all sides by investment information—whether they want it or not. Complex quantitative analysis, real-time stock quotes, and the like are available at any local library, if not through a personal computer. Investors now ask their mutual fund managers about their "alpha"; they want to know a fund's "Sharpe ratio"; they read articles about "complexity theory" and "behavioral finance."

Yet this barrage of information has not necessarily translated into better returns. Instead, we focus on the quantity of data. We want more sophisticated and complex information. Presumably it will enhance our returns. Our world may or may not be any more complex than it has ever been, but we have certainly made the investment process more complicated. In today's environment of a mind-numbing information flow that is at once electrifying and terrifying, where is the intelligent investor to turn?

*Turn to simplicity.* The great paradox of this remarkable age is that the more complex the world around us becomes, the more simplicity we must seek in order to realize our financial goals. Never underrate either the majesty of simplicity or its proven effectiveness as a long-term strategy for productive investing. Simplicity, indeed, is the master key to financial success. The old Shaker hymn got it just right:

> 'Tis the gift to be simple;
> 'Tis the gift to be free;
> 'Tis the gift to come down
> Where we ought to be.

I'd like to offer some precepts to help you "come down where [you] ought to be" in your quest for investment success. Let me begin by describing what I regard as the realistic epitome of investment success. Here is my definition of the nature of the task: *The central task of investing is to realize the highest possible portion of the return earned in the financial asset class in which you invest—recognizing, and accepting, that that portion will be less than 100 percent.*

Why? Because of cost. As we have already seen, we must pay the costs of the intermediaries involved in making the investments in each financial asset class—cash reserves, bonds, stocks, and so on—available to us. To state the obvious, we know intuitively that our certificates of deposit and our money market funds will inevitably earn less than the going market rate for short-term commercial paper, simply because the costs of financial intermediaries—transaction costs, information costs, and the cost of convenience—are deducted from the interest rates paid by the government or by the corporate borrower.

Similarly, we do not—nor should we—expect our bond funds to provide us with higher yields than the average yield of the bonds held in a fund's portfolio. In fact, because of excessive fund fees in bond mutual funds as a group, the gap between 100 percent of the market return and the return that filters down to the investor after cost is often distressingly large—so large that *nearly* all bond funds are distinctly inferior investments.

The proposition applies even in the equity arena, the third major class of liquid financial assets. It is a mathematical impossibility—a definitional contradiction—for all investors *as a group* to outpace the returns that are earned in the total stock market. Indeed, given the high costs of equity fund ownership, it is a mathematical certainty that, over a lifetime of investing, only a handful of fund investors will succeed in doing so by any significant margin.

## WHEN ALL ELSE FAILS, FALL BACK ON SIMPLICITY

I propose to challenge most of the conventional wisdom that you hear and read. A considerable amount of good common sense is available to investors. Pay attention to it. But a considerable amount of foolishness—investment wizardry, financial legerdemain, and tempting solutions—is also promoted, often by the apparently omniscient. Disregard it. No matter what you hear or read, do not forget that we live and invest today in an uncertain world of finance, of volatile and interrelated securities markets. You may have heard that we are living in a new era, but I strongly caution you that, in human history, many more "new eras" have been predicted than have ever come to pass.

Amid the cacophony of advice bombarding you, mine, I imagine, is the most basic: To earn the highest of returns that are *realistically* possible, you should invest with simplicity. Accepting this reality—that investors as a group will inevitably capture less than 100 percent of the rates of return provided in any asset class—is the first step toward simplifying investment decisions. What, then, is the optimal method of approaching the 100 percent target and accumulating a substantial investment account? Rely on the ordinary virtues that intelligent, balanced human beings have relied on for centuries: common sense, thrift, realistic expectations, patience, and perseverance. In investing, I assure you that those characteristics will, over the long run, be rewarded.

Where should you begin? Consider that the ultimate in simplicity comes with the additional virtue of low cost. The *simplest* of all approaches is to invest solely in a single balanced market index fund— just one fund. *And it works.* Such a fund offers a broadly diversified middle-of-the-road investment program for a typical conservative investor who is investing about 65 percent of assets in stocks and 35 percent in bonds. This portfolio is entirely "indexed"—that is, its stocks and bonds are not actively managed, but simply represent a broad cross-section of the entire U.S. stock market and bond market. Over the past half-century, such a fund would have captured 98 percent of the rate of return of the combined stock and bond markets. Investing doesn't get much better than that.

Let me prove the point by evaluating the cumulative returns of balanced mutual funds—a group whose portfolios tend to be quite homogeneous, composed as they are of stocks with both value and growth characteristics, and good-quality bonds with intermediate-to-long maturities (usually including a small cash reserve). I'll compare

the cumulative returns of the average balanced fund with a hypo-
thetical no-load balanced index fund weighted 35 percent by the
Lehman High-Grade Corporate Bond Index and 65 percent by the
Standard & Poor's 500 Stock Index (rebalanced annually), with
the annual return reduced by estimated costs of 0.2 percent. We'll
take a half-century retrospective, in order to gain a broad view
from the lessons of history.

Fifty years, to be sure, is a long time. The past 15 years may be
more relevant for appraising today's fund industry, so let's look at the
35 balanced funds that have survived that period. As it turns out, you
would have been wise not to waste your energy trying to find the best
manager. *Only two funds outpaced the low-cost index fund for the full
period.* During the past 15 years—including most of the bull market,
with stock returns near historic highs—the average return of the
actively managed balanced funds was 12.8 percent per year, compared
with 14.7 percent for the balanced index fund, without a noticeable
difference in risk. That 1.9 percent deficit may not matter to investors
when they still earn 12.8 percent net, but when stock returns recede
to more normal levels—as they are apt to—the deficit's significance
will be more apparent.

This 1.9 percent relative advantage in recent times was more than
double the 0.9 percent advantage over the half-century, and probably a
better portent of things to come. The net results: $10,000 grew to
$78,200 in the index fund versus $60,900 in the managed fund. The
index fund advantage alone was $17,300—almost double the initial
capital. And, this time, with the higher 14.9 percent return on the index
itself, the index *fund*, with an annual cost of 0.2 percent, captured fully
99 percent of the market rate of return. Investing in a single balanced

index fund represents not only the ultimate in simplicity, but a productive choice as well.

## SIMPLICITY IN YOUR STOCK PORTFOLIO

Like most people, you may well be an investor who would like to control your own investment balance. Fair enough. I turn now to a second example of the value of simplicity—a single *equity* index fund for your stock portfolio. Again, during the past 15 years, the record of indexing has been truly remarkable. The total stock market index (Wilshire 5000) has outpaced the average diversified equity fund by 2.5 percentage points per year. Again, the index fund captured 99 percent of the annual market return of 16.0 percent. The cumulative result is really quite imposing, with an *added* return of more than $23,500—more than two times the value of the initial investment. This difference arises largely because *total* fund costs (expense ratios plus portfolio transaction costs) themselves ran to about two full percentage points.

As was the case with the balanced funds (only more so), this 15-year equity fund comparison amply justified a simple index approach to capturing the highest realistically possible portion of the market's returns—albeit slightly less than 100 percent.

What I have described here is the very essence of simplicity: owning the entire U.S. stock market (and, for a balanced index fund, the entire U.S. bond market as well); making no effort to select the best manager; holding the asset allocation constant and making no attempt at market timing; keeping transaction activity low (and minimizing taxes as well); and eliminating the excessive costs of investing that characterize managed mutual funds. *And it worked.* Even if future outcomes of this approach are less successful, it's hard to imagine that they could provide markedly inferior wealth accumulation relative to comparable managed funds. The success of the index fund reaffirms a basic piece of investment wisdom: When all else fails, fall back on simplicity.

Ever the realist, I recognize that few expect that "all else will fail." In the real world, lots of all-too-human traits get in the way of a simple, all-encompassing index fund approach:

> *"Hope springs eternal.*
> *"I'm better than average."*
> *"Even if the game is expensive, it's fun."*
> *"That example is too good to be true."*
> *"It can't be* that *simple."*

These are common refrains in the words and thoughts of investors who choose to pursue the conventional strategy of relying entirely on actively managed funds to implement their investment strategies.

### *If You Decide Not to Index . . .*

But if the beginning of simplicity is the index fund, it need not be the end. History suggests that, in the long run, only one of every five actively managed funds is apt to outpace the market index (after taxes, only one of seven). And some simple commonsense principles should help you to select them and to earn a generous portion of the market's return—again, all too likely, less than 100 percent. If there are long odds against outpacing the market, going about the task of fund selection intelligently can at least help to guard against a significant failure. Even master investor Warren Buffett, a strong proponent of the index approach, concedes that there may be other ways to construct an investment portfolio:

*Should you choose . . . to construct your own portfolio, there are a few thoughts worth remembering. Intelligent investing is not complex, though that is far from saying that it is easy. What an investor needs is the ability to correctly evaluate selected businesses. Note the word "selected": You don't have to be an expert on every company, or even many. You only have to be able to evaluate companies within your circle of competence. The size of that circle is not very important; knowing its boundaries, however, is vital.*

The Prussian General Karl von Clausewitz once said, "The greatest enemy of a good plan is the dream of a perfect plan." And, though I believe that an index strategy is a good strategy, you may want to seek a better plan, if not a perfect plan, no matter how great the challenge, no matter how overpowering the odds against implementing it with extraordinary success. So, much as I would urge you to commit your investments to an all-index-fund approach—or at least to follow an approach using index funds as the core of your portfolio—I'm going to offer you another simple approach: eight basic rules that should help you to capitalize on the advantages that have accounted for the historical ability of an index to provide superior returns. These eight rules are not complex. But they should help you to make intelligent fund selections for your investment program.

### RULE 1: SELECT LOW-COST FUNDS

From much that I hear, I am known as a sort of fringe fanatic—an apostle of the message that costs play a crucial role in shaping long-term fund returns. I've said "Cost matters" for so long that one of my followers gave me a Plexiglas pillar inscribed with the Latin translation: *Pretium Refert*. But cost *does* matter. I've shown you the effect on returns and on asset allocation. I've been harping about costs for years, and it was with some delight that I read these words from Warren Buffett in the Berkshire-Hathaway Annual Report for 1996:

*Seriously, costs matter. For example, equity mutual funds incur corporate expenses—largely payments to the funds' managers—that average about 100 basis points,\* a levy likely to cut the returns their investors earn by 10 percent or more over time.*

Sadly, Mr. Buffett was too conservative in his calculations. The average equity fund now charges not 100, but 155 basis points, and also incurs portfolio transaction costs of at least another 50 basis points. Together, they comprise expenses of 200 basis points or more. If I may revise his comment, then, fund costs are "a levy likely to cut the returns their investors earn by *20 percent* or more over time." Again, sadly—and unbelievably—bond fund fees also average more than 1 percent, a grossly unjustified levy on *any* gross interest yield, especially today's nominal yield of about 5% percent on the long U.S. Treasury bond, which would be cut by almost 20 percent. I regard such costs as unacceptable.

A low expense ratio is the single most important reason why a fund does well. Therefore, carefully consider the role of expense ratios in shaping fund returns. If you select actively managed funds, emulate the index advantage by choosing low-cost funds. *The surest route to top-quartile returns is bottom-quartile expenses.* Using yet another period—the five years from 1991 to 1996—Table 4.1 gives the record for funds owning stocks with large market capitalizations.

---

\* 100 basis points equals 1 percent

Note that both groups *earned* similar preexpense returns. But the 1.2 percent cost advantage was largely responsible for the 1.9 percent performance advantage for the low-cost funds. The link is hardly accidental. Lower costs are the handmaiden of higher returns.

The costs that actively managed funds incur in buying and selling portfolio securities are hidden, but nonetheless real. Fund portfolio turnover averages some 80 percent annually. It is expensive, perhaps adding as much as 0.5 to 1.0 percentage points (or more) to the more visible cost of fund expenses. So, favor low-turnover funds, but not only because these costs are lower. They also provide substantial tax advantages. The longer that actively managed funds hold portfolio securities, the greater the extraordinary value of deferral of capital gains becomes to their shareholders. Many high-turnover funds are expensive as well as tax-inefficient, so it behooves you to consider *after-tax* returns, along with present unrealized gains, which could lead to potentially massive future capital gains distributions and the burden of unnecessary taxes. The odds against active managers' outpacing the *after-tax* returns of index funds rise even higher. So if you own any funds outside of a tax-deferred retirement plan, *don't forget that taxes are costs too.*

Enough said, except that I would like to justify not only my appraisal of the importance of low-cost funds as a guideline for selecting funds, but also my selection of this warning as Rule 1. I rely on the support of William F. Sharpe, Nobel Laureate in Economics, who in a recent interview said: "The *first* thing to look at is the expense ratio" (italics added). You should follow his advice and recognize that selecting among low-cost managed funds should maximize the unlikely possibility that you will earn returns in excess of a low-cost index fund (20 basis points or less) simply because minimizing the cost differential gives a fund a far greater chance to compete success-fully. After all, a low-cost fund with a 40-basis-point expense is fighting a 20-knot breeze in its efforts to win the sailing race, but a high-cost fund (150 basis points) is fighting a 130-knot typhoon.

**TABLE 4.1**

LARGE CAPITALIZATION STOCK FUNDS: RETURNS VS. EXPENSES (1991–1996)

|  | Total Return before Expenses | Expense Ratio | Total Return after Expenses |
|---|---|---|---|
| Lowest-cost quartile | 14.7% | 0.5% | 14.2% |
| Highest-cost quartile | 14.0 | 1.7 | 12.3 |
| Low-cost advantage | +0.7% | −1.2% | +1.9% |

## RULE 2: CONSIDER CAREFULLY THE ADDED COSTS OF ADVICE

Tens of millions of investors need personal guidance in allocating their assets and selecting funds. Other tens of millions do not. For those in the latter category, some 3,000 no-load funds, without sales commissions, are available to choose from, and it is the essence of simplicity for self-reliant, intelligent, informed investors to purchase shares without resorting to an intermediary salesperson or financial adviser. Assuming the funds are properly selected, buying no-load funds is the least costly way to own mutual funds, and costs will consume the lowest possible proportion of future returns.

For the many investors who require guidance, there are registered advisers and brokerage account executives, many of whom serve their clients ably at a fair price. Good advisers give you their personal attention, help you avoid some of the pitfalls of investing, and provide worthwhile asset-allocation and fund-selection services. But, like any of us, they must earn their keep, providing you with valuable services that make it worth your while to invest through them. But I do not believe that they can identify, *in advance*, the top-performing managers— no one can!—and I'd avoid those who claim they can do so. The best advisers can help you develop a long-range investment strategy and an intelligent plan for its implementation.

You should know exactly how much the adviser's services will cost. Advice may be provided by registered "fee-only" investment advisers, who usually charge annual fees beginning at 1 percent of assets. It may also be provided by brokerage firm representatives who receive sales commissions. Commissions represent a significant drag on a mutual fund's performance, especially if the fund's shares are held for only a short period. It would be foolish to pay a 6 percent load if you expect to hold the shares for only a few years. Over 10 years, on the other hand, such a load would cut your return by a more modest 0.6 percent per year. In all, paying a reasonable price for guidance—especially when the adviser helps minimize your "all-in" cost (his or her cost, *plus* the costs of the funds) by focusing on low-cost funds—may well be acceptable in light of the services you receive.

Beware of the many *apparently* no-load funds that charge a hidden load—a special kind of sales charge, known as a 12b-1 fee, that is deducted from your returns each year. This fee may reduce your annual return by an additional one percentage point. If regular fund expenses are also 1.5 percentage points, the combined fee could consume one-fourth of a long-term 10 percent return on your portfolio, reducing it to 7.5 percent. Deductions may be even larger if you liquidate your fund shares within five or six years. Other funds use these 12b-1 fees, not to pay the salespeople, but to promote sales of the fund's shares through aggressive advertising and marketing programs.

These fees provide no net benefit whatsoever to you, but they are paid out of your pocket. Be wary of funds that charge 12b-1 fees.

Most of all, beware of wrap accounts—packages of mutual funds assembled within a "wrapper" for which an additional fee is paid. They are usually expensive. Owning a package of managed funds may make sense under some circumstances, but paying 2 percent or more of assets per year for such a package defies reason. In my judgment, an investor who pays up to 4 percent a year in total costs (fund expenses plus the wrap fee) has destroyed any chance of approximating the total returns of the financial markets. Such a cost is simply too much dead weight—too great a handicap—on the return of *any* fund to enable it to be competitive. It cannot win the race.

## RULE 3: DO NOT OVERRATE PAST FUND PERFORMANCE

My third rule has to do with the first element that catches the eye of most investors, whether experienced or novice: the fund's past track record. (The analogy to a horse race implied by the phrase "track record" is presumably unintentional!) But track records, helpful as they may be in appraising how thoroughbred horses will run (and they may not be very effective there either) are usually hopelessly misleading in appraising how money managers will perform. There is no way under the sun to forecast a fund's future absolute returns based on its past record. Even if someone could accurately forecast the future *absolute* returns the stock market will deliver—no mean task!—there is no way to forecast the future returns that an individual mutual fund will deliver *relative* to the market. The only exception would be the relative returns of index funds.

Now, I must contradict myself ever so slightly. Two highly probable, if not certain, forecasts *can* be made:

1. *Funds with unusually high expenses are likely to underperform appropriate market indexes.*

2. *Funds with past relative returns that have been substantially superior to the returns of an appropriate market index will regress toward, and usually below, the market mean over time.*

Reversion to the mean—the law of gravity in the financial markets that causes funds that are up to go down, and funds that are down to go up—is clear, quantifiable, and apparently almost inevitable.

The two studies summarized in Table 4.2 show the deteriorating returns of top-quartile growth and growth and income funds relative to the market return over consecutive decades, as 99 percent of those funds reverted toward the mean. Note that only one fund was an exception to the rule. That fund—which ruled the world during both the 1970s and the 1980s and became the largest fund in the industry— reverted magnificently to the mean during the 1990s. Sometimes, reversion to the mean requires patience!

**TABLE 4.2**

REVERSION TO THE MEAN

| Period | Number of Funds in Top Quartile | Reversion Toward or Below Mean[*] Number | Percentage |
|---|---|---|---|
| 1970s to 1980s | 34 | 33 | 97% |
| 1987 to 1997 | 44 | 44 | 100 |
| Total | 78 | 77 | 99% |

[*] *Standard & Poor's 500 Index.*

The mutual fund industry is well aware that nearly all top performers eventually lose their edge. Why fund sponsors persist in the vigorous, expensive, and finally misleading advertising and promotion of their most successful past performers defies all reason—except one. Promotion of funds with high past returns brings in lots of new money from investors, and lots of new fees to the adviser. Managers are highly rewarded for their transitory past success. Have you ever seen the promotion of a fund that has had either a low absolute return or a subpar relative return? (During the past 15 years, 95 percent of all equity funds have failed to beat the Standard & Poor's 500 Stock Index.) Promotions of funds based on past performance lead you in the wrong direction. Ignore them.

### RULE 4: USE PAST PERFORMANCE TO DETERMINE CONSISTENCY AND RISK

Despite Rule 3, there *is* an important role that past performance can play in helping you to make your fund selections. While you should disregard a single aggregate number showing a fund's past long-term return, you can learn a great deal by studying the nature of its past returns. Above all, *look for consistency.* When I evaluate mutual funds (and I have looked carefully at many hundreds of them during my long career), I like to look at a fund's ranking among other funds with similar policies and objectives (i.e., I compare a large-cap value fund with other large-cap value funds, a small-cap growth fund with other comparable funds, and so on).

*Morningstar Mutual Funds* makes these comparisons easy. It shows, in a simple chart, whether a fund was in the first, second, third, or fourth quartile of its group during each of the preceding 12 years. The chart gives a fair reflection of *both* the consistency of a fund's policies *and* the relative success of its managers. For a fund to earn a top performance evaluation, it should have, in my opinion, at least six to nine years in the top two quartiles and no more than one or two years in the bottom quartile. I would normally reject funds with four or five years in the bottom quartile, even if offset by the same number in the top quartile. Figure 4.4 provides two examples of real-world funds that reflect the standards I've set forth.

The "good" fund was in the top half in 10 years, in the bottom quartile only once, and in the third quartile once. The "bad" fund was in the top half six times and in the bottom quartile four times, and it had two third-quartile appearances. I've taken the liberty of also showing in Figure 4.4 how an index fund stacks up. Remarkably—and I caution you not to expect the pattern to recur quite this favorably in the future—the S&P 500 index fund earned top-half ranking fully 11 times, without once finding its way into the bottom quartile. In any event, consistency is a virtue for a mutual fund. Intelligent investors will want to give it heavy weight in the fund selection process.

FIGURE 4.4

*MORNINGSTAR* PERFORMANCE PROFILES\*: CONSISTENCY

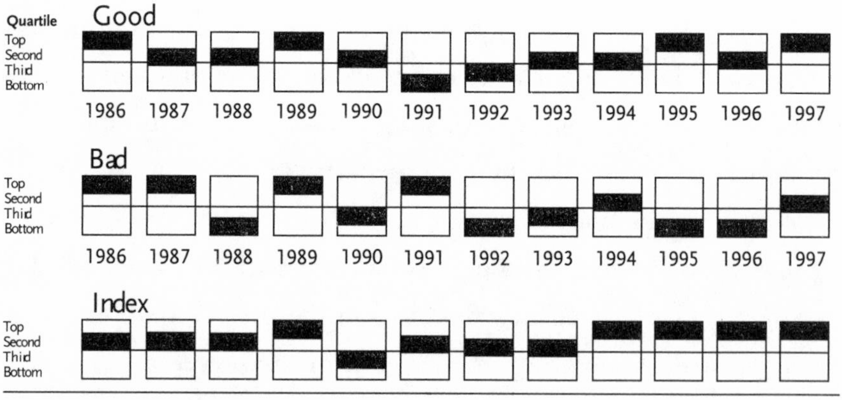

\* *Quartile within* Morningstar *category.*

In using the word *performance*, I am not limiting my interest solely to return. *Risk is a crucial element in investing.* I especially like to know a fund's *Morningstar* risk rating—based on a fund's returns in the months in which it underperformed the risk-free U.S. Treasury bill—relative to its peers with similar objectives and policies, and relative to all equity funds. That rating serves as a rough guide to how much relative risk the fund typically assumes. There is a difference! Indeed, the risk of the average large-cap value fund (22 percent *below* average) has carried only half of the risk of its small-cap growth fund counterpart (93 percent above average). Table 4.3 compares the *Morningstar* risk ratings for the nine basic investment styles. Risk matters. For while future fund returns are utterly unpredictable, large differences in relative risk among funds have proven to be highly predictable.

Risk—however measured and however elusive a concept, except in retrospect—should be given the most careful consideration by the intelligent investor. Markets, no matter what you may have come to think, do not *always* rise!

TABLE 4.3

RISK PROFILE* (AVERAGE FUND = 100)

| Capitalization | Style | | |
| --- | --- | --- | --- |
|  | Value | Blend | Growth |
| Large | 78 | 84 | 114 |
| Medium | 85 | 105 | 156 |
| Small | 104 | 140 | 193 |

* This matrix places each fund into one of nine categories. The vertical columns represent the size of the companies in the portfolio. The horizontal rows represent the investment style, focusing on value stocks (those with below-average price-earnings ratios and above-average yields), growth stocks (the reverse), or a blend of both styles. The S&P 500 Index fund is categorized as large-cap blend, and carries a relative risk of 85.

## RULE 5: BEWARE OF STARS

Here, I refer primarily to the recent emergence of fund portfolio managers as stars. Alas, the fact is that there are precious few, if any, mutual fund superstars who have had the staying power of Michael Jordan or Arnold Palmer or Robert Redford or Laurence Olivier. The few who may have fitted into this category were never, as far as I know, identified *in advance* of their accomplishments. Who had ever heard of Peter Lynch or John Neff or Michael Price in 1972, before they had achieved their splendid records?

Even though their light may shine brightly for a time, many super-stars seem to limit their association with a given fund. The average portfolio manager lasts only five years at the helm of a fund, and, in one of the largest, most aggressive—and formerly hottest—fund organizations, the average stint has been only two and a half years. (Turnover in the fund portfolio, which inevitably accompanies a change of managers, results in truly onerous cost penalties.) These superstars are more like comets: they brighten the firmament for a moment in time, only to burn out and vanish into the dark universe. Seek good managers if you will, but rely on their professionalism, experience, and steadfastness rather than on their stardom.

Be careful, too, about star *systems* (as distinct from star *managers*). The best-known stars are, of course, those funds awarded top five-star billing by *Morningstar Mutual Funds.* (I call these funds "Morning-stars.") The fund world has embraced—and has encouraged investors to invest on the basis of—a system in which a fund with four or five stars is a success. (One or two stars—sometimes even three—mark a failure.) But, as the editors of *Morningstar Mutual Funds* candidly acknowledge, their star ratings have little predictive value. *The Hul-bert Financial Digest* has demonstrated that buying five-star funds as they emerge, and redeeming them when they lose their top rating, produces below-market returns at above-market risk. Not a good combination! Based on the frequent fund switching implied by the Hulbert methodology, I accept that conclusion. But I would be more forgiving. I have little doubt that most of today's three-, four- and five-star funds, *if held over time*, will outpace their one-star peers. Even as you ignore star portfolio managers, then, be skeptical of funds with the lowest star ratings, and focus on funds with the higher star ratings. (But don't trade them!)

### RULE 6: BEWARE OF ASSET SIZE

Funds can get too big for their britches. It is as simple as that. Avoid large fund organizations that (1) have no history of closing funds— that is, terminating the offering of their shares—to new investors, or (2) seem willing to let their funds grow, irrespective of their investment goals, to seemingly infinite size, beyond their power to differentiate their investment results from the crowd.

Just what constitutes "too big" is a complex issue. It relates to fund style, management philosophy, and portfolio strategy. A few examples: a fund investing primarily in large-cap stocks can surely be managed successfully—if not for truly exceptional returns—even at the $20 billion or $30 billion (or higher) level. (*None* of today's funds of that size has outpaced the Standard & Poor's 500 Index over the past five years.) For a fund investing aggressively in tiny microcap stocks (usually market capitalizations of less than $250 million), $300 million of assets might be too large.

Often, checking the fund's quartile rankings over time (mentioned in Rule 4) will reveal whether growing size has had an impact on relative return. Figure 4.5 shows the performance pattern of a

FIGURE 4.5

PERFORMANCE PROFILE: PROBLEM FUND

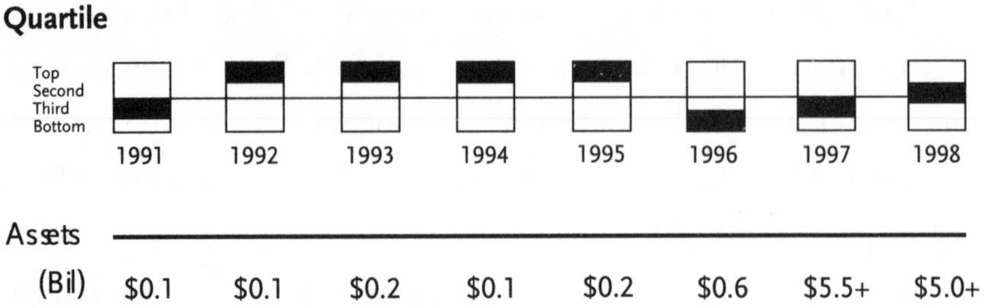

**Quartile**

| | 1991 | 1992 | 1993 | 1994 | 1995 | 1996 | 1997 | 1998 |
|---|---|---|---|---|---|---|---|---|
| Top<br>Second<br>Third<br>Bottom | | | | | | | | |

Assets

| (Bil) | $0.1 | $0.1 | $0.2 | $0.1 | $0.2 | $0.6 | $5.5+ | $5.0+ |
|---|---|---|---|---|---|---|---|---|

* June 1998

once-popular midcap growth fund whose record deteriorated severely as it grew. In 1991–1995, it earned top-quartile ratings in four of the five years, and its assets grew from a tiny $12 million to the $1 billion range. But the three years since its assets moved to $2 billion, and then to $6 billion, were spent in the bottom quartile. Its failed "momentum" strategy (buying stocks with powerful earnings thrust) may have accounted for part of the deterioration, but the clear message is that size has impeded return. It is not a positive message for investors considering the fund today.

Optimal fund size depends on many factors. A broad-based market index fund, for example, should be able to grow without size limits. A giant fund with very low portfolio turnover and relatively stable cash inflows from investors can be managed more easily than one with aggressive investment policies and volatile cash flows—in and out—that not only reflect, but are magnified by, its short-term performance. A multimanager fund—especially if it uses managers who are unaffiliated with one another—can be successful at larger asset levels than a fund supervised by a single management organization. But do not underestimate the challenge a fund faces in selecting two or three, or even four, truly excellent managers. There are no easy answers.

Size—present and potential—is a highly important concern. Excessive size can, and probably will, kill any possibility of investment excellence. The record is clear that, for the overwhelming majority of funds, the best years come when they are small. Small *was* beautiful, but "nothing fails like success." When these funds caught the public fancy—or, more likely, were vigorously hawked to a public that was unaware of its potential exposure to the problems of size—their best years were behind them. Unbridled asset growth in a fund should be a warning flag to intelligent investors.

## RULE 7: DON'T OWN TOO MANY FUNDS

A single *ready-made* balanced index fund—holding 65 percent stocks and 35 percent bonds, as shown in my earlier example—can meet the needs of many investors. A pair of stock and bond index funds with a *tailor-made* balance—a higher or lower ratio of stocks—can meet the needs of many more. But what is the optimal number of funds for investors who elect to use actively managed funds? I truly believe that it is generally unnecessary to go much beyond four or five equity funds. Too large a number can easily result in overdiversification. The net result: a portfolio whose performance inevitably comes to resemble that of an index fund. However, because of the higher costs of the non-index-fund portfolio, as well as its broadened diversification, its return will almost inevitably fall short. What is more, even though it may be overdiversified, such a portfolio (for example, one with two large-cap blend funds and two small-cap growth funds) may exhibit much more short-term variation around the market return. Therefore, according to the common definition of risk, it will be riskier than the index. To what avail?

A recent study by *Morningstar Mutual Funds*—to its credit, one of the few publications that systematically tackles issues like this one—concluded essentially that owning more than four randomly chosen equity funds didn't reduce risk appreciably. Around that number, risk remains fairly constant, all the way out to 30 funds (an unbelievable number!), at which point *Morningstar* apparently stopped counting. Figure 4.6 shows the extent to which the standard deviation of the various fund portfolios declined as more funds were added.

*Morningstar* noted that owning only a *single* large blend fund could provide a lower risk than any of the multiple-fund portfolios. I've added such a fund to Figure 4.6. But *Morningstar* did not note,

FIGURE 4.6

REDUCING RISK BY OWNING MULTIPLE FUNDS

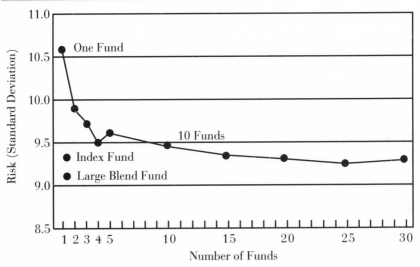

*Data from* Morningstar Investor.

though it might have, that a single all-market index fund provided as low a risk as did the 30-fund portfolio. I've added that too. *Morningstar* also failed to mention, though perhaps it should have, that the assumed initial investment of some $50,000, which would have grown to final values ranging from $85,000 to $116,000 in various fund combinations, would have grown to $113,000 in a single all-market index fund—right at the top of the range. The alleged virtues of multifund diversification and risk control hardly appear compelling.

I would add that I am not persuaded that international funds are a necessary component of an investor's portfolio. Foreign funds may reduce a portfolio's *volatility*, but their economic and currency risks may reduce *returns* by a still larger amount. The idea that a theoretically optimal portfolio must hold each geographical component at its market weight simply pushes me further than I would dream of being pushed. My best judgment is that international holdings should comprise 20 percent of equities *at a maximum*, and that a zero weight is fully acceptable in most portfolios.

What is the point of having as many as 20 diversified funds in a portfolio (i.e., 5 percent of assets in each fund), and thus—given the inevitable overlap of their holdings—owning as many as 1,000 individual common stocks? I'm not at all sure. Perhaps a simple five-fund portfolio like the one shown in Table 4.4 would suit the needs of investors seeking active equity management.

This portfolio would be clearly different from an all-market index fund—and somewhat riskier—but it could provide an opportunity to add value, assuming that the five funds were well chosen. Each fund selected should have a significant impact on fully diversifying the portfolio.

**TABLE 4.4**

A SIMPLE FIVE-FUND PORTFOLIO

| Fund | Percent of Investment |
|------|----------------------|
| Large-cap | 50% |
| Midcap | 10 |
| Small-cap | 20 |
| Specialty* | 10 |
| International | 10 |
| Total | 100% |

* Such as a health care, technology, or energy fund. Real estate funds might also be included, although my impression is that they are less apt to perform as a separate asset class than as a sector subject to the vagaries of the stock market.

## RULE 8: BUY YOUR FUND PORTFOLIO—AND HOLD IT

When you have identified your long-term objectives, defined your tolerance for risk, and carefully selected an index fund or a small number of actively managed funds that meet your goals, *stay the course*. Hold tight. Complicating the investment process merely clutters the mind, too often bringing emotion into a financial plan that cries out for rationality. I am absolutely persuaded that investors' emotions, such as greed and fear, exuberance and hope—if translated into rash actions— can be every bit as destructive to investment performance as inferior market returns. To reiterate what the estimable Mr. Buffett said earlier: "Inactivity strikes us as intelligent behavior." Never forget it.

The key to holding tight is buying right. Buying right is *not* picking funds you don't fully understand; it is *not* picking funds on the basis of past performance; it is *not* picking funds because someone tells you they're hot or because they have managers who have been stars, or even because they have been awarded five *Morningstars*; and it is most assuredly *not* picking high-cost funds. If you have avoided these fundamental errors, then simply keep an eye on how your fund performs. If you chose intelligently in the first place, an annual performance appraisal ought to be just fine. And patiently tolerate periodic nonextreme shortfalls relative to the fund's peers. A major event—an extended aberration in a fund's performance, a radical shift in its policy, a merger of its management company, a fee increase or the imposition of a 12b-1 fee—all should set off alarms. But, if I may modify the familiar phrase about investigating before you invest, I would urge: "Investigate before you divest."

Don't select funds as if they were simply individual common stocks, to be discarded and replaced as they face the inevitable ebb and flow of performance. Select a fund with the same thoughtful consideration you would give to appointing a trustee for your assets and establishing a lifetime relationship. That approach is the very essence of simplicity. Decades ago, many of America's wealthiest families chose a single trustee or investment adviser to look after their entire estates and to remain with them ever after. An investment account in a broadly diversified mutual fund is, in truth, neither more nor less than a diversified trust fund (except that the mutual fund is usually even more diversified). Suppress the temptation to add redundant layers of diversification. While you're at it, demand that the industry provide you with mutual funds that measure up to a high level of trusteeship responsibility. You deserve it.

### Simplicity . . . Or Complexity?

*The opposite of simplicity is complexity. In recent years, according to Charles T. Munger, Warren Buffett's partner at Berkshire Hathaway, many large foundations and college endowment funds, have "tried to become better versions of Bernie Cornfield's 'Fund of Funds,' drifting toward more complexity, with not few but many investment counselors, chosen by an additional layer of consultants to decide which counselors are best, allocating funds to various categories, including foreign securities. . . . There is one thing sure about all of this complexity. The total costs can easily reach 3 percent of net worth per annum, paying the croupiers 3 percent of starting wealth. If the average gross real return from equities goes back, say, to 5 percent over some long future period, and the croupiers' take remains the same as it has always been, the average intelligent player will be in a prolonged, uncomfortable shrinking mode. For obvious reasons . . . I think indexing is a wiser choice for the average foundation than what it is now doing." Mr. Munger has clearly cast his lot with simplicity.*

## THE PARADIGM OF SIMPLICITY

Simplicity will help you to come down to where you ought to be. Buy right and hold tight. Follow these eight basic rules for investing. In this complex world, stick with simplicity. To the extent you decide that indexing is not for you, these rules should still afford you considerable advantage in the quest for solid long-term returns. My approach to investing is simple in concept, but it is far from easy in implementation. You will find, I fear, a fairly small number of funds that filter through my screens. There ought to be lots more.

I would emphasize that each of the eight rules I have offered is designed to help you select a portfolio of funds that may give you the very advantages that have elevated the index fund—the paradigm of simplicity—to its present prominence and acceptance among individual and institutional investors alike. That parallelism is not an accident. So, as you consider your strategy, you cannot afford to ignore the low-cost index fund.

Don't forget that the central task of investing is to capture the maximum possible portion—even though it's almost certain to be less than 100 percent—of the market's rate of return. To an important degree, however, that comparison understates the importance of the task. Remember that because of the impact of compounding, the gap between the capital that is attainable and the capital that is actually created increases rapidly. For example, capturing even 90 percent of the market's annual return—9 percent versus 10 percent—produces only 86 percent of the capital increase over a decade and 76 percent of the increase over 25 years. Once again, little things mean a lot.

Indexing will probably never rule the *entire* world—only part of it! But indexing works so well only because most funds—burdened by excessive costs, promoted with claims of past performance success that is highly unlikely to be sustained, and managed with strategies that call for a short-term focus—*don't* work very well. For that reason, the index fund—which works very well indeed—has proved to be the optimal way to realize the highest possible portion of the return earned in the stock market. But it need not be the *only* way.

In this chapter, I have tried to present both the value of passively managed market index funds and the rudiments of how to select actively managed funds simply and successfully. Whichever route you decide to follow—and, happily, you have the ability to follow both routes—you will have acquired "the gift to be simple" from an investment standpoint, and "the gift to be free" of the cacophony of information that assaults us, seemingly without remission. I am confident that if you follow these basic standards, you will have acquired "the gift to come down to where you ought to be" in implementing your long-run financial plans.

Wharton professor **Jeremy Siegel**'s research on stocks'
past performance is a key element in the case for stocks
as long-term investments.

# PERSPECTIVES ON STOCKS
# AS INVESTMENTS
by Jeremy J. Siegel

from *Stocks for the Long Run* (1994)

*It was only as the public came to realize, largely through the writings of Edgar*
*Lawrence Smith, that stocks were to be preferred to bonds during a period of dollar*
*depreciation, that the bull market began in good earnest to cause a proper valua-*
*tion of common shares.*
—Irving Fisher, 1930[*]

*The "new-era" doctrine—that "good" stocks (or "blue chips") were sound invest-*
*ments regardless of how high the price paid for them—was at the bottom only a*
*means of rationalizing under the title of "investment" the well-nigh universal*
*capitulation to the gambling fever.*
—Benjamin Graham and David Dodd, 1934[**]

I T WAS A seasonally cool Monday evening on October 14, 1929 when
Irving Fisher arrived at the Builders' Exchange Club at 2 Park
Avenue in New York City. Fisher, a professor of economics at Yale

---

[*] Irving Fisher, *The Stock Market Crash and After*, New York: MacMillan Co., 1930, p. 99.
[**] Benjamin Graham and David Dodd, *Security Analysis*, 1934, p.11.

University and the most renowned economist of his time, was scheduled to address the monthly meeting of the Purchasing Agents Association.

Irving Fisher, the founder of modern capital theory, was no mere academic. He actively analyzed and forecast financial market conditions, wrote dozens of newsletters on topics ranging from health to investments, and created a highly successful card indexing firm based on one of his own patented inventions. Despite hailing from a modest background, his personal wealth in the summer of 1929 exceeded $10 million.*

Members of the association and the press crowded into the meeting room. Fisher's speech was mainly designed to defend investment trusts, the forerunner of today's mutual funds. But the audience was most eager to hear his views on the stock market.

Investors had been nervous since early September when Roger Babson, businessman and market seer, predicted a "terrific" crash in stock prices.** Fisher had dismissed this pessimism, noting that Babson had been bearish for some time. But the public sought to be reassured by the great man who had championed stocks for so long.

The audience was not disappointed. After a few introductory remarks, Fisher uttered a sentence that, much to his regret, became one of the most quoted phrases in stock market history: "Stock prices have reached what looks like a permanently high plateau."***

On October 29, two weeks to the day after Fisher's speech, stocks crashed. Fisher's "high plateau" transformed into a bottomless abyss. The next three years witnessed the most devastating market collapse in history. Like Neville Chamberlain's proud claim that the "agreement"

---

* Robert Loring Allen, *Irving Fisher: A Biography*, Cambridge: Blackwell, 1993, p. 206.

** *Commercial and Financial Chronicle*, September 7, 1929.

*** "Fisher See Stocks Permanently High," *New York Times*, October 16, 1929, p. 2.

Adolph Hitler signed in Munich in September 1938 guaranteed "peace in our time," Fisher's prediction about the stock market stands as a memorial to the folly of great men who failed to envision impending disaster.

After the crash, Fisher's reputation as a forecaster was shattered. It made little difference that he was right in many of his other economic predictions. He had correctly forecast the rising bull market in the 1920s, rightly emphasized the importance of the Federal Reserve in creating a favorable economic climate, and properly defended investment trusts, the forerunners of today's mutual funds, as the best way that the public could participate in the stock market.

Fisher was also right that October evening when he pointed out that the increase in stock prices at the time largely stemmed from a rise in earnings. Fisher noted, "Time will tell whether the increase will continue sufficiently to justify the present high level. I expect that it will."[*]

Time did eventually justify stock levels in 1929. But the time frame was far longer than Irving Fisher, or for that matter anyone else, believed. The truth that stocks were in fact better investments after their prices had *dropped* from their highs held no interest for investors. The proven long-term superiority of equity investing, which served as the rationale during the stock market advance, was roundly ignored as investors dumped stocks regardless of their intrinsic value.

### EARLY VIEWS OF STOCK INVESTING

Throughout the nineteenth century, stocks were deemed the province of speculators and insiders, but certainly not conservative investors. It was not until the early twentieth century that researchers came to realize that stocks, as a class, might be suitable investments

---

[*] *New York Times*, Ibid, p.2.

under certain economic conditions. At that time, Irving Fisher himself maintained that stocks would indeed be superior to bonds during inflationary times, but that common shares would likely underperform bonds during periods of declining prices.[*] That stocks were better investments during inflation but inferior during deflation became the conventional wisdom of the early twentieth century.

This popular conception, however, was exploded by Edgar Lawrence Smith, a financial analyst and investment manager of the 1920s. Smith was the first to demonstrate that accumulations in a diversified portfolio of common stocks outperformed bonds not only in times of rising commodity prices, but also when prices were falling. Smith published his studies in 1924 in a book entitled *Common Stocks as Long-Term Investments.* In the introduction he stated:

*These studies are a record of a failure—the failure of facts to sustain a preconceived theory. [The theory] that high-grade bonds had proved to be better investments during periods of [falling commodity prices].[**]*

By examining stock returns back to the Civil War, Smith found that not only did stocks beat bonds whether prices were rising or falling, but there was a very small chance that you would have to wait a long time (which he put at 6 and, at most, 15 years) before having an opportunity to liquidate your stocks at a profit. He concluded:

*We have found that there is a force at work in our common stock*

[*] Irving Fisher, *How to Invest When Prices Are Rising*, Scranton, Pa.: G. Lynn Sumner & Co., 1912.

[**] Edgar L. Smith, *Common Stocks as Long-Term Investments*, New York: Macmillan, 1925, p. v.

*holdings which tends ever toward increasing their principal value . . .*
*unless we have had the extreme misfortune to invest at the very peak*
*of a noteworthy rise, those periods in which the average market value*
*of our holding remains less than the amount we paid for them are of*
*comparatively short duration. Our hazard even in such extreme cases*
*appears to be that of time alone.*[*]

Smith's conclusion was right, not only historically, but also prospec-
tively. It took just over 15 years to recover the money invested at the
1929 peak, following a crash far worse than Smith had ever examined.
And since World War II, the recovery period for stocks has been
better than Smith's wildest dreams. The *longest* it has even taken since
1945 to recover an original investment in the stock market (including
reinvested dividends) was the 3½-year period from December 1972 to
June 1976.

### INFLUENCE OF SMITH'S WORK

Smith wrote his book at the onset of one of the greatest bull markets in our history. Its conclusions caused a sensation in both academic and investing circles. The prestigious weekly, *The Economist*,
stated, "Every intelligent investor and stockbroker should study Mr.
Smith's most interesting little book, and examine the tests individ-
ually and their very surprising results."[**]

Irving Fisher saw Smith's study as a confirmation of his own
long-held belief that bonds were overrated as safe investment in a
world with uncertain inflation. Fisher summarized:

---

[*] Edgar L. Smith, Ibid., p. 81.

[**] "Ordinary Shares as Investments," *The Economist*, June 6, 1925, p. 1141.

*It seems, then, that the market overrates the safety of "safe" securities and pays too much for them, that it underrates the risk of risky securities and pays too little for them, that it pays too much for immediate and too little for remote returns, and finally, that it mistakes the steadiness of money income from a bond for a steadiness of real income which it does not possess. In steadiness of real income, or purchasing power, a list of diversified common stocks surpasses bonds.\**

Smith's ideas quickly crossed the Atlantic and were the subject of much discussion in Great Britain. John Maynard Keynes, the great British economist and originator of the business cycle theory that became the accepted paradigm for generations, reviewed Smith's book with much excitement. Keynes stated:

*The results are striking. Mr. Smith finds in almost every case, not only when prices were rising, but also when they were falling, that common stocks have turned out best in the long-run, indeed, markedly so. . . . This actual experience in the United States over the past fifty years affords* prima facie *evidence that the prejudice of investors and investing institutions in favor of bonds as being "safe" and against common stocks as having, even the best of them, a "speculative" flavor, has led to a relative over-valuation of bonds and under-valuation of common stocks.\*\**

---

\* From foreword by Irving Fisher in Kenneth S. Van Strum, *Investing in Purchasing Power*, New York: Barrons, 1925, p. vii. Van Strum, a writer for Barron's weekly, followed up and confirmed Smith's research.

\*\* J. M. Keynes, "An American Study of Shares versus Bonds as Permanent Investments," *The Nation & The Athenaeum*, May 2, 1925, p. 157.

Money managers were quick to realize the impact of Smith's work. Hartley Withers wrote in *The London Investors Chronicle* and *Money Market Review*:

*Old-fashioned investors and their old-fashioned advisers have so long been in the habit of looking on all holdings of ordinary shares or common stocks as something rather naughty and speculative, that one feels a certain amount of hesitation in even ventilating the view that is now rapidly gaining acceptance that ordinary shares, under certain conditions, are really safer than [bonds], even though the latter may be of the variety which is commonly called "gilt-edged."*[*]

Smith's writings were published in such prestigious journals as the *Review of Economic Statistics* and the *Journal of the American Statistical Association*.[**] Further research confirmed his results. Smith acquired an international following when Siegfried Stern published an extensive study of returns in common stock in 13 European countries from the onset of World War I through 1928. Stern's study showed that the advantage of investing in common stocks over bonds and other financial investments extended far beyond America's financial markets.[***]

---

[*] Quoted by Edgar Lawrence Smith in *Common Stocks and Business Cycles*, New York: The William-Frederick Press, 1959, p. 20.

[**] Edgar Lawrence Smith, "Market Value of Industrial Equities," *Review of Economic Statistics*, IX, pp. 37–40, January, 1927 and "Tests Applied to an Index of the Price Level for Industrial Stocks," *Journal of the American Statistical Association*, supplement (March 1931), pp. 127–35.

[***] S. Stern, *Fourteen Years of European Investments, 1914–1928*, The Bankers' Publishing Co., 1929.

## COMMON STOCK THEORY OF INVESTMENT

The research demonstrating the superiority of stocks became known as the "Common Stock Theory of Investment."[*] Smith himself was careful to not overstate his findings. He wrote:

> Over a period of years *the principal value of a* well-diversified holding *of common stocks of* representative *corporations in* essential *industries tends to increase in accordance with the operation of compound interest. . . . Such stock holding may be relied upon over a term of years to pay an average income return on such increasing values of something more than the average current rate on commercial paper.*[**]

Yet Chelcie C. Bosland, a professor of economics at Brown University in the 1930s, claimed that the common stock theory was often misused to justify any investment in stocks no matter what the price. Bosland stated:

> *The purchase of common stocks after 1922 was more likely to result in profit than in loss. Even though this was largely a cyclical up-swing, many believed that it was a vindication of the theory that common stocks are good long-term investments. Participation in this profit-making procedure became widespread. The "boom psychology" was everywhere in evidence. No doubt the "common stock theory" gave even to the downright speculator the feeling that his actions were based upon the solid rock of scientific finding.*[***]

---

[*] Chelcie C. Bosland, *The Common Stock Theory of Investment, Its Development and Significance*, New York: The Ronald Press Co., 1937.

[**] Edgar Lawrence Smith, op. cit., p. 79, emphasis added.

[***] Chelcie C. Bosland, *The Common Stock Theory of Investment*, by Assoc. Prof. of Economics, Brown University, New York: The Ronald Press, 1937, p. 4.

## A RADICAL SHIFT IN SENTIMENT

But the glorious days for common stocks did not last. The crash pushed the image of stocks as good investments into the doghouse, and with it the credibility of Smith's contention that stocks were the best long-term investments. Lawrence Chamberlain, an author and well-known investment banker, stated, *"Common stocks, as such, are not superior to bonds as long-term investments, because primarily they are not investments at all. They are speculations."*[*]

The common-stock theory of investment was attacked from all angles. In 1934 Benjamin Graham, an investment fund manager, and David Dodd, a finance professor at Columbia University, wrote *Security Analysis*, which became the bible of the value-oriented approach to analyzing stocks and bonds. Through its many editions, the book has had a lasting impact on students and market professionals alike.

Graham and Dodd clearly blamed Smith's book for feeding the bull market mania of the 1920s by proposing plausible sounding but fallacious theories to justify the purchase of stocks. They wrote:

> *The self-deception of the mass speculator must, however, have its element of justification. . . . In the new-era bull market, the "rational" basis was the record of long-term improvement shown by diversified common-stock holdings. [There is] a small and rather sketchy volume from which the new-era theory may be said to have sprung. The book is entitled* Common Stocks as Long-Term Investments *by Edgar Lawrence Smith, published in 1924.*[**]

---

[*] Lawrence Chamberlain and William W. Hay, *Investment and Speculations*, New York: Henry Holt & Co., 1931, p. 55. Emphasis his.

[**] Benjamin Graham and David Dodd, *Security Analysis*, 2nd edition, New York: McGraw-Hill, 1940, p. 357.

## POST-CRASH VIEW OF STOCK RETURNS

The crash left the impression that stocks could not be worthy long-term investments. So much had been written about so many who had been wiped out by the market that the notion that stocks could still beat other financial assets was regarded as ludicrous.

In the late 1930s, Alfred Cowles III, founder of the Cowles Commission for economic research, constructed capitalization-weighted stock indexes back to 1871 of all stocks traded on the New York Stock Exchange. Cowles examined stock returns including reinvested dividends and concluded:

*During that period [1871–1926] there is considerable evidence to support the conclusion that stocks in general sold at about three-quarters of their true value as measured by the return to the investor.*[*]

Yet Cowles placed the blame for the crash of 1929 squarely on the shoulder of the government, claiming that increased taxation and government controls drove stock prices downward.

As stocks slowly recovered from the depression, their returns seemed to warrant a new look. In 1953, two professors from the University of Michigan, Wilford Eiteman and Frank P. Smith, published a study of the investment returns on all industrial companies with trading volume over one million shares in 1936. By regularly purchasing these 92 stocks without any regard to the stock market cycle (a strategy called "dollar cost averaging"), they found that the returns over the next 14 years, at 12.2 percent per year, far exceeded those in

---

[*] Alfred Cowles III and Associates, *Common Stock Indexes 1871–1937*, Bloomington, Indiana: Pricipia Press, 1938, p. 50.

fixed-income investments. Twelve years later they repeated the study, using the same stocks they used in their previous study. This time the returns were even higher, despite the fact they made no adjustment for any of the new firms or new industries that had surfaced in the interim. They wrote:

> *If a portfolio of common stocks selected by such obviously foolish methods as were employed in this study will show an annual compound rate of return as high as 14.2 percent, then a small investor with limited knowledge of market conditions can place his savings in a diversified list of common stocks with some assurance that, given time, his holding will provide him with safety of principal and an adequate annual yield.*\*

Many dismissed the Eiteman and Smith study because it did not include the great crash of 1929–32. But in 1964, two professors from the University of Chicago, Lawrence Fisher and James H. Lorie, examined stock returns through the stock crash of 1929, the Great Depression, and World War II.\*\* Fisher and Lorie concluded that stocks offered significantly higher returns (which they reported at 9.0 percent per year) than any other investment media during the entire 35-year period, 1926 through 1960. They even factored taxes and transaction costs into their return calculations and concluded:

> *It will perhaps be surprising to many that the returns have consistently*

---

\* Wilford J. Eiteman and Frank P. Smith, *Common Stock Values and Yields*, Ann Arbor, Michigan: University of Michigan Press, 1962, p. 40.

\*\* "Rates of Return on Investment in Common Stocks," *Journal of Business*, 37 (January 1964), pp. 1–21.

*been so high. . . . The fact that many persons choose investments with a substantially lower average rate of return than that available on common stocks suggests the essentially conservative nature of those investors and the extent of their concern about the risk of loss inherent in common stocks.*[*]

Ten years later, Roger Ibbotson and Rex Sinquefield published an even more extensive review of returns in an article entitled, "Stocks, Bonds, Bills, and Inflation: Year-by-Year Historical Returns (1926–74)."[**] They acknowledged their indebtedness to the Lorie and Fisher study and confirmed the superiority of stocks as long-term investments. Their summary statistics, which are published annually in yearbooks, are frequently quoted and have often served as the return benchmarks for the securities industry.[***]

### INVESTMENT PHILOSOPHY AND THE VALUATION OF EQUITY

The high prices that stocks reach during bull markets, which historians often characterize as filled with "undue" or "unwarranted" optimism, are in fact often justified on the basis of the *long-term record* of corporate earnings and dividend growth. Unfortunately, this long perspective does not interest most players in the market. Most investors roundly ignore forecasters who analyze the long run, but do not predict the direction of the market in the short run.

Over 60 years ago, John Maynard Keynes lamented the lack of

---

[*] Ibid., p. 20.

[**] *Journal of Business*, 49 (January 1976), pp. 11–43.

[***] *Stocks, Bonds, Bills, and Inflation Yearbooks, 1983–1997*, Ibbotson and Associates, Chicago, Illinois.

long-term investors in the securities market. He ascribed it to human psychology, stating:

*Life is not long enough; human nature desires quick results, there is a peculiar zest in making money quickly, and remoter gains are discounted by the average man at a very high rate.*[*]

Yet these "remote gains," which accrue so assuredly to the long-run stockholder, must be the center of most people's investment strategy. The doctrine that common stocks provide the best way to accumulate long-term wealth, first expounded by Edgar Lawrence Smith nearly 75 years ago, has been reconfirmed in all subsequent research.

[*] John Maynard Keynes, *The General Theory of Employment, Interest and Money* (originally published in 1936), New York: Harcourt Brace and World, 1965 edition, p. 157.

Investors who try to forecast stock market fluctuations generally fail to prosper. **Roger Gibson**, a money manager in Pittsburgh, made the case against market timing in this passage from his 1990 book.

# MARKET TIMING
## by Roger C. Gibson

from *Asset Allocation* (1990)

COMMON STOCKS HAVE volatile returns. One consequence of that volatility is that investors have historically suffered negative annual returns approximately 30 percent of the time. Obviously, if there were a way to avoid the stock market's bad years, wealth would accumulate much more rapidly. Assume, for example, that it is December 31, 1925, and we are consulting a market timer who has made forecasts of 1926 security returns for Treasury bills, long-term government bonds, long-term corporate bonds, common stocks, and small stocks. He correctly predicts that of these five investment alternatives, common stocks will produce the best total return for 1926. We invest $1.00, which by the end of 1926 grows to be worth $1.12. Impressed with our market timer's predictive abilities, we again meet with him on December 31, 1926, for his advice as to where to position our money for the following year. Year after year our market timer, with perfect predictive accuracy, advises us concerning which investment alternative is appropriate for our market-timed portfolio.

Through compounding our wealth in this manner, our initial $1.00

investment would have grown to be worth approximately $2,650,000 by the end of 1988. This compares very favorably with the best-performing investment alternative, small stocks, with its ending value of $1,478, and with the more modest ending value of approximately $9 for Treasury bills! To contextualize this phenomenal result, consider the outcome had $1 million been initially invested at the end of 1925. By the end of 1988, the portfolio would have been worth $2.65 trillion—slightly more than the market value of all outstanding shares of all publicly traded common stocks in the United States. In essence, our 1925 millionaire would now own substantially all of corporate America!

Clearly, such market timing ability does not exist. Why then the persistent interest in market timing? People want to believe it is possible. Its appeal is truly seductive. When clients look at the long-term historical performance of common stocks, the hope of market timing is reinforced by what appears to be predictive trends—sustained periods of either rising or falling prices. The resolution of this seeming contradiction lies in the recognition that a random series of numbers does not always look random! A simple experiment will verify this. Take a coin, flip it 100 times and record the pattern of heads and tails produced. As you reach the end of the experiment, you will quite likely notice occasional runs of heads or runs of tails. Your knowledge of the nature of the coin flipping process prevents you, however, from inappropriately presuming the existence of predictive trends of either heads or tails. Each flip is independent of the preceding one.

When we examine the pattern of returns for common stocks, we see the same phenomenon. The run of heads in our coin flipping experiment becomes a prolonged period of rising stock market prices, classified as a bull market. The run of tails corresponds to the bear market. As we experience a prolonged bear market, such as occurred in 1973–1974, we tend to punish ourselves after the fact by concluding that we should have known that the bear market would have continued once prices started falling. This is particularly true in the midst of a bear market, when the public is reminded day by day in the financial press and on the evening news about how foolish it is to own common stocks. Similarly, common stock prices bottomed out during the summer of 1982, prior to one of the biggest bull markets in history. With the benefit of retrospect, people tend to conclude that everyone should have known that stocks were cheap during the summer of 1982 and poised for a big rise. The fact is that investors, in the aggregate, did not know stocks were a great bargain, otherwise their prior buying activity would have prevented the stocks from becoming such bargains in the first place. On the eve of this bull market, the financial press was filled with gloom and doom, with only an occasional voice crying in the wilderness regarding outstanding stock values.

An efficient market incorporates into current security prices relevant known information, as well as consensus expectations regarding the unknown. Thus, when it comes to predicting stock market movements, it is not of any value to know whether we are at war or peace, have a Republican or Democrat in the White House, or have been in an economic expansion or contraction. What then moves the market? It is measured by new information relevant to the pricing of investments, which was not previously known. In essence, it is the surprises that no one sees coming which trigger price movements to establish new equilibriums in the markets. These surprises themselves are random events. Occasionally there are more good surprises than bad, and we have a bull market. Other times the reverse is true, and we have a bear market. There will always be bulls and bears, but the evidence indicates that there is no consistent way to predict the turning points.

Before engaging in a review of the research studies on market timing, it is helpful to review some statistics on stock market cycles, as summarized in a research paper by Trinity Investment Management Corporation. The data covers the nine peak-to-peak cycles since World War II. The first cycle began May 29, 1946, and the last cycle ended August 25, 1987. Trinity observed:

1. *There are about 1.7 times as many up months as down months: 309 versus 187.*

2. *The average bull market is up 104.8 percent versus the average bear market's drop of −28.0 percent.*

3. *Bull markets last nearly three times as long as bear markets: 41 months for the up legs versus 14 for the down legs.*

4. *Even within the bear markets, on average about 3 to 4 months out of 10 are up months.*

Trinity makes the further observation that during bull markets, on average, only 8 months (out of the 41-month average bull market duration) accounted for more than 60 percent of the total return achieved.

Clearly, the average advance in a bull market is more than sufficient to regain the ground lost during a typical bear market. The fact that, in bear markets, 3 to 4 months out of 10 are up months reinforces the notion that it is often difficult to know that a bear market is occurring, until one is looking back after the fact. According to a research study by William F. Sharpe,

*. . . a manager who attempts to time the market must be right roughly three times out of four, merely to match the overall performance of those competitors who don't. If he is right less often his relative performance will be inferior. There are two reasons for this. First, such a manager will often have his funds in cash equivalents in good market years, sacrificing the higher returns stocks provide in such years. Second, he will incur transaction costs in making switches, many of which will prove to be unprofitable.*

Regarding the potential gains from market timing, Sharpe concluded that,

*Barring truly devastating market declines similar to those of The Depression, it seems likely that gains of little more than four percent per year from timing should be expected from a manager whose forecasts are truly prophetic.* [*]

A study by Robert H. Jeffrey concluded:

*No one can predict the market's ups and downs over a long period, and the risks of trying outweigh the rewards.*

He goes on to comment:

*The rationale for being a full-time equity investor is not that there are more positive real return periods than negative ones in most time frames, but rather that most of the "positive action" is compressed into*

---

[*] William F. Sharpe, "Likely Gains from Market Timing," *Financial Analysts Journal,* March–April, 1975, pp. 60–69.

*just a few periods, which (perversely but understandably) tend to follow particularly adverse times for stocks.* [*]

With reference to Ibbotson Associates' examination of security returns from 1926 through 1988, suppose that a common stock investor had missed the six best years for common stocks, during which time he alternatively had invested in Treasury bills. By being on the sidelines in cash equivalents during this critical 10 percent of the time period, $1 initially invested in stocks at the end of 1925 would have declined from what would have been $406 with continuous investment in the S&P 500 to only $45 as a consequence of having missed these six superlative years.

Consider a market timer who has a 50/50 forecasting ability—that is, he is wrong in his predictions as often as he is right. Depending on which years he is wrong, his investment experience will vary widely. If he is lucky, he will be in the wrong place at the wrong time when the spread between Treasury bills and the S&P 500 is narrow, thereby not suffering significantly from the error. If, however, his mistakes more often than not occur during time periods when the spread is quite large, then the results can be disastrous. Based on the capital market experience 1926 through 1982, Jeffrey concluded:

> . . . *if the theoreticians are correct about the inefficiency of market timing (that is, it will generally be accurate only 50% of the time), the probable outcome is a best-case real dollar return only about two times greater than what would come from continuous*

---

[*] Robert H. Jeffrey, "The Folly of Stock Market Timing," *Harvard Business Review*, July–August, 1984, pp. 102–10.

*investment in the S&P, while the worst case produces about one*
*hundred times less!*

*The point of these . . . statistics is simply to emphasize that a market-*
*timing strategist has tremendous natural odds to overcome, and that*
*these odds increase geometrically with the length of the time frame and*
*with the frequency of the timing interval. There is probably no situa-*
*tion where* caveat emptor *is more apropos for the portfolio owner than*
*in interviewing prospective timing managers.*[*]

Much of the problem with market timing concerns the fact that a
disproportionate percentage of the total gain from a bull market tends
to occur very rapidly at the beginning of a market recovery. If a
market timer is on the sidelines in cash during this critical time, he is
apt to miss too much of the action.

In another study, Jess S. Chua and Richard S. Woodward
approached the subject from another angle in attempting to ascertain
whether it is an inability to avoid bear markets or the tendency to miss
the early part of a market recovery that accounts for the poor results
achieved from market timing. They concluded:

*Overall, the results show that it is more important to correctly fore-*
*cast bull markets than bear markets. If the investor has only a 50%*
*chance of correctly forecasting bull markets, then he should not prac-*
*tice market timing at all. His average return will be less than that*
*of a buy-and-hold strategy even if he can forecast bear markets*
*perfectly.*

---

[*] Jeffrey, "The Folly of Stock Market Timing," pp. 107–8.

These researchers concluded that for market timing to pay:

*Investors require the forecast accuracies of at least:*
*80% bull and 50% bear;*
*70% bull and 80% bear; or*
*60% bull and 90% bear . . .*\*

This is particularly interesting because professional market timers most often stress capital preservation and the ability to avoid bear markets as the major benefit to be derived from their services.

In his wonderful book, *Investment Policy*,\*\* Charles D. Ellis referred to an unpublished study of 100 large pension funds:

*. . . their experience with market timing found that while all the funds had engaged in at least some market timing, not one of the funds had improved its rate of return as a result of its efforts at timing. In fact, 89 of the 100 lost as a result of "timing"—and their losses averaged a daunting 4.5 percent over the five-year period.*

Although long-term gains from market timing are highly unlikely, there will always be investors who have positive results from timing activities—particularly in the short-run. This is because over any single period, there will be a wide dispersion of investor experiences,

---

\* Jess H. Chua and Richard S. Woodward, *Gains from Stock Market Timing*, Monograph 1986–2 of *Monograph Series in Finance and Economics*, ed. Anthony Saunders (New York: Salomon Brothers Center for the Study of Financial Institutions at the Graduate School of Business Administration of New York University), pp. 12–13.

\*\* Charles D. Ellis, *Investment Policy* (Homewood, Ill.: Dow Jones-Irwin, 1985), p. 13.

with some investors doing well and some doing very poorly. Statistically, this is what we expect. The danger is the leap of logic which presumes that the good market timing result is caused by superior predictive ability. In the aggregate, market timing does not work, and most investor experiences have been and will be negative. Those market timers who have most recently made the right moves, however, are written up in financial publications and interviewed on television. This fuels the hopes of those who wish there were a way to get the advantage of a bull market while avoiding the pain of a bear market. Meanwhile, unsuccessful market timing firms fade away as clients reallocate what is left of their portfolios to the newly identified market timing guru. Many investors prefer to live with false hope, rather than critically examine whether market timing is possible at all. As Aristotle observed: "A plausible impossibility is always preferable to an unconvincing possibility." To face the question of whether market timing is possible forces an investor to acknowledge that he may have to either periodically face the pain of a bear market, or alternatively forego investing in common stocks altogether and thereby sacrifice the possibility of real capital growth. There is a pervasive human tendency to reinterpret one's experience to fit preconceptions. This is often the case with market timing, where hope springs eternal that somewhere, someone will somehow be able to consistently catch the bull while safely avoiding the bear.

The alternative to market timing is to simply buy and hold common stocks. As William Sharpe points out:

*A manager who keeps assets in stocks at all times is like an optimistic market timer. His actions are consistent with a policy of predicting a good year every year. While such a manager may know that such* *predictions will be wrong roughly one year out of three, such an attitude is nonetheless likely to lead to results superior to those achieved by most market timers.* [*]

I would like to close the discussion with an observation from Charles D. Ellis:

*In investment management, the real opportunity to achieve superior results is not in scrambling to outperform the market, but in establishing and adhering to appropriate investment policies over the long term—policies that position the portfolio to benefit from riding with the main long-term forces in the market.* [**]

---

[*] Sharpe, "Likely Gains from Stock Market Timing," p. 67.

[**] Ellis, *Investment Policy*, pp. 22–23.

Money manager **John Train** is a careful student of stock-picking and investment strategy. This piece originally ran in *Forbes* in 1978.

# THE MAN WHO NEVER LOST
by John Train

EVERYBODY WHO FINALLY learns how to make money in the stock market learns in his own way.

I like this tale of his own personal enlightenment sent by Melvid Hogan, of Houston.

"Right after I was discharged from the Army at the close of World War II and went into the drilling-rig building business, I began buying and selling stocks on the side, at first as a hobby. At the end of each year I always had a net loss. I tried every approach I would read or hear about: technical, fundamental and combinations of all these . . . but somehow I always ended up with a loss.

"It may sound impossible that even a blind man would have lost money in the rally of 1958—but I did. In my in-and-out trading and smart switches I lost a lot of money.

"But one day in 1961 when, discouraged and frustrated, I was in the Merrill Lynch office in Houston, a senior account executive sitting at a front desk whom I knew observed the frown on my face that he had been seeing for so many years and motioned me over to his desk.

" 'Would you like to see a man,' he asked wearily, 'who has never lost money in the stock market?'

*245*

" 'Never had a loss?' I stammered.

" 'Never had a loss on balance,' the broker drawled, 'and I have handled his account for near 40 years.' Then he gestured to a hulking man dressed in overalls sitting among the crowd of tape watchers.

" 'If you want to meet him, you'd better hurry,' the broker advised. 'He only comes in here once every few years except when he's buying. He always hangs around a few minutes to gawk at the tape. He's a rice farmer and hog raiser from down at Baytown.'

"I worked my way through the crowd to find a seat by the stranger in overalls. I introduced myself, talked about rice farming and duck hunting for a while (I am an avid duck hunter) and gradually worked the subject around to stocks.

"The stranger, to my surprise, was happy to talk about stocks. He pulled a sheet of paper from his pocket with his list of stocks scrawled in pencil on it that he had just finished selling and let me look at it.

"I couldn't believe my eyes! The man had made over 50% long-term capital-gain profits on the whole group. One stock in the group of 30 stocks had been shot off the board, but others had gone up 100%, 200% and even 500%.

"He explained his technique, which was the ultimate in simplicity. When during a bear market he would read in the papers that the market was down to new lows and the experts were predicting that it was sure to drop hundreds of points more on the Dow, the farmer would look through a Standard & Poor's Stock Guide and select around 30 stocks that had fallen in price below $10—solid, profit-making, unheard of little companies (pecan growers, home furnishings, etc.)—and paid dividends. He would come to Houston and buy a $50,000 'package' of them.

"And then, one, two, three or four years later, when the stock market was bubbling, and the prophets were talking about the Dow soaring to new highs, he would come to town and sell his whole package. It was as simple as that.

"During the subsequent years as I cultivated Mr. Womack (and hunted ducks on his rice fields) until his death last year, I learned much of his investing philosophy.

"He equated buying stocks with buying a truckload of pigs. The lower he could buy the pigs, when the pork market was depressed, the more profit he would make when the next seller's market would come along. He claimed that he would rather buy stocks under such conditions than pigs because pigs did not pay a dividend. You must feed pigs.

"He took a farming approach to the stock market in general. In rice farming there is a planting season and a harvesting season; in his stock purchases and sales he strictly observed the seasons.

"Mr. Womack never seemed to buy a stock at its bottom or sell it at its top. He seemed happy to buy or sell in the bottom or top range of its fluctuations. When he was buying he had no regard whatsoever for the old cliché, 'Never Send Good Money After Bad.' For example, when the bottom fell out of the market in 1970, he added another $50,000 to his previous bargain-price positions and made a virtual killing on the whole package.

"I suppose that a modern stock market technician could have found a lot of alphas, betas, contrary opinions and other theories in Mr. Womack's simple approach to buying and selling stocks. But none I know put the emphasis on 'buy price' that he did.

"I realize that many things determine if a stock is a wise buy. But I have learned that during a depressed stock market, if you can get a cost position in a stock's bottom price range it will forgive a multitude of misjudgments later.

"During a market rise, you can sell too soon and make a profit, sell at the top and make a very good profit, or sell on the way down and still make a profit. So, with so many profit probabilities in your favor, the best cost price possible is worth waiting for.

"Knowing this is always comforting during a depressed market, when a 'chartist' looks at you with alarm after you buy on his latest 'sell signal.'

"In sum, Mr. Womack didn't make anything complicated out of the stock market. He taught me that you can't be buying stocks every day, week or month of the year and make a profit, any more than you could plant rice every day, week or month and make a crop. He changed my investing lifestyle and I have made a profit ever since."

I remind the reader that although this feeling for the rhythm of markets is a useful one to acquire, it's not the only strategy or even the best strategy. Probably Mr. Womack would have done as well by just buying and holding growth stocks.

Higher returns will help your investments grow faster—
but your savings rate is the real key to your investment
portfolio. **Joe Dominguez** and **Vicki Robin**, leading proponents of a movement toward living simply, make a
compelling case for saving more, and suggest creative
ways to do it.

# THE AMERICAN DREAM—
# ON A SHOESTRING
by Joe Dominguez and Vicki Robin

*from Your Money or Your Life* (1992)

IT IS BOTH sad and telling that there is no word in the English
language for living at the peak of the Fulfillment Curve, always
having plenty but never being burdened with excess. The word
would need to evoke the careful stewarding of tangible resources
(time, money, material possessions) coupled with the joyful expansion
of spiritual resources (creativity, intelligence, love). Unfortunately,
you can't say, "I'm enoughing," or "I'm choosing a life of enoughness," to explain that mixture of affluence and thrift that comes from
following the steps of this program. The word "frugality" used to
serve that function, but in the latter half of the twentieth century frugality has gotten a bad reputation.

How did frugality lose favor among Americans? It is, after all, a
perennial ideal and a cornerstone of the American character. Both
Socrates and Plato praised the "golden mean." Both the Old Testa-
ment ("Give me neither poverty nor wealth, but only enough") and
the teachings of Jesus ("Ye cannot serve both God and money") extol

the value of material simplicity in enriching the life of the spirit. In American history well-known individuals (Benjamin Franklin, Henry David Thoreau, Ralph Waldo Emerson, Robert Frost) as well as groups (Amish, Quakers, Hutterites, Mennonites) have carried forward the virtue of thrift—both out of respect for the earth and out of a thirst for a touch of heaven. And the challenges of building our nation required frugality of most of our citizens. Indeed, the wealth we enjoy today is the result of centuries of frugality. As we said earlier, the "more is better" consumer culture is a Johnny-come-lately on the American scene. Our bedrock is frugality, and it's high time we made friends with the word—and the practice.

Let's explore this word "frugality" to see if we can't redeem it as the key to fulfillment in the nineties.

### THE PLEASURES OF FRUGALITY

We looked up "frugal" in a 1986 Merriam-Webster dictionary and found "characterized by or reflecting economy in the expenditure of resources." That sounds about right—a serviceable, practical and fairly colorless word. None of the elegance or grace of the "enoughness" that FIers experience. But when we dig deeper, the dictionary tells us that "frugal" shares a Latin root with *frug* (meaning virtue), *frux* (meaning fruit or value) and *frui* (meaning to enjoy or have the use of). Now we're talking. Frugality is enjoying the virtue of getting good value for every minute of your life energy and from everything you have the use of.

That's very interesting. In fact, it's more than interesting. It's transforming. Frugality means we are to *enjoy* what we have. If you have ten dresses but still feel you have nothing to wear, you are probably a spendthrift. But if you have ten dresses and have enjoyed wearing all of them for years, you are frugal. Waste lies not in the number of possessions but in the failure to enjoy them. Your success at being frugal is measured not by your penny-pinching but by your degree of enjoyment of the material world.

Enjoyment of the material world? Isn't that hedonism? While both have to do with enjoying what you have, frugality and hedonism are opposite responses to the material world. Hedonism revels in the pleasures of the senses and implies excessive consumption of the material world and a continual search for more. Frugal people, however, get value from everything—a dandelion or a bouquet of roses, a single strawberry or a gourmet meal. A hedonist might consume the juice of five oranges as a prelude to a pancake breakfast. A frugal person, on the other hand, might relish eating a single orange, enjoying the color and texture of the whole fruit, the smell and the light spray that comes as you begin to peel it, the translucence of each section, the flood of flavor that pours out as a section bursts over the tongue . . . and the thrift of saving the peels for baking.

To be frugal means to have a high joy-to-stuff ratio. If you get one unit of joy for each material possession, that's frugal. But if you need ten possessions to even begin registering on the joy meter, you're missing the point of being alive.

There's a word in Spanish that encompasses all this: *aprovechar*. It means to use something wisely—be it old zippers from worn-out clothing or a sunny day at the beach. It's getting full value from life, enjoying all the good that each moment and each thing has to offer. You can "*aprovechar*" a simple meal, a flat of overripe strawberries or a cruise in the Bahamas. There's nothing miserly about *aprovechar*; it's a succulent word, full of sunlight and flavor. If only "frugal" were so sweet.

The "more is better and it's never enough" mentality in North America fails the frugality test not solely because of the excess, but because of the lack of enjoyment of what we already have. Indeed, North Americans have been called materialists, but that's a misnomer.

All too often it's not material things we enjoy as much as what these things symbolize: conquest, status, success, achievement, a sense of worth and even favor in the eyes of the Creator. Once we've acquired the dream house, the status car or the perfect mate, we rarely stop to enjoy them thoroughly. Instead, we're off and running after the next coveted acquisition.

Another lesson we can derive from the dictionary definition of "frugal" is the recognition that we don't need to possess a thing to enjoy it—we merely need to *use* it. If we are enjoying an item, *whether or not we own it*, we're being frugal. For many of life's pleasures it may be far better to "use" something than to "possess" it (and pay in time and energy for the upkeep). So often we have been like feudal lords, gathering as many possessions as possible from far and wide and bringing them inside the walls of our castle. If we want something (or wanted it in the past, or imagine we might want it in the future), we think we must bring it inside the boundaries of the world called "mine." What we fail to recognize is that what is outside the walls of "mine" doesn't belong to the enemy; it belongs to "the rest of us." And if what lies outside our walls is not "them" but "us," we can afford to loosen our grip a bit on our possessions. We can gingerly open the doors of our fortress and allow goods (material and spiritual) to flow into and out of our boundaries.

Frugality, then, is also learning to share, to see the world as "ours" rather than as "theirs" and "mine." And, while not explicit in the word, being frugal and being happy with having enough mean that more will be available for others. Learning to equitably share the resources of the earth is at the top of the global agenda, and some creative frugality in North America could go a long way toward promoting that balance.

Frugality *is* balance. Frugality is the Greek notion of the golden mean. Frugality is being efficient in harvesting happiness from the world you live in. Frugality is right-use (which sounds, appropriately, like "righteous")—the wise stewarding of money, time, energy, space and possessions. Goldilocks expressed it well when she declared the porridge "not too hot, not too cold, but just right." Frugality is something like that—not too much, not too little, but just right. Nothing is wasted. Or left unused. It's a clean machine. Sleek. Perfect. Simple yet elegant. It's that magic word—enough. The peak of the Fulfillment Curve. The jumping-off point for a life of being fulfilled, learning and contributing to the welfare of the planet.

"Frugal, man." That's the cool, groovy way to say "far out" in the nineties. Surfers will talk about frugal waves. Teenage girls will talk about frugal dudes. Designers will talk about frugal fashions. Mark our words!

Keep this in mind as we explore ways to save money. We aren't talking about being cheap, making do or being a skinflint or a tightwad. We're talking about *creative* frugality, a way of life in which you get the maximum fulfillment for each unit of life energy spent.

In fact, now that you know that money is your life energy, it seems foolish to consider wasting it on stuff you don't enjoy and never use. If you are 40 years old, actuarial tables indicate that you have just 329,601 hours of life energy in your bank. That may seem like a lot now, but those hours will feel very precious at the *end* of your life. Spend them well now and you won't have regrets later.

In the end, this creative frugality is an expression of self-esteem. It honors the life energy you invest in your material possessions. Saving those minutes and hours of life energy through careful consuming is the ultimate in self-respect.

## NINE SURE WAYS TO SAVE MONEY

### 1. Don't go shopping

If you don't go shopping, you won't spend money. Of course, if you really need something from the store, go and buy it. But don't just go shopping. According to Carolyn Wesson, author of *Women Who Shop Too Much*, "59 million persons in the U.S. are addicted to shopping or to spending." About 53 percent of groceries and 47 percent of hardware-store purchases are "spur of the moment." When 34,300 mall shoppers across the country were asked the primary reason for their visit, only 25 percent said they had come in pursuit of a specific item. About 70 percent of all adults visit a regional mall weekly. The number of U.S. shopping centers has grown from 2,000 in 1957 to more than 30,000 today, according to the International Council of Shopping Centers. The number of shopping malls recently surpassed the number of high schools in the United States.

Indeed, shopping is one of our favorite national pastimes. More than the simple act of acquiring needed goods and services, shopping attempts to fill (but obviously fails, since we have to shop so often) myriad needs: for socializing and time structuring, for a reward after a job well done, for an antidepressant, for esteem-boosting, self-assertion, status and nurturing. A Martian anthropologist might conclude that the mall is our place of worship, and shopping the central ritual of communion with our deity. Lewis Lapham observes, "We express our longing for the ineffable in the wolfishness of our appetite. . . . The feasts of consumption thus become rituals of communion." Consumption seems to be our favorite high, our nationally sanctioned addiction, the all-American form of substance abuse.

So don't go shopping. And while you're at it, stay away from advertising that whets your appetite for stuff you don't want. And for pity's sake don't tune in to the Home Shopping Network. You may be saving more than money. You may be saving your sanity, not to speak of your soul.

## 2. Live within your means

This notion is so outmoded that some readers might not even know what it signifies. To live within your means is to buy only what you can prudently afford, to avoid debt unless you have an assurance that you will be able to pay it promptly and always to have something put away for a rainy day. It was quite a fashionable way to live one short generation ago, before we started living beyond our means. There are two sides to the coin of living beyond your means. The shiny side is that you can have everything you want right now. The tarnished side is that you will pay for it with your life. Buying on time, from cars to houses to vacations, often results in paying three times the purchase price. Is going to Hawaii for two weeks this year worth working perhaps four additional months next year to pay it off? This doesn't mean you have to cut up all your credit cards—you just have to avoid using them.

Living within your means suggests that you wait until you have the money before you buy something. This gives you the benefit of avoiding interest charges. It also gives you a waiting period during which you may well discover that you don't want some of those things after all. He who hesitates saves money. The bright side of living within your means is that you will use and enjoy what you have and harvest a full measure of fulfillment from it, whether it's your old car, your old coat or your old house. It also means that you can weather the economic bad times when they come—which they will. Alfred Malabre, economics editor of *The Wall Street Journal*, published a book in 1987 whose title says it all: *Beyond Our Means: How America's*

*Long Years of Debt, Deficits and Reckless Borrowing Now Threaten to Overwhelm Us.* In it he says:

> *In brief, the jig is about up and, for all the accumulated wisdom of all the eminent economists of the various schools, painless extrication from our predicament just isn't going to be possible.*

Now that's a pitch for living within your means if there ever was one!

### 3. Take care of what you have

There is one thing we all have that we want to last a long time—our bodies. Simple attention to the proven preventive practices will save you lots of money. Brushing your teeth, for example, could save thousands in dental bills. And eating what you know agrees with your body (judging by your energy, not by your taste buds) may save you thousands in expensive procedures, not to speak of your life.

Extend this principle to all your possessions. Regular oil changes are known to extend the life of your car. Cleaning your tools extends their life. (How many hair dryers and vacuum cleaners have choked on hair balls?) Dusting your refrigerator coils saves energy and could save your refrigerator. One big difference between living beings and machines is that machines are not self-healing. If you ignore a headache it will probably go away. If you ignore a funny noise in your engine you could throw a rod, burn out a water pump or otherwise incur major (and costly) damage.

Many of us have lived with excess for so many years that it no longer occurs to us to maintain what we have. "There's always more where that came from," we tell ourselves. But more costs money. And more may not, in the long run, be available.

## 4. Wear it out

What's the last item you actually wore out? Americans discard 1,455 pounds of garbage every year (here is one area where we're still the world's leader), and much of that was probably still perfectly usable. Synthetic fibers are extremely durable. It's hard to actually wear out clothing these days. If it weren't for the fashion industry (and boredom) we could all enjoy the same basic wardrobe for many years. Survey your possessions. Are you simply upgrading or duplicating last year's electronic equipment, furniture, kitchenware, carpeting and linens, or are you truly wearing them out? Think how much money you would save if you simply decided to use things even 20 percent longer. If you usually replace your towels every two years, try replacing them every two and a half years. If you trade in your car every three years, try extending that to four. If you buy a new coat every other winter, see whether every third winter would do just as well. And when you're about to buy something, ask yourself, "Do I already have one of these that is in perfectly usable condition?"

Another way to save money is to ask, before trashing something, whether there might be another way to use part or all of it. Old letters become scrap paper. A chipped cup becomes a pencil holder. A broken toaster oven becomes an assortment of screws, plus an electrical cord, Nichrome wire, a small metal tray and a heat-resistant handle. Old furniture can provide the wood for your next carpentry job. The frugality experts from the 1930s (and before) always kept a pile of wood scraps and assorted junk out back and had a knack for cobbling together what was needed out of available materials. All it takes is the recognition that everything is useful and the creativity to see what those uses might be. Then instead of buying something you can ask yourself, "Do I already have this item in some other form? If so, what would it take to make it serve my current needs?"

A word of caution to the already frugal. Using something until you wear it out does not mean using it until it wears *you* out. If you must continually fiddle with a lamp to make it work and you've already tried repairing it, it may not be worth your life energy to coax it along for another year. If your car is taking you for a ride, costing more hours in tinkering (or more money in repairs) than it's giving you in service, do buy a newer one. If your knee joints are suffering from running shoes that have lost their bounce, it would be cheaper to buy a new pair (on sale) than to have knee surgery.

## 5. Do it yourself

Can you tune your car? Fix a plumbing leak? Do your taxes? Make your own gifts? Rewire a toaster? Change the tire on your bicycle? Bake a cake from scratch? Build a bookshelf? Repair your roof? Clean your chimney? Sew a dress? Cut your family's hair? Form your own nonprofit corporation? It used to be that we learned basic life skills from our parents in the process of growing up. Then the Industrial Revolution put our parents in factories and, after the passing of child labor and mandatory public education laws, put us in schools. Next our grandparents were put in rest homes, removing the people who traditionally taught life skills to the children while the parents worked. Eventually home economics and shop classes had to be incorporated in the curriculum as supplements to the ever-decreasing skill-nourishment we got at home. By the 1970s it was no longer fashionable for mothers to stay at home with their children. By the 1980s many couples assumed it wasn't even possible, economically, for mothers to stay home with their children. Is it any wonder that the only way we know how to take care of ourselves in the 1990s is to be consumers of goods and services provided by others? To reverse that trend, just ask yourself, when you're about to hire an expert: "Can I do this myself? What would it take to learn how? Would it be a useful skill to know?"

Basic living and survival skills can be learned through adult education classes, extension agents, summer rural residential programs and, last but not least, books. Every breakdown can be used as an opportunity for learning and empowerment. What you can't do, or choose not to do, you can hire others to do, and tag along for the ride. Every bit of your energy invested in solving these breakdowns not only teaches you something you need to know for the next time but helps prevent mistakes and reduces the bill. One FIer tells the story of how her heating system failed one winter. Three companies sent out repair people to assess the problem and make a bid. Each one told her with absolute certainly what the problem was. Unfortunately, each told her a different story. So she cracked the books, meditated on the Rube Goldberg maze of pipes, came to an educated guess and chose the company that came closest to her analysis, thus saving herself hundreds of dollars of unnecessary and possibly destructive work. By staying with the repairman and observing his work she also was able to avert a few more expensive mistakes and to save (expensive) time by doing some of the simpler tasks. A typical working couple might have paid ten times what she did to have the job done and then felt fortunate to have two paychecks "since the cost of living in the modern world is so high."

## 6. Anticipate your needs
Forethought in purchasing can bring tremendous savings. With

enough lead time you will inevitably see the items you need go on sale by the time you need them—at 20 to 50 percent under the usual price. Keep current on catalogs and sale flyers of national and local catalog merchandisers. Read the sale ads in the Sunday paper. Be aware of seasonal bargains such as January and August "white sales," holiday sales (such as Memorial Day and Labor Day) and year-end clearance sales.

By simply observing the poor condition of your car's left rear tire while it still has some life left, you can anticipate a need. By simply being aware of this need you will naturally notice the phenomenal tire sale that will appear in the sports section of your Sunday newspaper three weeks from now—and you'll *know* it's a phenomenal sale because you have been watching prices.

In the shorter term, shopping at the corner convenience store can be expensive. Anticipating your needs—that you'll be wanting evening snacks, that you'll run out of milk midweek or that there's some taping you want to do and you're all out of blank cassettes—can eliminate running out to the corner store to pick up these items. Instead you can purchase them during your supermarket shopping or on a run to the discount store. This can result in significant savings.

Anticipating your needs also eliminates one of the biggest threats to your frugality: impulse buying. If you haven't anticipated needing something when you leave your house at 3:05, chances are you don't need it at 3:10 when you're standing at the gazingus-pin counter at the corner store. We're not saying you should only buy things that are on your premeditated shopping list (although that isn't such a bad idea for compulsive shoppers); we *are* saying that you must be scrupulously honest when you're out and about. Saying, "I anticipate needing this," as you're drooling over a left-handed veeblefitzer or cashmere sweater is not the same as having *already* anticipated needing one and recognizing that this particular one is a bargain. Remember the corollary to Parkinson's Law ("The work expands to fit the time allowed for its completion"): "Needs expand to encompass whatever you want to buy on impulse."

### 7. Research value, quality, durability and multiple use

Research your purchases. *Consumer Reports* and other publications give excellent evaluations and comparisons of almost everything you might buy—and they can be fun just to read. Decide what features are most important to you. Don't just be a bargain junkie and automatically buy the cheapest item available. Durability might be critical for something you plan to use daily for twenty years. One obvious way of saving money is to spend less on each item you buy, but it's equally true that spending $40 on a tool that lasts ten years instead of buying a $30 one that will need to be replaced in five years will save you $20 in the long run. Multiple use is also a factor. Buying one item for $10 that will serve the purpose of four different $5 items will net you a savings of $10. One heavy-duty kitchen pot can (and perhaps should) replace half a dozen specialty appliances like a rice cooker, a popcorn popper, a Crockpot, a deep-fat fryer, a paella pan and a spaghetti cooker. So, if you really expect to be using an item, buying for durability and for multiple purposes can be a good savings technique. But if you'll be using the item only occasionally you may not want to spend the extra dollars on a high-quality product. Knowing what your needs are and knowing the whole range of what is available will allow you to choose the right item.

Besides reading consumer magazines, you can evaluate quality by developing a sharp eye and carefully examining what you are buying.

Are the seams in a piece of clothing ample? Are the edges finished? Is the fabric durable? Is it washable or will you be paying dry-cleaning bills to keep it clean? Are the screws holding the appliance together sturdy enough for the job? Is the material strong or flimsy? Is the furniture nailed, stapled or screwed? Here is where you will become an expert materialist—knowing materials so well that you can read the probable longevity of an item the way a forester can read the age and history of a fallen tree. This is the opposite of crass materialism. This is as much honoring the wonder of creation as standing in a redwood grove. Everything you purchase has its origin in the earth. Everything. Knowing the wear patterns of aluminum versus stainless steel is honoring the earth every bit as much as lobbying for stronger environmental protection laws.

## 8. Get it for less

There are numerous ways to bargain-hunt. Here are few:

1. *Mail-order discounters:* When you know exactly what you want, including make and model, you can cut out the middleman and order through discount catalogs. Discounts in film and photographic equipment, in computers and associated paraphernalia, in tapes and in stereo and video equipment are huge; see ads in photography, computer and stereo magazines. Get specialized discounters' catalogs; these are available not only for photography, computer, audio and video supplies but also for tools, automobile parts and equipment, sporting goods and much more. Besides being money-savers, catalogs are a great education in conscious consuming. Ponder those enigmatic left-handed veeblefitzers. What are they for? Why are they in the doohickey section? Were there veeblefitzers in last year's catalog or is this a technological breakthrough? Will one veeblefitzer save me

the headache of replacing those @#!$@!!*$$!!! framus-pinders every year? *We* are catalog-reading addicts—everything from J. C. Penney to J. C. Whitney—and we would have to say that we have acquired more of a general education from this activity than from our years in college.

2. *Discount chain stores:* Just because you buy something at "the best store in town" doesn't mean it's of any better quality than the same item bought at a discount chain store. The discounters and warehouse stores carry many high-quality, name-brand products at a discount, but you have to know your prices. So even if you prefer to browse at high-priced emporium because you trust their buyers to select only the best equipment, do your buying at a discount chain store. One word of warning, however: just because the stereo you want is available at Harry's Low-Cost Cash-and-Carry doesn't mean it's a bargain. Harry's price may indeed be cheaper, if he is passing on his low overhead to you, or if the item is overstocked, discontinued or being used as a loss leader (an item priced at or below cost to lure you into the store for a buying binge). But on the other hand, it may not. *Know your prices.* How can you know when and where to buy what? See number 3 below.

3. *Comparison-shop by phone:* Where do you shop and how did you choose it? Is it where you've always shopped? At the mall closest to your home? Where your friends shop? Where advertising or status seeking has told you is the *only* place to shop? *We* shop via the telephone. Once we know what we want, we phone around for the best price. The more educated you are about the product and the more specific you can be about the exact make or model you want, the more successful your bargain-hunting will be. You will be amazed at the range of prices quoted for the same item. If you prefer doing

business with a particular store or supplier, phone-shop for the best price and then ask your favorite vendor if he or she can match it. In 1984, after much research, we decided we wanted a Toyota Tercel with four-wheel drive. We then called every dealership within 100 miles—and shaved $4,000 (33 percent) of the highest bid by purchasing a demonstrator (a deluxe model with everything but air-conditioning) that had 3,600 miles on it. Seven years and 100,000 miles later, *nothing* has gone wrong.

4. *Bargain:* You can ask for discounts for paying cash. You can ask for discounts for less-than-perfect items. You can ask for the sale price even if the sale begins tomorrow or ended yesterday. You can ask for further discounts on items already marked down. You can ask for discounts if you buy a number of items at the same time. You can ask for discounts anywhere, anytime. Nothing ventured, nothing gained. Haggling is a time-honored tradition. The list price of any consumer item is usually inflated. As soon as you hear the words, "The list price is . . ." you should say, "Yes, but what is *your* price?" According to Jim Dacyczyn you should be able to shave 24 percent off the sticker price for a car, but this strategy applies to more than houses, cars and other major purchases. You have nothing to lose by asking for a discount at any store—from your local hardware store to a clothing emporium. A case in point was our recent outing to buy new running shoes. A $60 (list price) pair was sitting on the manager's special rack with no price. They fit perfectly. We asked a salesman what they would cost. "24.99," he replied. "Would you take $19.99?" we asked. Surveying what he had left, he said, "Eighteen dollars." We could have pointed out that haggling etiquette suggests that his counteroffer be higher, not lower, than ours. But we were astute enough just to shut our mouths, open our wallet and take advantage of a great bargain. A

reporter for *The Wall Street Journal*, researching an article on the increase in haggling precipitated by the 1990–91 recession, tried bargaining in his New York neighborhood. From hardware stores to antique boutiques to major retail department stores, the majority of retailers were willing to shave substantial amounts off the asking price. So bargain. What have you got to lose?

### 9. Buy it used

Reexamine your attitudes about buying used items. If you are a thrift-store or garage-sale addict, look at whether you are really saving money or whether you are buying items that you don't need just because they're "such a bargain." But if you wouldn't be caught dead in a musty Salvation Army thrift store, look around your town: thrift stores have become fashionable emporiums. Even *Newsweek* says so. In "I Can Get It for You Resale" the magazine declared that "Secondhand shopping is chic as well as thrifty. . . . The change reflects the new national Zeitgeist. . . . Quality and value are more important than flash and cash." Clothing, kitchenware, furniture, drapes—all can be found in thrift stores, and you may be surprised at the high quality of many of them. As a matter of fact, donating brand-new items to thrift stores is one way that shopaholics justify excess purchases. If you just can't bring yourself to shop at thrift stores, consider consignment shops. The prices are higher, but the quality is consistently higher as well. In our experience, thrift stores are best for clothing but garage sales are cheaper (and more reliable) for appliances, furniture and household items. If you're an early bird (arriving before the sellers have even had their morning coffee) you can often find exceptional buys. On the other hand, the later in the day you go to a garage sale, the more eager the people will be to get rid of the stuff for a song. "Swap meets" and "flea markets" are two names for the same event—weekend open-air bazaars where you'll find merchants of every stripe displaying their wares: shrewd hucksters, collectors of every kind and families hoping to unload their excess before moving across country. Just as when you shop at discounters, you have to know your prices. There are some clever nomads working the flea-market circuit who will sell you tools, imported peasant clothing, crystals and other items for *more* than you'd pay at the shopping mall.

James H. Gipson has managed the Clipper Fund since
1984, compiling a superb record. The book he published
that year ncluded this summary of characteristics
investors should cultivate.

# THE VIRTUES OF INVESTING
## by James H. Gipson

from *Winning the Investment Game* (1984)

VIRTUE IS MORE than its own reward in investing; it adds to
an investor's bottom line and prevents withdrawals from it.
Adopting the following virtues will not guarantee a successful result, since money management is one business without a
money-back guarantee. The virtues will, however, significantly
increase the odds of obtaining that successful result.

CONTRARY THINKING

Fashion is fine for clothing, but a guarantee of loss for investing. The
investor has the unpleasant choice of doing the fashionable and
comfortable thing which will lose money or the uncomfortable and
contrary thing which will make money.

Assets become overpriced precisely because they are popular and
comfortable to own. Common stocks were very popular in 1969, just
as real estate and gold were very popular in 1979. All three assets
were grossly overpriced because large numbers of investors bought
them on the soon-to-be-mistaken belief that they could go nowhere
but up.

The belief that an asset can only go up, quaint as it seems with the benefit of hindsight, was supported by plausible arguments at the time. Stocks could only go up in 1969 because corporate profits would grow forever in a Keynesian-led economy which had banished the business cycle. Gold and real estate could only go up in 1979 because they were the best inflation hedges in a world with per-petual double-digit inflation. The plausible arguments are endless, and they always sound convincing.

Often the most convincing argument is "X is going up. Buy it now before it goes higher." Jumping on the bandwagon can be irresistibly appealing when everyone else seems to be making money in the favored asset. The seldom-stated premise of bandwagon psychology is that the profitable trend of the immediate past will persist into the indefinite future, or at least far enough into the future for the investors and their friends to retire rich.

In practice, it seldom works that way. Investment trends often per-sist longer than is rationally justifiable, but they never persist indefi-nitely. Trends change, often abruptly, causing great pain to investors with linear minds who assume that the future will duplicate the past. There is no scientific way to predict when an overvalued asset will begin to fall like a rock, but the long-term odds strongly favor an investor who avoids investing in the asset which is most popular in cocktail party conversations.

The cocktail party test is an unscientific but useful test of conven-tional wisdom. If everyone is saying, "I just made a mint in stocks (or real estate, gold coins, Tiffany lampshades, etc.)," then the favored asset is probably near its peak of popularity. If everyone thinks that any asset can only go up in the immediate future because it has only gone up in the past, then it should be sold rather than bought. Large profits are for the few, not for the many, and the sight of many people bragging about making profits in any single asset generally means that those profits are coming to an end.

The cocktail party test also illustrates why a contrary approach to investing is so hard to practice. When everyone is bragging about the money they are making in asset X, no one wants to be a wet blanket by saying that they are likely to lose their shirts and possibly the rest of their wardrobes too. That kind of public contrary opinion is more likely to make enemies than friends, even if it turns out to be true. The best investment policy is to avoid what everyone else is buying, the best social policy is to be discreet about it. Going along with the crowd is a far easier course of action; most people want to belong to the group.

In addition to the natural desire to join the group, a major obstacle to contrary thinking is lack of confidence. Deep down, many people do not have much confidence in their own opinions, particularly on a complex subject such as investing. The volatility of asset prices in recent years has given almost everyone the opportunity to be wrong some of the time, diminishing whatever confidence may have existed before. A corollary of this lack of confidence is the belief that others' opinions must be superior, regardless of whether or not they are. Lack of confidence impels investors to substitute other people's opinions for their own, often with unhappy results.

Nonprofessional investors who feel insecure when faced with the specter of competing with professionals can take a great deal of comfort from knowing that the professionals are usually wrong too. Mutual fund managers have a remarkably good record of raising cash at market bottoms and then investing it at market tops. Pension fund managers have a similarly poor record, best illustrated by the lunacy of 1971 to

1973. They invested over 100 percent of their net cash flow in stocks (the excess over 100 percent came from reducing cash and liquidating bonds), which left them very exposed to the disastrous bear market of 1973 to 1974. Worse yet, the stocks they bought heavily were the "nifty fifty," a few large-growth companies (e.g., IBM, Pfizer, Polaroid, Avon, and McDonald's) whose price/earnings multiples were raised to 60 to 70 times; a few years later many of those multiples were less than 10 times and many of the losses exceeded 75 percent.

Professional investment analysts have a similarly dismal track record. Surveys of the top-rated analysts' favorite stocks show an uncommonly good tendency to reflect those stocks which have done well over the last year. Not surprisingly, those same favorites also show an uncommonly good tendency to produce dismal results in the following year. Professional investors also are afflicted with the malady of projecting the profitable trend of the immediate past into the indefinite future, with the same results which insecure nonprofessionals experience.

Too much confidence can be as dangerous as too little. Just as an insecure investor is prone to rely on consensus thinking, an overconfident investor is liable to think he can do no wrong after a period of unusually good profits. The euphoric feeling that "I have this investing game down pat" generally occurs to novices who have no personal experience of being wrong but are about to have one. Investing can be a humbling experience for an overconfident investor since everyone is wrong occasionally over a long period of time. The investor who runs a little scared and is prepared to question assumptions, recheck analyses, and recognize mistakes early is likely to fare better. In investing, as in other aspects of life, pride goeth before the fall.

Perhaps the best way to overcome psychological obstacles to contrary investing is to recognize from the start that investing requires a different mode of thought from the mode of thought appropriate to everyday living. Being a joiner is fine when it comes to team sports, fashionable clothes, and trendy restaurants. When it comes to investing, however, the investor must remain aloof and suppress social tendencies. When it comes to making money and keeping it, the majority is always wrong.

Once investors decide on the general idea of contrary investing, they usually adopt at least one of these particular approaches:

*Avoiding stocks with high P/E ratios.* A high P/E ratio is a good measure of a stock's popularity, just as a low P/E ratio is a good measure of its disfavor. Bargains are more likely to be found in low P/E stocks. Since high and low are relative concepts, an investor should compare the P/E ratio of his stocks with that of the stock market as a whole. The financial sections of most large Sunday newspapers contain the P/E ratio for Standard and Poor's 500 stock index.

*Recognizing that most people are playing the wrong game most of the time.* When everyone is buying stocks to capitalize on noninflationary growth, then the likely denouement is a recessionary decline of growth or a takeoff of inflation. If everyone is buying gold or real estate to hedge against inflation, then inflation is probably nearing a temporary (or maybe permanent) halt. If tulip bulbs, Tiffany lampshades, or some other asset of marginal economic value is registering major financial gains, then cash is a better place to be.

*Looking for bargains in keeping with the Burmese adage that a man fears the tiger which bit him last, not the tiger which will bite him next.* Fear of stocks is greatest when leveraged speculators have gone to the wall in a bear market, creating a buying opportunity for an investor with both ready cash and a cool head. Fear of real estate is at its greatest after a long period of high interest rates and weak property prices, forcing leveraged speculators to throw their properties on the market at distress prices. One of the early Rothschilds said that the time to buy is when blood is running in the streets, and a modern version of that is to buy an asset when the current owners of it are drowning in red ink. What causes fear in the seller is likely to cause apprehension at a minimum in the buyer, so contrary investors should accept the fact that they will never feel completely comfortable when they make their best buys.

*Selling to the optimists and buying from the pessimists.* Belief that the future will be completely wonderful or completely awful leads most investors to buy at high prices and to sell at low ones. The contrary investor should be on the other side of those transactions. Reality generally falls somewhere in between the worst and best that investors imagine, so betting against either extreme is usually a good policy.

Contrary investing will not produce instant profits. Nothing will. Improving the odds in their favor is the best that investors reasonably may expect. If practiced over a long period of time, however, contrary investing will keep investors out of trouble and point them toward bargains. The long-term period is critical to success, which suggests another virtue of investing—patience.

## PATIENCE
Patience is a virtue with a strange distribution among investors. Young investors have all the time in the world to enjoy the long-term benefits of patient investing, but they generally are the least patient. They want

instant gratification and immediate results. They want everything right now, including instant investment performance. Young investors who own stocks are likely to check their prices on a daily or hourly basis even when they are not actively buying and selling.

Old investors do not have much time left and are actuarially unlikely to enjoy the long-term results of patient investing. Their lives are entering their twilight years, yet they invest as if there will be an infinite number of tomorrows. Old investors tend to be patient investors despite the apparent lack of payoff from that patience.

For both young and old, temperament plays a larger role in their investing than most care to acknowledge. The young in a hurry in their business and social lives are likely to be in a hurry to see investment results too. The old who are patient in most other aspects of life are likely to be patient in investing too.

For the investors of any age who can rise above their own temperaments and choose rational courses of action which are most likely to enrich them, there are compelling arguments for choosing patience.

Patience is necessary simply by nature of the investing game itself. Over short periods of 1 to 2 years, luck is probably more important than skill. Stock prices have a large random element to them, analogous to Brownian motion in physics. That random motion of stock prices is a more important determinant of profits and losses than are skill and strategy in the short run. Only over periods of 3 to 5 years do the random movements of stock prices cancel each other out, leaving the net result of the investor's intelligence and diligence.

Luck can play a dominant role in short-term real estate results too. Perhaps a new shopping center will build adjacent to the investor's property; better yet, on the property. Perhaps a rich couple will fall in love with the house an investor is selling and will pay handsomely in order to get it. Perhaps the solid citizen to whom the investor sold a house suddenly defaults on a second trust deed, declares bankruptcy, and ties up the investor in lengthy and expensive court proceedings. Such events can have a major impact on a property owner's short-term results. But in the long run, the good luck and bad luck cancel each other out, leaving a net result which is due primarily to an investor's own efforts.

Patience focuses an investor's attention on the goal of compounding money over a long period. Compounding can be magic, even when the compounding rate is modest. Investors who compound their money in real terms at 7 percent per year will double it in 10 years; in 40 years they will have 16 times their original amount. If the Indians and their descendants who sold Manhattan for $24 had been successful in compounding their money at 7 percent after taxes for the last 350 years, they would have about $30 billion today.

That $30 billion demonstrates more than the magic of compounding at even moderate rates of return. The complete absence of any pools of private capital remotely approaching $30 billion suggests that long-term compounding is an extraordinarily difficult feat. Even if one or two generations of investors are capable enough to accumulate and compound a respectable pool of assets, one of the heirs is likely to dissipate or lose it all.

The mortal enemy of compounding is the wipeout. A respectable rate of compounding for a lifetime can be lost with a single bad investment decision. The odds are that an investor will make that decision, or one of the investor's heirs will. Reducing the odds of a wipeout and raising the rate of compounding are the twin goals of this book.

Patience has more than the long-term advantage of focusing an investor's attention on the goals of long-term compounding and avoiding a wipeout. Patience also helps control short-term brokerage costs as well. The patient investor is less likely to buy and sell often, thereby reducing the 6 percent that a real estate broker charges or the roughly 3 to 4 percent that a normal stockbroker charges for a round trip to sell one stock and buy another (discount brokers charge much less, and a stockholder should use one). A toll charge of 3 to 6 percent may seem small in relation to the total amount of an investor's principal, but it is large in relation to the annual income and profit received. If, for example, an impatient stockholder makes 10 percent per year in profits and turns over his portfolio twice a year at an average cost of 3 percent per turn, then 60 percent of his annual profits go to his broker! At the end of each year investors should add up their brokerage commissions along with their net profits, and then compare the two figures to see whether it is they or their brokers who are making the most money off the investments.

## DILIGENCE, OR KNOWLEDGE IS PROFIT

There is no point in playing an investing game without an unfair advantage. Games such as tennis and golf are structured to avoid giving an advantage to any one player, which is the way it should be to achieve a sporting competition. Unlike tennis or golf, the investing game is not played for sporting competition; it is played to make and keep money. The investor's odds of making and keeping money increase in proportion to the advantages the person can accumulate over other investors. One of the most important advantages is superior knowledge about the asset one is buying or selling.

That advantage of superior knowledge generally is obtained by diligence. In real estate that advantage is obtained by knowing more about the property than the person on the other side of the transaction.

Recent sales of comparable property, zoning and assessment changes, plans for nearby developments, current financing available, and many other details go into making a knowledgeable real estate investor. That knowledge does not come easily; an investor has to work to obtain it and to keep current about it.

Superior knowledge confers a comparable advantage on a stockholder in a positive sum investing game. Stockholders who are not willing or able to work very hard to become knowledgeable about their securities are best advised to find a good mutual fund run by portfolio managers who do work hard. Stockholders who are willing to work hard should be willing to read a good many annual reports, utilize investment advisory information such as that provided by Value Line and Standard & Poor, and learn about securities research and accounting. Accounting in particular is both difficult and dry, but it is the language of finance; an investor who cannot read that language is at a significant disadvantage.

Knowledge is not only power, but profit as well. The investor's goal should be to know more about the asset being bought or sold than the investor on the other side of the transaction. This advantage of superior knowledge does not come cheaply; it takes work.

There is a temptation for intellectually brilliant people to believe that their brains can substitute for knowledge. To a degree that is true, but, often, brilliant people overestimate that degree of substitutability as well as the degree of their own brilliance. Superior knowledge almost always requires some effort.

Superior knowledge is a relative concept; adequate knowledge is an absolute one. There are many investment opportunities where no reasonable amount of research will give most investors knowledge adequate to make an intelligent decision. This is particularly true for high-technology companies whose products and processes require a level of evaluative expertise which few people possess. High technology is exciting and sexy, but also impenetrable except to investors with the specialized knowledge to understand it. A good rule of thumb: Buy only what you understand.

## VALUE ORIENTATION

Once an investor adopts a contrary, patient, and diligent approach toward finding investment opportunities, the obvious next step is to find out what those opportunities look like. Value orientation is another investment virtue which increases the investor's odds of compounding money.

Value is as protean as it is important. It comes in many forms, but its common denominator is this: Buy assets at a discount from what rational buyers are willing to pay for the entire company or property. The *private buyer rule* will help an investor avoid such manias as the "nifty fifty" stocks of 1972 and 1973 (no sane private buyer would have paid those prices) and will point toward investments which are likely to offer better returns.

Determining what private buyers are paying takes only a moderate amount of work in real estate. Benchmarks of value are common to the industry, and a little time with a good broker will produce benchmarks such as the following:

*Motels sell at three to five times gross.* Since expenses generally amount to about 65 percent of gross revenues, debt service should not exceed one-third of gross. Motels can be extraordinary tax shelters, thanks to IRS regulations which allow buildings to be depreciated over 15 years and furniture and fixtures to be depreciated over 3 to 5 years.

*Apartments are priced at six to seven times gross revenues in areas where expenses are heavy and eight times gross in areas of moderate expenses.* If the landlord pays tenant utility bills, then multiples of gross revenues are accordingly lower.

*Condominiums in a given area may sell for $200 to $300 per square foot, with adjustments for the character of the building, height (i.e., ground floor versus penthouse), view, and physical condition.*

Once a real estate investor knows the benchmarks of value for his particular interest, he is in a position to search for a property at less than its value to a private buyer. Examples of wise investment procedure include:

*Looking for an apartment house with a normal return on the investor's investment, but where that return is based on below-market rents because the current owner has not been vigorous enough in raising them.* The investor who buys the apartment house and then raises the rents (never a pleasant task, and occasionally an impossible one where rent control applies) will realize an immediate increase in both the rental income and the market value of the property.

*Finding the "fixer-upper" which is often underpriced, whether it is an old house or an old office building.* Investors generally pay a premium for the newest and the best, so older properties often generate higher returns. Fixing up an older property can add significant value over and above the costs of restoration. But an investor who takes that approach should be very careful about estimating both the time and the costs necessary for restoration. Most restoration projects come in over budget and behind schedule.

*Taking the patient-vulture approach of waiting for the desperate seller.* Desperate sellers usually accumulate around the bottom of a recession when they have to sell their highly leveraged properties to pay off their loans. Desperate sellers can pop up any time, however, particularly when they have moved from the area and their objective has changed from getting the best price for their home to simply getting rid of it. A good sign of a desperate seller is a property which has been on the market for some time and has taken at least one price cut. Patiently waiting like a vulture for a seller to get in trouble may sound like a hardhearted tactic, but it produces bargains.

*Avoiding negative cash flow situations.* Particularly near a speculative top in real estate, properties often change hands at prices so high that there is no cash return to the buyer. Buyers accept minimal or negative returns because they believe that future inflation will raise those returns to high positive levels or because they believe that a greater fool will buy the property at a greater price. Occasionally a bet on a property with a negative cash flow will be profitable, but that is a bet only for those who can afford high risks. If inflation does not raise rents fast enough, then the temporary negative cash flow becomes a permanent one; a permanent negative cash flow is a good prescription for personal bankruptcy.

A value approach to stocks is more complex than a value approach to real estate. The real estate investor buys the whole property, but the shareholder buys only a small portion. Determining value to a rational private buyer may be difficult in some cases and impossible in others. Despite the additional complexities, a value approach to stocks is much the same in purpose.

Some kinds of corporate assets sell often enough to develop benchmarks of value to a private buyer. Television stations and monopoly newspapers generally sell for 8 to 10 times their pretax profits, with stations in growth markets commanding premium prices. Oil in the ground either sells for about $10 per barrel or sells on a discounted cash flow basis using a 25 percent discount rate. Most real estate investment trusts publish the current market value of their assets in their annual reports, based on independent appraisals. Tender offers (i.e., offers by one company to buy another) also provide a good source of value to a private buyer. The investor with a good estimate of the private transactions value of a company's assets has a ceiling on what should be paid and also has a target to use in attempting to buy assets at a large discount from their fair values.

Most corporate assets do not trade often enough to establish good benchmarks of value. For large companies such as General Motors and IBM there simply is no private market. In this case investors will have to do their own valuation based on price/earnings ratios, growth rates, balance sheets, etc. (as discussed in the section on contrary thinking).

One of the most important valuation decisions is whether stocks are cheaper than bonds. Stocks were cheaper than bonds or cash equivalents for 30 years until the Fed began its new operating policy in October 1979. Since then, interest rates have gone high enough to provide real competition for equity returns. A quick test is to compare the yield to maturity on long-term treasury bonds with the earnings yield on common stocks. The financial sections of most large Sunday newspapers give the P/E ratio for the Standard and Poor's 500 stock index; dividing that ratio into 1 gives the earnings yield on stocks. Unless the earnings yield exceeds the yield to maturity on bonds, stocks should be avoided, as shown in the accompanying table.

| P/E ratio onS&P 500 | Earning yield(1/PE), % | Bond yield, % | Cheaper asset |
|---|---|---|---|
| 8 | 12.5 | 9.0 | Stocks |
| 15 | 6.7 | 9.0 | Bonds |

Shareholders do not buy an entire company; they buy only shares in it. In practice that is a very mixed blessing. The blessing arises from the shareholders' passive position which enables them to receive dividends without the nuisance of running the business. (Any owner of a small apartment who has tried to evict a tenant for non-payment of rent knows very well how much nuisance there can be in active ownership.) That passive position can be a real problem, however, when management of a company has a different set of priorities from the shareholders'. Few managements run their companies to maximize the long-term returns of their shareholders; most managements view themselves like politicians who try to please many different constituencies, and shareholders are only one constituency (others include employees, suppliers, customers, the government, etc.). Managements with this constituency approach generally aim for a satisfactory level of profits to deflect shareholder complaints, then turn to other goals. This creates only a medium-level problem for shareholders since its effect is already included in the level of profits and their growth. The real problem arises when management's interests are directly opposed to those of the shareholders; in those cases, management usually decides in its own favor. If a management team is incompetent or even senile, it is very difficult to remove and replace with a better or more vigorous management team. If the company receives a generous tender offer, management may fight tooth and nail to retain its own power and prerequisites even though the shareholders would be better off to enjoy a 50 to 80 percent premium over the market value of their stock. The separation of managers and shareholders in modern corporations drives a wedge between actual and potential profits to the shareholders. Generally that wedge is small, but in exceptional cases such as tender offers it can be very large.

Even a shareholder who buys only a tiny share of a large company should still ask the final question: Would I buy the entire company at this price if I had the means? Assuming the perspective of a long-term owner helps an investor separate the latest investment fads from solid reasons to own a business. Taking an owner's perspective helps focus an investor's attention on issues such as: Do I understand the business? Does it seem like a business with a good long-term future? What are the business risks and who are the competitors? Does the stock's price seem reasonable in relation to the value of the business and in relation to other investment opportunities?

The investor who understands the company and buys its stock at a discount from the private transactions value of its assets has gone a long way toward assuming an owner's perspective. There is a tendency for many investors, particularly institutional ones who manage pension funds and trust departments, to view a stock as just a piece of paper with a few numbers attached (e.g., P/E ratio, yield, etc.). Adopting an owner's perspective helps avoid that unfortunate tendency.

Other assets are far more difficult to value than property and stocks in terms of their worth to a private buyer. Gold is not amenable to the private buyer technique, despite its industrial uses in electronics. Commodities such as copper and silver have their primary value to industrial users for construction, power transmission, and photography, but that value varies sharply over a business cycle.

## CLEARLY DEFINED OBJECTIVES

Few investors really know their own objectives, strange as that may seem. They generally define their objectives only in fuzzy terms and then change them at the wrong time. When a bull market is near its peak, conservative investors frequently become aggressive in hope of cashing in on the bonanza. When a bear market has inflicted severe losses, aggressive investors often turn so conservative that they miss the opportunities in front of them. Investors who clearly define their objectives and stick to them stand a good chance of avoiding those mistakes.

Objectives do not start with how much money an investor hopes to make; they start with how much the investor can afford to lose. The risk an investor can afford to take depends both on finances and on temperament. A serious appraisal of finances should be a first step. How much money can be lost without severely impacting the investor's standard of living? What major expenses (e.g., a house, college tuition for a child) can be expected in the near future? A careful appraisal of income, expenses, and assets is essential to defining an investor's risk tolerance.

A careful appraisal of an investor's temperamental tolerance for risk is just as essential. There are wealthy investors who can afford large losses but who become extremely upset over even small ones. Most pension funds can afford to take a very long-term view which looks beyond the short term, but most pension fund managers are mesmerized by short-term losses. They focus on relative performance in bull markets (Is my portfolio doing better than the S&P 500?) and on absolute performance during bear markets (Am I losing any money at all?). A good test of an investor's psychological risk tolerance is to imagine losing increasing amounts of money until he gets to the point where he would wake up at night scared stiff.

An investor's risk tolerance is set by either his finances or his temperament, whichever is lower. That risk tolerance neither can nor should be defined too rigorously, but can be divided into three simple categories: low, medium, and high. Once investors begin to think in those terms, they have a useful guide as to which investments are right for them.

Writing down investment objectives is often a useful step. When a low-risk investor's friends are making a bundle of money in highly leveraged real estate, high speculative stocks, and volatile commodities, he should pull out his written objectives as a way to keep his perspective and help avoid getting caught up in the mania of the moment. When a high-risk investor sees other investors staggered by declining asset prices, he should pull out his written objectives as a reminder that now is the time to take those high risks.

Investors should not select investments *above* their risk tolerance, but frequently should select investments *below* them. Just because an investor is financially and psychologically prepared to take high risks does *not* mean that he always should have high-risk investments in his portfolio. He should take high risks only when the available opportunities pay him well to do so, and should join low-risk investors when he is not so well paid. There are times when high-risk investments become so overpriced (e.g., common stocks in 1969 and real estate in 1979) that aggressive investors are better off avoiding risks they are not well-paid to take.

## A Cool Head, or Fear and Greed Overcome

"If you can keep your head when all about you are losing theirs" was one of Rudyard Kipling's required virtues for becoming a mature adult. It is also a required virtue for becoming a successful investor.

Keeping one's head is easier said than done because emotions are far more powerful motivating forces than cool, rational thoughts. The relevant emotions are greed and fear, the eternal yin and yang of investing. Understanding one's own impulse toward greed and fear, overcoming it, and then capitalizing on other investors' greed and fear are the three stages of an investor's progress.

Understanding greed and fear begins with the recognition that everyone has those two emotions. Becoming aware of those emotions, particularly when one is becoming ascendent over the other, is the first step toward overcoming them. Mark Twain once observed that "courage is resistance to fear, mastery of fear—not absence of fear." Overcoming greed and fear is something no one does completely, but some do better than others. One useful method is to maintain a certain physical and psychological distance from other investors. Greed and fear are insidiously contagious even for intelligent persons, but the degree of contagion diminishes sharply with the amount of contact with other investors who are caught in the vise of either one of those emotions.

The perspective of distance in 1929 helped a professor at Harvard Business School recognize how vastly overpriced the stock market was, a recognition which he frequently conveyed to his students. When his students graduated in June, he left his teaching post and went to Wall Street to become research director at a brokerage firm. Once immersed in the mania, he lost his perspective and allowed his greed to overcome his recognition of how overvalued the stock market was. When the stock market crashed in October, the former professor and his clients were fully invested and fully exposed to the losses which followed.

A certain distance helps prevent contagious infection by greed and fear, and so does a clear discipline. If real estate investors follow the discipline of avoiding properties with negative cash flows, they are less likely to lose their assets. If stockholders avoid stocks when bonds are cheaper, as discussed earlier in this chapter, then they are less likely to be vulnerable to bear markets. Benjamin Graham, often regarded as the father of security analysis, once observed that the discipline of a greater reliance on hard numbers and a lesser reliance on judgment (which is likely to be influenced by the emotions of greed and fear) will enhance an investor's chances of success.

Graham also had another idea with the purpose of enabling investors to capitalize on other people's greed and fear. The idea was that an investor does business with an emotionally volatile fellow named Mr. Market. At times Mr. Market is in a euphoric mood and is willing to pay large amounts of money for companies, often far larger amounts than private buyers are willing to pay. At times Mr. Market is gloomy and despondent enough to sell stocks at far less than what private buyers are paying and often at far less than Mr. Market himself bought them not long before. The investor with a cool head has an obvious advantage when he sells to Mr. Market's euphoric mood and buys from his gloomy one.

Kipling's poem goes further into the virtues of keeping a cool head:

*If you can trust yourself when all men doubt you*
*But make allowance for their doubting too.*

Friends, acquaintances, and coworkers probably will not appreciate a cool head who throws a wet blanket on their euphoric and greedy mania, however much a wet blanket is needed. Those same people will not appreciate a cheery, chipper person talking about the wonderful bargains available when they are gloomy and despondent over the large losses they have suffered in creating those bargains. The emotional Mr. Market is not some distant lunatic, but a cross-section of the investor's friends and coworkers. If an investor wants to keep his relationships intact, he is better off keeping his own counsel about how their emotional behavior creates opportunities for cooler and more rational minds.

# TRUST NO ONE
## by Andrew Tobias

from *The Only Investment Guide You'll Ever Need* (1978)

*Trust everybody, but cut the cards*
—Finley Peter Dunne

I F YOU OR anyone you know is over fifty, I *urge* you to get pencil and paper ready."

So begin the celebrity life insurance commercials you may have seen on TV. Dick Van Dyke does them. Ed McMahon does them. Even Gavin MacLeod—good ol' Murray on the *Mary Tyler Moore Show*—does them.

Murray, Murray, Murray.

But the plans sound good, don't they? No matter how bad your health, *you cannot be turned down* for this "top-quality, big-dollar" protection. Yet amazing as it seems—well, this is why I told you to get your pencil and paper ready—Murray's plan costs just $5 a month. And—get this!—your premiums are guaranteed never to rise as you get older.

Says Murray: "I can't tell you what a relief it is to know that we won't be a burden on our children." Here the kids thought they stood

*289*

to inherit a pretty penny—Murray did go on to captain the *Loveboat*, after all—but had it not been for this insurance, they'd have been left with nothing but the funeral bill. *Thank heavens for this insurance.*

If you're 50, Murray says, just $5 a month buys you $10,000 in protection.

Catch #1: If you die of an illness, your heirs get $2,800, not $10,000. The bulk of the insurance benefit is for *accidental* death only. Yet accidents are a minor cause of death among older people. (Dick Van Dyke's pitch calls them "one of the leading causes of death for people over forty-five." But actually, fewer than 3% of deaths among people over 45 are caused by accidents. So more than 97% of the time the payoff would be $2,800, not $10,000.)

It's true, you can't be turned down for this coverage; but—Catch #2—only after you've paid premiums for two years are you actually covered. Die of an illness before then, and your heirs get nothing but a refund of the premiums you've paid.

True, too, your rates are guaranteed not to rise (well, sort of) but— Catch #3—as you get older, your coverage falls. Say you pay $5 a month, month after month, for 25 years. Then, at 75, having paid in a total of $1,500, you have a heart attack and die. This policy pays your heirs a grand total of $225. Period. (Die after age 79 and they get no benefit at all.) This is what Murray endorses as BIG-DOLLAR protection. He can't tell you what a relief it is to know that $225 will be there when his loved ones need it.

If at age 79 you died not of an illness but, say, hang gliding into a utility pole, your heirs would get an extra $775, except that—Catch #4—death while hang gliding doesn't qualify for the accidental death bonus. Neither does death in a war (declared or undeclared), in a private plane, by suicide, during surgery, or while intoxicated, if intoxication caused the accident. (If you were merely three sheets to the wind in the bar car of your commuter train when it derailed and flew off a cliff, you'd be okay.)

Catch #5: Your rates are guaranteed never to rise *only so long as the insurance company doesn't raise them.* If it decides everybody should pay $6 a month instead of $5, or to cancel all the policies altogether because it's not making money on them, the company is free to do so.

Catch #6: Five bucks a month is the least you can pay; but this is portrayed as *such* a good deal for "folks like us," as Murray puts it— you know, warm, bald guys who make $80,000 an episode—that many folks sign up for the full $40-a-month's worth, to cover both them and their spouses four times over. Five dollars a month is nothing. But $40 a month, in the budgets of many older Americans—$480 a year—is a hefty sum.

The pitchmen freely acknowledge they're paid to endorse these insurance plans, but Dick Van Dyke says, in his follow-up letter: "P.S. I'm sure you know I would never speak out for anything I didn't personally believe in." Gavin MacLeod, in *his* P.S., writes: "I want you to know I would never speak out for anything I didn't believe in with my whole heart." The cash Continental American Life paid him to endorse this plan has nothing to do with it.[*]

Trust no one. It kills me to say that, and I'll admit there are exceptions—but the list is shorter than you think. I mean, my God: if you can't trust Murray!

---

[*] MacLeod and Van Dyke were both reportedly paid $25,000 to do the television commercials, plus a commission on each toll-free call the commercials produced. An executive close to the arrangement estimates the final take for each man to have been between $100,000 and $200,000.

Here is an ad for the Oppenheimer Special Fund. Oppenheimer is no slouch of an investment firm, and this is its *special* fund. In fact, says the ad, this fund has appreciated at a rate of 21.5% a year for the last 10 years. Compare *that* with what your local bank is paying. You're smart enough to know performance like that can't necessarily be repeated (if only you had thought to invest 10 years ago!). And you imagine, given that they're trying pretty hard to sell this to you, there may be a sales commission involved (there is: only $4,575 of the $5,000 you were thinking of investing actually goes to work for you—the rest is an immediate loss). But never mind that. We're talking about 21.5% annual growth—enough, if it continued for another two decades, to turn a single $2,000 IRA contribution into $90,000!

You are all set to send in your money, when you come across Jane Bryant Quinn's column in *Newsweek*. She has studied the prospectus—you could have studied it, too, but you would have been a rare investor if you did—and she has noticed that "the big gains that Oppenheimer packs into its alluring yield of 21.5% came long ago. Between 1974 and 1980, share values rose an average of 39% a year. But zigzag performance from 1980 to 1984 brought an average annual loss of 4%."

No place in the ad do you see anything about an average annual loss of 4%.*

Trust no one. You've got to take responsibility for your own affairs. Many people wish they could turn the whole mess over to someone

---

* In the hot stock market of 1985, the fund did jump 16.8%, but that performance placed the fund in the bottom fifth of the mutual funds ranked by Lipper Analytical Services. In the decade since, the Oppenheimer Growth Fund, as it's now called, grew smartly, but underperformed the averages.

else. Widows particularly express this wish, having in some cases been made to feel over many years of marriage that they can't possibly understand anything having to do with money. But the folks who do understand money, while many have your best interests at heart, have their own interests at heart, too. You have to take responsibility for your own money because no one cares about it as much as you. That doesn't mean you can't rely on a variety of experts to help—a good accountant, a good mutual fund manager, perhaps a good real estate or insurance agent, financial planner or attorney. But ultimately it's you who is in charge.

If you don't understand what you're investing in, or haven't formed a broad spending/borrowing/saving/insuring/investing plan yourself, it's unlikely things will work out terribly well. (Most people wind up with nothing, says financial adviser Venita Van Caspel, "not because they plan to fail, but because they fail to plan.") What's more, you *can* do it. The simple investments are very often the best. And that goes, too, for the simple loans, the simple insurance, and the simple financial plans.

(I had a friend who earned $2 million a year at Merrill Lynch executing a very complex, computer-assisted trading strategy. Around 1990, he went out on his own and offered me and others the chance to do it with him. He labored mightily to explain exactly *what* he was doing, but all any of us could understand—even the head of an investment bank who also went in on this—was that a 50% annual gain was essentially guaranteed unless interest rates rose or fell more than 700 basis points in a single year. Which never happens—and didn't. Don't you wish you could get into deals like this? Don't you wish you knew what basis points are?* It was the most sophisticated, complex deal

---

* Each basis point equals one-hundredth of one percent. When the prime rises from 7% to 8% it's climbed "100 basis points."

I've ever invested in. It sure wasn't available to "the Little Guy." And it lost money. Big time. My friend wasn't trying to fleece us. He meant well. He was just wrong—for reasons I could understand no better than what it was he was doing in the first place.)

It's not enough to respond to advertising headlines or the salesperson's enthusiasm or the lavishly illustrated brochure. You've got to read between the lines—or at least read the prospectus. And since you won't—most prospecti are unreadable—you've got to stick to sensible investments recommended by competent, disinterested parties. Not competent *or* disinterested, competent *and* disinterested—which certainly leaves out Murray, may very likely leave out tips from your hair stylist, and may even leave out advice from your accountant or financial planner, who could be getting a commission for steering you into a particular deal. ("Your purpose," a well-known San Francisco financial planner was quoted in the *Wall Street Journal* as having told a group of fellow financial planners, "is to get up before [potential clients] and confuse them. And step two is to create a dependency." Step three, in many cases, is to start selling them things.)

If only you had access to an expert you could *trust*. Someone who did know how to read a prospectus.

With that in mind, pour yourself a beer and get out your letter opener, for what we have here—delivered by hand to our door—is a fat manila envelope from nothing less than the United States Trust Company, one of the oldest, classiest, most exclusive banks in the country. ("When you do something very well," its ads say, "you simply cannot do it for everyone.")

Inside is everything you'll need to evaluate and sign up for the Samson Properties 1985-A Drilling Program. U.S. Trust—which actually is a very fine institution, this ancient episode notwithstanding—

describes Samson 1985-A as "a quality oil and gas investment with relatively moderate risk, inherent tax benefits, and the potential for significant upside economic gains." (As opposed, one presumes, to downside economic gains.)

The bank's cover letter outlines the deal and encloses a colorful Samson sales brochure, a deadly 165-page Samson prospectus, a huge U.S. Trust business reply envelope for your signed papers, and a form you sign agreeing to pay the bank a 5% "advisory fee" for bringing the deal to your attention. (There is already a 7.5% sales commission built into the deal, but the bank can't touch it—it's illegal for banks to sell securities like these—so, instead, it charges this 5% advisory fee. The bank's not *selling* anything—merely sending sales materials, recommending that you buy it and enclosing all the papers you need to sign to send in with your check. See the difference?)

By paying the "advisory fee," you are in effect getting the deal at 105% of retail. You could avoid the fee by purchasing Samson units directly through a stockbroker, but when you deal with a classy bank—this is not a bank that's out hawking car loans—you should show a little class yourself.

Participations in Samson 1985-A run $25,000 and up.

THESE ARE SPECULATIVE SECURITIES AND INVOLVE A HIGH DEGREE OF RISK, cautions the front page of the prospectus. The S.E.C. makes 'em say stuff like that. The bank prefers to describe it as "relatively moderate risk."

The brochure explains that by mid-1984, "Samson's 1973–1981 Programs had distributed cash equal to 127% of total cash invested" and would distribute a further 226% over the life of those programs. The brochure says you shouldn't count on future programs all doing so well, but, hey, 127% and 226%—that's like three and a half times your money! Plus, U.S. Trust likes the program, and Samson must be getting more experienced each year, and drilling costs *are* really low these days, and boy, could I ever use the tax deduction—where do I sign?

At least that was my reaction.

The brochure does say, "These figures assume an equal investment in each of the programs offered from 1973 through 1981," but that sounds innocuous enough.

It turns out that its very first program, a teeny-tiny deal in 1973 that involved a total of just $325,000 and 11 investors, has paid off like gangbusters. But all its subsequent programs, ranging from 3 to 30 times as big, have mostly tanked. (Funny how often that first deal, which helps sell all subsequent deals, is a lot more successful than the rest.)

If you don't assume "an equal investment in each of the programs," but assume instead the amounts that were *actually* invested, the return on those 1973–81 programs by mid-1984 would have been not 127% (all your money back and then some), but 45% (less than half your money back).

Of the nearly $30 million that investors handed Samson in 1981 (not to mention the $70 million in 1982, 1983, and the first part of 1984), less than $1 million had been paid back by September 30, 1984.

Of the three 1980 deals—one private, two public—one had paid back 74%, two had paid 17% and 9% respectively. Guess which one was the private deal.

And understand, these numbers are not return *on* investment (with luck, that comes later), they're return *of* investment.

If there were a cynic in the room—and I trust there's not—he might suggest that Samson raised $100 million in drilling investments from 1981 through 1984 on the strength of one crummy little $325,000 program it had drilled ten years earlier.

In fact, as it turns out, *that first deal wasn't drilled by Samson at all.* It was drilled by May Petroleum. Samson merely purchased the producing wells at $2-a-barrel-era oil prices and kept pumping as oil prices shot sky-high, apparently realizing that it had the makings of a great brochure.

Having said all this, it's important to be clear that there are many drilling companies whose records are at least as uninspired (I've been in several) and that Samson's 1973–81 programs still have a lot of hydrocarbons in the ground. The brochure says that those programs are projected to return yet a further 226% of investors' money.

But what were these projections based on? What was Samson figuring, and U.S. Trust apparently buying, as a reasonable projection for the price of that oil still in the ground?

Right there on page 78 of the prospectus, paragraph 3, is your answer, plain as day. The 226% return yet to come is based not only on the fabulous results of that first teeny-tiny program Samson didn't drill, but also on the assumption that oil will continue (continue?) to sell for $29.50 a barrel through 1986 (it actually dropped to $10 at one point) and then climb, over the following sixteen years, to $75.

One of the nice things about going through the bank is that you get the benefit of its independent analysis. "In addition to the information contained in the enclosed Offering Prospectus, supplied by [Samson]," writes the bank in its cover letter, "certain other facts should be made known to you."

Oh, boy, I thought: the dirt.

"In particular, our analysis has established [Samson's competence and its track record]." Whereupon the bank simply restates the assertion of Samson's brochure: "through June 30, 1984," the bank writes unquestioningly, "Samson's 1973–1981 programs have distributed cash equal to 127% of total cash invested and had estimated future cash distributions equal to 226% of cash invested."

Somebody at U.S. Trust should have read the prospectus.

Yet if you can't blindly rely on U.S. Trust in such matters—truly one of the finest fiduciary institutions in the country, to which I owe a *lot* of money—on whom *can* you blindly rely?

No one.

# ACKNOWLEDGMENTS

Many people made this anthology.

At Thunder's Mouth Press and Avalon Publishing Group:
Thanks to Tracy Armstead, Will Balliett, Sue Canavan, Kristen Couse, Maria Fernandez, Linda Kosarin, Shona McCarthy, Dan O'Connor, Neil Ortenberg, Paul Paddock, Susan Reich, David Riedy, Michelle Rosenfield, Simon Sullivan, and Mike Walters.

At The Writing Company:
Nate Hardcastle helped with editorial research and oversaw permissions research and negotiations. Nat May, Mark Klimek, Taylor Smith and Wynne Parry took up slack on other projects.

At the Portland Public Library in Portland, Maine:
The librarians helped collect books from around the country.

I also am grateful to the writers whose work appears in this book.

Finally, my thanks are due to scores of money managers and journalists who shared their knowledge of finance, investing and prose. Some of them also have been my friends. I am thinking in particular of Garry Belsky, Mark Boyar, Chuck Carlson, Jerry Edgerton, Carla Fried, Roger Gibson, Ken Gregory, Diane Harris, Peter Kadzis, Craig Litman, Lani Luciano, Tom Marsico, Baie Netzer, Eric Schurenberg, Michael Sivy, Paul Sloan, and Ellen Stark—but there are others.

# PERMISSIONS

# BIBLIOGRAPHY

The selections used in this anthology were taken from the editions listed below. In some cases, other editions may be easier to find. Hard-to-find or out-of-print titles often are available through interlibrary loan services or through Internet booksellers.

Belsky, Gary and Thomas Gilovich. *Why Smart People Make Big Money Mistakes—and How to Correct Them*. New York: Simon & Schuster, 1999.

Bogle, John C. *Common Sense on Mutual Funds: New Imperatives for the Intelligent Investor*. New York: John Wiley & Sons, 1999.

Dominguez, Joe and Vicki Robin. *Your Money or Your Life: Transforming Your Relationship with Money and Achieving Financial Independence*. New York: Penguin Books, 1992.

Ellis, Charles D. and James R. Vertin, eds. *Classics II: Another Investor's Anthology*. Homewood, Ill.: Business One Irwin, 1991. (For "Mistakes of the First Twenty-five Years" and "Ben Graham: Ideas as Mementos".)

Gibson, Roger C. *Asset Allocation: Balancing Financial Risk*. Homewood, Ill.: Business One Irwin, 1990.

Gipson, James H. *Winning the Investment Game: A Guide for All Seasons*. New York: McGraw-Hill, 1984.

Graham, Benjamin. *The Intelligent Investor: A Book of Practical Counsel*. New York: HarperBusiness, 1985. (For "The Superinvestors of Graham-and-Doddsville".)

Hagstrom, Robert G. *The Warren Buffett Way: Investment Strategies of the World's Greatest Investor*. New York: John Wiley & Sons, 1994.

Kazanjian, Kirk. *Value Investing With the Masters*. New York: New York Institute of Finance, 2002.

Lynch, Peter with John Rothchild. *One Up on Wall Street*. New York: Penguin Books, 1990.

Mackay, Charles. *Extraordinary Popular Delusions and the Madness of Crowds*. New York: L. C. Page & Company, 1932.

Malkiel, Burton G. *A Random Walk Down Wall Street*. New York: W. W. Norton & Company, 1973.

Siegel, Jeremy J. *Stocks for the Long Run*. New York: McGraw-Hill, 1998.

Tobias, Andrew. *The Only Investment Guide You'll Ever Need*. New York: Harcourt, 1978.

Train, John. *The Craft of Investing*. New York: HarperBusiness, 1994.